Society in Freefall
There Is a Safety Net!

Wayne Kablanow

World rights reserved. This book or any portion thereof may not be copied or reproduced in any form or manner whatever, except as provided by law, without the written permission of the publisher, except by a reviewer who may quote brief passages in a review.

The author assumes full responsibility for the accuracy of all facts and quotations as cited in this book. The opinions expressed in this book are the author's personal views and interpretations, and do not necessarily reflect those of the publisher.

This book is provided with the understanding that the publisher is not engaged in giving spiritual, legal, medical, or other professional advice. If authoritative advice is needed, the reader should seek the counsel of a competent professional.

Copyright © 2021 Wayne Kablanow
Copyright © 2021 TEACH Services, Inc.
ISBN-13: 978-1-4796-1384-7 (Paperback)
ISBN-13: 978-1-4796-1385-4 (ePub)
Library of Congress Control Number: 2021917665

All Scriptures, unless otherwise stated, are taken from the New King James Version®. Copyright © 1982 by Thomas Nelson. Used by permission. All rights reserved.

Photo Credits:
©Wayne Kablanow - page 59

©Steve Creitz - pages 12, 15, 40, 44, 45, 46, 50, 88, 92, 110, 116, 122, 167, 168, 173, 177, 189, 202, 207, 212, 244

©Lars Justinen - pages 24 and 111

Published by

TEACH Services, Inc.
PUBLISHING
www.TEACHServices.com • (800) 367-1844

Acknowledgements

I am supremely indebted to God the Father, His Son Jesus Christ, and the Holy Spirit for the insights in this book.

I am also indebted to my loving wife, Jeanine Kablanow, for helping me express my thoughts in a smooth and understandable flow of words.

I greatly appreciate S. T. Morton for encouraging me to write this Bible study in a book format.

I also am very thankful to the many friends who read the rough draft and gave insightful suggestions.

Foreword

On January 5, 1975, a shocking accident occurred in the beautiful city of Hobart, the capital of the Australian island state of Tasmania. A fully laden cargo ship making its way up the Derwent River struck a pylon on the Tasman Bridge, which connects Hobart with its eastern suburbs. A section of the bridge plunged 150 feet into the water below. For motorists crossing the bridge at the time, the collapse was a nightmare come true. Four cars carrying a total of five people plunged off the bridge. There were no survivors. Today, Planet Earth finds itself in a very similar predicament. Our world has been ravaged by 6,000 years of sin. We have sown the wind and are now reaping the whirlwind (see Hosea 8:7).

In *Society in Freefall*, author Wayne Kablanow traces some of the most remarkable events in the history of the world to reveal the hopeful future God promises the human family. History and prophecy, combined with solid scholarship, unite to provide a richly detailed understanding of the mysteries of the Bible and offer hope for a world that often seems to have passed the point of no return. Such a book is desperately needed at this time. Clear, straightforward, and thoroughly biblical, *Society in Freefall* offers hope for today and bright hope for tomorrow.

The religious landscape is littered with theories, predictions, assumptions, and speculations. *Society in Freefall* cuts through the clutter and delivers a much-needed analysis of the Bible's great, overarching themes, connecting the reader with a reliable understanding of the vital subjects relevant to where we are in the stream of history. Although time is running out for Planet Earth, eternity beckons. This book will provide you with an explanation, encouragement, and inspiration as you journey towards the future God has prepared for you.

John Bradshaw
President, It Is Written

Introduction

Society is in a political, moral, social, and religious freefall. No one has been able to reverse the trend. Politicians and religious leaders, separately and together, have failed to change the direction in which society is heading.

One leader after another has stepped forward with a message of change for the purpose of saving our nation and the world at large. However, they have made huge moral blunders that have only hastened the demise of our society. Wanting to be of help, they instead become part of the problem.

One of the biggest issues we face is where to find truth. Is there any voice left that is reliable? With dozens of news sources (many new within the last decade), all contradicting and criticizing each other, how is anyone to know what is true? "Fake news" is the newly coined, politically accepted term for blatant lies.

> **Society is in a political, moral, social, and religious freefall. No one has been able to reverse the trend. Politicians and religious leaders, separately and together, have failed to change the direction in which society is heading.**

Is there any place people can go today and know they are getting the full truth and nothing but the truth?

Trust is the foundation upon which a society is built, but trust is being replaced by suspicion, fear, rebellion, and social unrest. The COVID-19 pandemic has only added to this atmosphere of distrust. With neighbors reporting on neighbors and co-workers reporting on co-workers, our society is quickly becoming a police state based on fear and control instead of on trust and freedom.

Current statistics could easily be quoted here, but as soon as statistics are put on paper, they are out of date. You are so painfully aware of current trends that you do not need them rehashed here. That is not the purpose of this book.

The purpose of this book is not only to reveal society's freefall but also show there is a safety net for those who are willing to trust it. This safety net is woven into every chapter of this book. However, in order to understand both the freefall and the safety net, we have to go back in history.

After we have a historical understanding of the freefall and the safety net, we will be able to understand the current and future dangers and opportunities our world faces. This is not a quick-read book. The further you read, the more you will realize it is a study volume.

If there exists somewhere in the universe an all-knowing, all-powerful, and all-present God who has a message for you and everyone on planet earth during the final plunge of earth's history, would you want to know that message? The reality is God does exist, and His heart is filled with love and compassion for you. Out of His heart of love, He has sent a message of hope to the entire world today. That message is found in the fourteenth chapter of the book of Revelation[1]. It is the purpose of this book to unpack that message. On the surface, it seems scary because it is filled with judgment and symbolic representations. However, when it is understood, it is filled with love and hope.

When you finish reading this entire book, you will have gained an understanding that will give you peace, even during the troublous times in which we find ourselves. You will have confidence in the only source of truth that is trustworthy and reliable. Fear will be replaced by love, suspicion by trust, and anxiety by hope.

With that said, let us begin the journey!

---

[1] See Revelation 14:6–12

Table of Contents

Acknowledgements iii

Foreword. v

Introduction vii

    1. Background of the Freefall 11

    2. The Conflict and the Safety Net 24

    3. The Conflict Turned Global. 38

    4. The Attack of the Antichrist 50

    5. God's Counterattack. 73

    6. The Vision of Truth's Fall and Rise Again 91

    7. The Most Exciting Prophecy 104

    8. The Blessed Hope. 122

    9. Who Is Able to Stand? 137

    10. God's Mark 150

    11. A Counterfeit Mark 166

    12. Three, No, Four Angels Shout! .188

    13. Satan's 1,000-year Vacation 209

    14. The End of Sin. 228

    15. Society's Rebirth 243

Appendix A—Why Antiochus IV Epiphanes Is Not the
               Little Horn of Daniel 8 255

Appendix B—Some Critical Hebrew Words in Understanding
               and Connecting Daniel 8 and 9 260

Chapter 1

Background of the Freefall

For thousands of years, the Middle East was the center of civilization. It was there that some of the greatest societies our world has ever seen thrived and built structures at which we marvel today.

Even though the Hanging Gardens of Babylon no longer exist, we know enough about them to be inspired. King Nebuchadnezzar built them to satisfy his wife Amytis, for she was raised in an area where there was a lot of vegetation, but the area around Babylon was very dry and arid. The Hanging Gardens of Babylon were known as one of the Seven Wonders of the World.

Nebuchadnezzar built more than three hundred magnificent temples throughout the city, the greatest of these being the temple of Marduk, which was three hundred feet high. The outside was covered with blue glazed tile, which made it glisten in the sun, and the inside was overlaid with gold. It contained eighteen tons of gold in all, the throne and altar alone made of eight-and-one-half tons of gold.

Babylon was not the only place where fabulous structures were built. The temple in Jerusalem was the most stunningly beautiful building the world has ever seen. It was not large, but its beauty was beyond compare. It was made of huge, pure, white marble blocks, and the inside was covered with pure gold, with angels engraved in the gold. All the furnishings were made of pure gold, silver, or bronze. King Solomon, who built the temple, received tribute of almost four thousand pounds of gold yearly from neighboring nations. In fact, the biblical record states of him that "King Solomon surpassed all the kings of the earth in riches and wisdom."[2] "The king made silver as common in Jerusalem as stones."[3]

What if those structures from antiquity existed today in America? How long would it be until all the gold, silver, and precious stones would be looted and gone? Yet, in ancient times, these were places of worship and social interaction, freely opened to the public. I hope you are beginning to catch a glimpse of the stark contrast between society today and ancient times. Today, we like to boast of our great technological advances, but what about society as a whole?

---

[2] 2 Chronicles 9:22
[3] 2 Chronicles 9:27

Around 600 years before Christ was born, Babylon (in Iraq today) was equivalent to the present-day United States. It was not the only kingdom on earth, but it was the strongest and most dominant. King Nebuchadnezzar had extended its borders and made it a great nation. The city of Babylon was ten miles around—larger than Rome, which, at that time, was only six miles in circumference, and Athens, which was four miles.

Babylon had an economic engine that the world has not witnessed since. For example, they had a twenty-year food supply stored within the city, and the river Euphrates, their water supply, ran through the city. It had double walls so thick that they held chariot races on top of them (one, twelve feet, and the other, twenty-two feet thick). The Babylonians were confident they could outlast any enemy who would besiege them. The city had eight gates, the most famous being the Ishtar Gate, which was excavated and reconstructed in the Pergamon Museum in Berlin. The walls leading up to this gate were covered with the images of 120 lions with eagle's wings. This detail will re-surface when we get to Daniel 7.

One night, Nebuchadnezzar, the king of Babylon, lay awake considering the future of his kingdom, and the God of heaven gave him an impressive dream (people in the Middle East still hold dreams in high regard). However, when Nebuchadnezzar awoke, he could not remember the dream, even though he had a strong impression that it was significant for himself and his kingdom.[4]

The king did the only thing he knew to do: He ordered his wise men (magicians, astrologers, sorcerers, and Chaldeans) to tell him his dream and its interpretation. Magicians, astrologers, and sorcerers are understood in our world today, but who were the Chaldeans? They were an ancient Semitic people that became so dominant in Babylonia that, during the time of Nebuchadnezzar, the residents of Babylon were called

---

[4] See Daniel 2:1–3

Chaldeans. There was a special group of them who helped compose the inner circle of Nebuchadnezzar's cabinet.

Of course, none of them could tell the king what he had dreamed the night before. It was an absurd demand. They responded by saying:

> There is not a man on earth who can tell the king's matter; therefore no king, lord, or ruler has *ever* asked such things of any magician, astrologer, or Chaldean. *It is* a difficult thing that the king requests, and there is no other who can tell it to the king except the gods, whose dwelling is not with flesh.[5]

Put yourself in the place of these wise men. If the king told you the dream and asked for an interpretation, you could come up with an interpretation that was believable. However, they were commanded to reveal the dream as well as the interpretation.

On the other hand, the king thought this was a very reasonable request, since it would prove his wise men (his brain trust) were connected to reliable sources of truth. It would demonstrate he could trust their interpretation.

The king was beginning to realize his usual source of truth was not as trustworthy as he thought. Therefore, he became angry and ordered that all the wise men of Babylon be executed.

Daniel and his three friends (Hananiah, Mishael, and Azariah) were captives from Jerusalem, whom Nebuchadnezzar had brought to Babylon when he conquered the Jews in the year 605 BC.[6] These young men were likely still in their teens and of royal heritage, with "no blemish, good-looking, gifted in all wisdom, possessing knowledge and quick to understand."[7]

Nebuchadnezzar did not kill off the talented people of the nations he conquered. Instead, he retrained them and employed them in the leadership of his government. Accordingly, Daniel and his friends were in training to be part of the king's wise men—his brain trust.

Therefore, when the decree went out to kill all the wise men of Babylon, Daniel and his friends were sought with them. However, Daniel asked for time to seek the God of heaven in order to reveal the king's dream and its interpretation. It is very interesting that, though Nebuchadnezzar refused to give the other wise men time, he was

---

[5] Daniel 2:10, 11
[6] See Daniel 1:1
[7] Daniel 1:4

merciful to Daniel and granted his request. Obviously, the king had grown fond of Daniel.

Subsequently, Daniel did what was natural to him—what he was accustomed to doing three times a day: He and his friends had a prayer meeting and sought the God of heaven to save their lives. Remember, it was the God of heaven who had given the dream to the king, so we begin to see His plan in this whole event. He was trying to direct the king to the only reliable source of truth.

That night, God gave Daniel the same dream he had given Nebuchadnezzar, along with the interpretation. The next morning, Daniel came to the king and declared, "There is a *God in heaven who reveals secrets*, and He has made known to King Nebuchadnezzar what will be in the *latter days*."[8] This was the same message the prophet Isaiah had proclaimed years before:

> Remember the former things of old, For I am God, and there is no other; I am God, and there is none like Me, *Declaring the end from the beginning*, and from ancient times things that are not yet done, saying, "*My counsel shall stand*, and I will do all My pleasure."[9]

Additionally, Jesus reiterated the same message many years later: "And now I have told you *before it comes*, that when it does come to pass, you may *believe*."[10]

Daniel continued to assure the king that God had answered his unasked prayer—his questions about the future of his kingdom. He was trying to show the king that the God of heaven is the only reliable source of truth—not the magicians, astrologers, sorcerers, or Chaldeans.

Let us note how the wise men of Babylon claimed to receive their information:

- Magicians professed the ability to interpret the future by the shape of an animal's liver
- Astrologers attempted to interpret the future by the placement of the stars in the heavens
- Sorcerers tried to foretell the future by consulting the dead
- Chaldeans attempted to forecast future events by the way numbers fell together

---

[8] Daniel 2:28 (emphasis added)
[9] Isaiah 46:9, 10 (emphasis added)
[10] John 14:29 (emphasis added)

Background of the Freefall

Daniel demonstrated a very different attitude from what the other wise men demonstrated. He took no credit for himself. He was humble and gave all the glory to God. This humble spirit intrigued the king and opened his heart to receive God's message through Daniel.

Daniel relayed to the king his dream:

> *You, O king, were watching; and behold, a great image! This great image, whose splendor was excellent, stood before you; and its form was awesome. This image's head was of fine* gold, *its chest and arms of* silver, *its belly and thighs of* bronze, *its legs of* iron, *its feet partly of* iron *and partly of* clay. *You watched while a* stone was cut out without hands, which struck the image on its feet of iron and clay, and broke them in *pieces.* Then the iron, the clay, the bronze, the silver, and the gold were crushed together, and became like chaff from the summer threshing floors; the wind carried them away so that no trace of them was found. And the stone that struck the image became a great mountain and filled the whole earth.[11]

One can only imagine the king leaning forward on the edge of his throne, enraptured with every detail as Daniel related the dream, saying, "Yes, yes, that is what I saw!" As Daniel concluded the dream, he again turned the king's mind to the God of heaven who gave both of them the same dream. He said, "This is the dream. Now *we* will tell the interpretation."[12] Daniel was emphatic that he was only the mouthpiece through which God was communicating truth to the king.

Since Daniel had been able to accurately relate to the king his dream, the king's heart was open to receive the interpretation, even though it

---

[11] Daniel 2:31–35 (emphasis added)
[12] Daniel 2:36 (emphasis added)

was not what he hoped to hear. From there, Daniel began to reveal the interpretation:

> You, O king, are a king of kings. For the God of heaven has given you a kingdom, power, strength, and glory; and wherever the children of men dwell, or the beasts of the field and the birds of the heaven, He has given them into your hand, and has made you ruler over them all—*you are this head of gold*.[13]

That great kingdom of Babylon that Nebuchadnezzar had built was fitly represented by the head of gold, not only because of all the gold that was in the city, but also because their civilization was of valuable quality. It is interesting that the dream depicted the value of each society decreasing as time progressed.

If the interpretation had ended there and the entire image had been made of gold, the king would have been delighted. However, the interpretation continued: "But after you shall arise *another kingdom inferior to yours*."[14] Babylon did not last forever like Nebuchadnezzar wanted. The Bible and secular historians agree on what happened.[15] Daniel records what kingdom conquered Babylon: "That very night Belshazzar, king of the Chaldeans, was slain. And *Darius the Mede* received the kingdom, being about sixty-two years old."[16]

This took place on October 12, 539 BC. The chest and arms of the image being made of silver is a fit symbol of the Medo-Persia Empire. The Medes and Persians were blood relatives, but the Medes arose to dominant power first. However, the Persians joined forces with them, and jointly, they conquered the entire Babylonian empire and expanded it even further, forming the Medo-Persian kingdom. Eventually, the Persians became stronger and more dominant to the point that many historians now call it the Persian Empire.

> *Since Daniel had been able to accurately relate to the king his dream, the king's heart was open to receive the interpretation, even though it was not what he hoped to hear.*

---

[13] Daniel 2:37, 38
[14] Daniel 2:39a (emphasis added)
[15] See Jeremiah 51:37, 64
[16] Daniel 5:30, 31 (emphasis added)

There is an interesting detail that is too fascinating to pass over: It appears that Darius the Mede co-reigned with Cyrus the Persian when they conquered Babylon, and 150 fifty years before Cyrus was born, God had predicted, through the prophet Isaiah, not only that Cyrus would conquer Babylon, but also how it would happen.[17] It is truly amazing how God can see the future even more clearly than we can see the past. His word is trustworthy and powerful!

The Medo-Persian kingdom demonstrated they were stronger than Babylon was, but the quality of their society was inferior to that of Babylon. Contrary to popular assumptions, the Bible depicts the reality that society was and is declining.

Daniel continued to unfold the rise and fall of world-ruling empires as outlined by the dream. In 331 BC, Medo-Persia fell as Alexander the Great, the first king of Greece, rapidly swept through the Middle East and parts of Europe. Alexander was just thirty years old when he conquered Medo-Persia and extended his kingdom beyond their borders. Nebuchadnezzar's dream pictured it this way: "A third kingdom of bronze, which shall rule over all the earth."[18]

This prediction of the rise of the Grecian Empire was again given to Daniel a few years after God gave Nebuchadnezzar his dream and before Babylon fell. In this dream, He gave Daniel a vision of future events involving world-ruling powers. In his dream, God employed the imagery of a ram and goat. Then He gave the interpretation regarding them: "The ram which you saw, having the two horns—they are the kings of *Media and Persia*. And the male goat is the kingdom of *Greece*. The large horn that is between its eyes is the first king."[19]

It is also interesting that Alexander's army had bronze helmets. The belly and thighs of bronze was a fit representation of Greece. Two hundred years after Nebuchadnezzar's dream, Greece conquered Medo-Persia and became the next world-ruling kingdom; but even though he conquered the world, Alexander could not conquer or rule himself:

> He who rose to the highest position the world could offer, fell equally as suddenly. He had conquered kingdoms, but was not master of his own passions. His love of praise led him to have himself proclaimed Son of Jupiter-Ammon in Egypt, and his love of drink

---

[17] See Isaiah 44:27, 28; 45:1–3
[18] Daniel 2:39b (emphasis added)
[19] Daniel 8:20, 21 (emphasis added)

caused his death at the age of thirty-two years, after a universal reign of only two years. Such was the fate of one who feared neither God nor man.[20]

After Alexander died, his four generals (Cassander, Lysimachus, Ptolemy, and Seleucus) vied for the control of the Grecian Empire, but none of them were able to succeed. Eventually, the kingdom was split into four divisions. In this weakened condition, they were vulnerable to foreign powers and taken over by another kingdom.

Daniel continued relating to the king the interpretation of his dream and introduced the next world-ruling kingdom, symbolized by the legs of iron: "And the *fourth kingdom* shall be as strong as *iron*, inasmuch as iron breaks in pieces and shatters everything; and like iron that crushes, that kingdom will break in pieces and *crush all the others*."[21]

At this point, the prophecy had established a solid pattern outlining one world-ruling kingdom followed by the next, hundreds of years before it happened, and exactly as history records. The next world-ruling power was none other than the Roman Empire, which conquered the splintered Grecian kingdom in 168 BC. Rome not only conquered the Grecian territories, but most of Europe as well.

Iron is a fit symbol of the strength and ruthless nature of the Roman Empire. We might note the helmets that the Roman army used were made of iron. Rome was in power when Jesus lived on this earth. It was a Roman governor who ordered Christ's crucifixion, and it was Roman soldiers who carried out that cruel execution. Rome not only participated in killing the Son of God, but also set their hearts and all their harsh powers toward annihilating the early Christian church.

Christ and His followers displayed a character in stark contrast to that of Rome. Instead of physical force, their power was found in their self-sacrificing love. This was a power the Roman armies were not able to conquer. The church had been molded into the likeness of Christ's loving character, as a potter molds a vessel out of ceramic clay. Isaiah talked about God's relation to His people this way: "But now, O LORD, You are our Father; *We are the clay*, and *You our potter*; And all we are the work of Your hand."[22]

In this context, let us see how the interpretation of Nebuchadnezzar's dream continues: "Whereas you saw the *feet* and *toes*, partly of potter's

---

[20] S.N. Haskell, The Story of Daniel the Prophet (South Lancaster, MA: New England Tract Society, 1903), p. 108
[21] Daniel 2:40 (emphasis added)
[22] Isaiah 64:8 (emphasis added)

clay and partly of iron, the kingdom shall be *divided*; yet the strength of the iron shall be in it, just as you saw the *iron mixed with ceramic clay*."[23]

The accuracy of Nebuchadnezzar's dream, hundreds of years in advance of its fulfillment, is absolutely astounding. If anyone could guess Babylon would be followed by Medo-Persia, who would be followed by Greece, who would then be followed by Rome, it would only be natural to guess that Rome would be followed by another world-ruling kingdom. However, that is not what the dream predicted, nor is it what history reveals.

Instead of another world-ruling power conquering Rome, it fell apart, largely from internal corruption, and, by AD 476, disintegrated into ten small nations in Europe. The dream specifically mentions the ten toes, graphically portraying the splintering of Rome into ten separate nations (Anglo-Saxons, Franks, Alamanni, Lombards, Ostrogoths, Burgundians, Visigoths, Suevi, Heruli, and Vandals).

Next, in just a few short words, Daniel gave Nebuchadnezzar a picture of the struggle that would take place between those ten European nations:

> And as the *toes of the feet* were partly of iron and partly of clay, so the kingdom shall be *partly strong* and *partly fragile*. As you saw iron mixed with ceramic clay, they will mingle with the seed of men; *but they will not adhere to one another*, just as iron does not mix with clay.[24]

The history of the European nations could not be more accurately summarized. There have been many attempts to reunite Europe into the old Roman Empire and regain its strength and status in the world. At various times through the centuries, all the royal families of Europe were blood relatives, as demonstrated by a mural on the wall of the Frederiksborg Castle in Denmark, depicting the relationships of all the kings and queens of Europe. They intermarried, thinking if they were all one family, they would be united; but all attempts for unity proved futile. God had said "they will not adhere to one another," and they have not.

Also, one military campaign and political attempt after another has tried, without success, to reunite Europe:

- Charlemagne (April 2, 748–January 28, 814)
- Charles V (February 24, 1500–September 21, 1558)
- Napoleon (August 15, 1769–May 5, 1821)
- Stalin (December 18, 1878–March 5, 1953)

---

[23] Daniel 2:41 (emphasis added)
[24] Daniel 2:42, 43 (emphasis added)

- Hitler (April 20, 1889–April 30, 1945)
- The European Union, which was officially established in 1993, is yet another attempt to reunite Europe, but events in recent years suggest it may be facing an unstable future.

Napoleon wrote his goals in his journal as follows: "There will be one Europe. There will be one currency. There will be one language. There will be one government over all of Europe." However, after his defeat at Waterloo, he said, "God Almighty is too much for me." He knew he was fighting against the Word of God, and he lost.

Hitler's goal was the same as Napoleon's was: "One people, one empire, one leader." And, even though he caused untold pain, sorrow, suffering, and death, he did not defeat God's word, for God has said, "they will not adhere to one another."

Another interesting aspect of this metal man is that the iron of the legs is also found in the feet and toes, indicating there is an aspect of Rome that continues even after it divided into the ten nations of Europe. However, the iron is now mixed with ceramic clay. As we saw earlier, ceramic clay represents God's people—His church.[25] This would indicate that, following the year AD 457, when Rome divided into ten nations, Europe would experience the mingling of church and state. This fact is focused on more fully in other prophecies in Daniel and Revelation, as we will see.

In Daniel's prayer of thanks to God for revealing Nebuchadnezzar's dream and its interpretation, he stated a truth that shines out through the unfolding of the dream:

> Blessed be the name of God forever and ever, for wisdom and might are His. And He changes the times and the seasons; *He removes kings and raises up kings*; He gives wisdom to the wise and knowledge to those who have understanding. He reveals deep and secret things; *He knows what is in the darkness, And light dwells with Him.*[26]

Ultimately, God is in control of the rise and fall of kings and nations. History clearly displays this truth. Let us look at some examples.

When the kingdom of Israel fell into deep apostasy, God sent them prophet after prophet to draw them back to Him, but they continued to backslide into darkness. Among many other abominations, they sacrificed

---

[25] See Isaiah 64:8
[26] Daniel 2:20–22 (emphasis added)

their innocent children to the pagan god Moloch and worshipped the sun god, Baal. Therefore, in 605 BC, God chose Babylon to execute corrective punishment upon Israel for redemptive purposes. Through the prophet Jeremiah, God called Nebuchadnezzar His "servant" to execute His punishment.

> Therefore thus says the LORD of hosts: "Because you have not heard My words, behold, I will send and take all the families of the north," says the LORD, "and *Nebuchadnezzar* the king of Babylon, *My servant*, and will bring them against this land, against its inhabitants, and against these nations all around, and will utterly destroy them, and make them an astonishment, a hissing, and perpetual desolations."[27]

In the same way, God had chosen Cyrus 150 years before he was born to execute judgment upon Babylon when Nebuchadnezzar's grandson, Belshazzar, was on the throne, leading his kingdom into open rebellion and immoral living against God.[28] God had chosen Medo-Persia not only to conquer Babylon, but also to let His people Israel return to Jerusalem to rebuild the temple, walls, and city.

Therefore, in 539 BC, Medo-Persia conquered Babylon, but they also became proud and corrupt. Then, in 331 BC, Greece came to power and conquered Medo-Persia, but they corrupted the temple of God in Jerusalem, attacked His people, and filled up the cup of their iniquity. Therefore, in 168 BC, Rome conquered the western world and ruled with an iron fist until they filled up their cup of iniquity by crucifying the Son of God and trying to annihilate His faithful followers.

After Rome disintegrated into the ten nations of Europe (by AD 476), the Church of Rome established her power over the European countries, beginning in AD 538, and ruled brutally throughout the next 1,260 years until removed by Napoleon's General Berthier in 1798. We will learn more about that in a later chapter.

What is clearly depicted by this prophecy in Daniel 2 is that society has been declining in value ever since ancient times. Gold, the most precious metal, was replaced by silver, which was replaced by brass, then iron, and finally iron mixed with clay. Even though technology and knowledge have greatly increased over the last 200 years, the quality of society has been declining, turning into a chaotic freefall in the last few years. The

---
[27] Jeremiah 25:8, 9 (emphasis added)
[28] See Daniel 5 and Jeremiah 25:12

destruction of successive kingdoms were employed by God to hold back the speed in which society has fallen over the centuries.

Nebuchadnezzar's dream, however, does not end with this world imploding upon itself. It does not end with World War III or a nuclear holocaust. It does not even end in a pandemic; it ends with the glorious second coming of Jesus Christ in the clouds of heaven, represented by the stone that strikes the image on its feet and toes and grinds it into powder.

> And *in the days of these kings the God of heaven will set up a kingdom which shall never be destroyed*; and the kingdom shall not be left to other people; it shall break in pieces and consume all these kingdoms, and it shall stand forever. Inasmuch as you saw that the stone was cut out of the mountain without hands, and that it broke in pieces the iron, the bronze, the clay, the silver, and the gold—the great God has made known to the king what will come to pass after this. *The dream is certain, and its interpretation is sure.*[29]

Outline of Nebuchadnezzar's Vision

605 BC	538 BC	331 BC	168 BC		476 AD		Christ's 2nd Coming
Babylon	Medo-Persia	Greece	Rome			Divided Nations of Europe	

So far, every detail of Nebuchadnezzar's dream has taken place exactly as predicted hundreds and thousands of years in advance. This gives us confidence that the final event of the dream will also take place exactly as predicted. We will dig into this more in a future chapter.

When Daniel finished relating the interpretation, Nebuchadnezzar fell on his face and acknowledged the supremacy of the God of heaven. "The king answered Daniel, and said, 'Truly *your God* is the *God of gods, the Lord of kings*, and a revealer of secrets, since you could reveal this secret.'"[30]

There are at least four points Daniel 2 eloquently illustrates:

1. God's Word can be trusted. The Bible is the only trustworthy source of truth.
2. God is intimately acquainted with the affairs of our lives and in pursuit of a loving, trusting relationship with each of us, as He had with Daniel.

---

[29] Daniel 2:44, 45 (emphasis added)
[30] Daniel 2:47 (emphasis added)

3. The next major event to take place is Christ's second coming.
4. Society has been declining for hundreds and thousands of years instead of rising to a higher state. This chapter gives a broad prophetic and historical outline of that decline. In future chapters, we will see how this decline turns into a global freefall just before Jesus returns.

In the next chapter, we will study Daniel 3 and 4 and begin discovering the spiritual battlefield in which we all live, as well as God's safety net. Without further ado, let us move forward to the only solution to our human predicament.

Chapter 2

The Conflict and the Safety Net

Daniel 3 and 4 were written specifically for us who are living in the time of the toenails of the image in Nebuchadnezzar's dream. Here we find an image being erected and all the world leaders forced to worship the image or be killed. The implications for the book of Revelation are too plain to be ignored.

In Revelation 13, we read about an end-time world power that tells "those who dwell on the earth to make an *image* to the beast who was wounded by the sword and lived. He was granted power to give breath to the *image* of the beast, that the *image* of the beast should both speak and cause as many as would not *worship* the image of the beast to be *killed*."[31]

We must first lay a solid foundation so we can clearly understand what this end-time image is and how to make sure we do not worship it. More than that, we need to know how to have the inner strength to resist wor-

shipping it, even at the threat of death. This is not human strength but inner strength that is produced by our willing submission to an outside power, Jesus Christ and the Holy Spirit. That is what this chapter and entire book demonstrate.

In Daniel 3 and 4, we find a battle waging over Nebuchadnezzar's heart. In chapter 3, Nebuchadnezzar makes a frontal attack against the interpretation of the dream revealed in chapter 2. He also reverses his acknowledgment that the God of heaven is the Supreme Ruler

---

[31] Revelation 13:14, 15 (emphasis added)

of the universe. "Nebuchadnezzar the king made an *image of gold*, whose height was sixty cubits and its width six cubits. He set it up in the plain of Dura, in the province of Babylon."[32]

A cubit is approximately eighteen inches, so Nebuchadnezzar's image was massive ninety feet tall and nine feet wide, and made of solid gold. Notice the difference between this image and the one Nebuchadnezzar saw in his dream. Rather than being made of differing metals, this image was pure gold. He did not want his kingdom to be replaced by any other kingdom, as revealed in God's interpretation of the dream. He wanted his kingdom to last forever, so he attempted to change God's prophecy. He was fighting against God's word. His pride had been humbled only for a short time, then he fell back into his old way of thinking.

Can you identify with Nebuchadnezzar? Do you ever struggle with pride and self-centered thoughts? This story illustrates how intense this battle can be, how patient and persistent God is, and how wonderful it is when we gain the victory through Jesus!

I cannot help but wonder if Nebuchadnezzar ordered the image to resemble his own appearance; but whatever it looked like, it was erected for his glory and praise. Its purpose was to unite the kingdom more fully under his control and power, and he was using worship as the means to accomplish his aim. In other words, he was uniting religion and state to accomplish his goals. As we continue this study, you will see how the adulterous mixture of church and state has been used repeatedly in the past and will be used again at the end of time.

After ordering all the government officials from the 120 provinces of his kingdom to gather at the foot of the image, Nebuchadnezzar had a herald proclaim:

> To you it is commanded, O peoples, nations, and languages, that at the time you hear the sound of the horn, flute, harp, lyre, and psaltery, in symphony with all kinds of music, you shall *fall down* and *worship* the *gold image* that King Nebuchadnezzar has set up; and whoever does not *fall down* and *worship* shall be cast immediately into the midst of a *burning fiery furnace*.[33]

It was a command to worship or die! Some form of the word "worship" is used eleven times in Daniel 3. Clearly, the issue at stake was worship. We are not told where Daniel was at this time, but his three friends

---
[32] Daniel 3:1 (emphasis added)
[33] Daniel 3:4–6 (emphasis added)

(Hananiah, Mishael, and Azariah, whom Nebuchadnezzar had renamed Shadrach, Meshach, and Abed-Nego) were present. And when the music played (notice how music plays a role in false worship), all those present were commanded to bow and worship the golden image.

What would you have done if you were there? Would you have stooped to tie your shoestring? Would you have decided you would bow just this once in order to save your life, thinking you could be a better witness alive, rather than dead? This is not just an interesting story from antiquity!

The issue of worship will also be the central issue that distinguishes those who receive the mark of the beast from those who are faithful to God at the end of time. In fact, the issue of worship is mentioned twenty-three times in Revelation.[34] Therefore, Daniel 3 is very instructive to us who live at the very end of time just before Jesus returns. We will pick up that theme later in this book.

Shadrach, Meshach, and Abed-Nego, rather than compromising the Word of God, refused to bow down to the image, and the report came back to the king:

> *Can you identify with Nebuchadnezzar? Do you ever struggle with pride and self-centered thoughts? This story illustrates how intense this battle can be, how patient and persistent God is, and how wonderful it is when we gain the victory through Jesus!*

"There are certain Jews whom you have set over the affairs of the province of Babylon: Shadrach, Meshach, and Abed-Nego; these men, O king, have *not paid due regard to you*. They do *not serve your gods or worship the gold image* which you have set up." Then Nebuchadnezzar, in *rage* and *fury*, gave the command to bring Shadrach, Meshach, and Abed-Nego. So they brought these men before the king.[35]

After threatening these three young men with death and defying the God of heaven by saying, "Who is the god who will deliver you from my hand,"[36]

---

[34] See Revelation 3:9; 4:10; 5:14; 7:11; 9:20; 11:1, 16; 13:3, 4, 8, 12, 14–17; 14:6–12; 15:4; 16:2; 19:4, 10, 20; 20:4; 22:8, 9
[35] Daniel 3:12, 13 (emphasis added)
[36] Daniel 3:15

Nebuchadnezzar gave them another chance. However, a second chance was not what they wanted.

> Shadrach, Meshach, and Abed-Nego answered and said to the king, "O Nebuchadnezzar, we have no need to answer you in this matter. If that is the case, *our God whom we serve is able to deliver* us from the burning fiery furnace, and He will deliver us from your hand, O king. *But if not,* let it be known to you, O king, that we do not serve your gods, *nor will we worship the gold image* which you have set up."[37]

What was it that gave these young men the courage and strength to make such a bold statement before the most powerful man in the world? It was their trust, confidence, and faith in the God of heaven. They had a deep and abiding love for the true God. Their love was so deep that they would rather die than dishonor Him or sacrifice their loyalty to Him in the slightest degree. This is exactly the type of love relationship about which Jesus spoke when He said, "If you *love Me*, keep My commandments."[38]

They had been taught the Scriptures from childhood, and as they were standing before that golden image, these words kept ringing in their ears: "You shall *love* the LORD your God with all your *heart*, with all your *soul*, and with all your *strength*. And *these words which I command you today* shall be in your *heart*."[39]

The "words" that God had commanded His people to keep were the Ten Commandments, and as Shadrach, Meshach, and Abed-Nego faced that fiery furnace, they could not help but remember the first two commandments:

1. You shall have *no other gods before Me*.[40]
2. You shall not make for yourself a *carved image*—any likeness of anything that is in heaven above, or that is in the earth beneath, or that is in the water under the earth; you shall *not bow down* to them nor serve them. For I, the LORD your God, am a jealous God, visiting the iniquity of the fathers upon the children to the third and fourth generations of those who hate Me, but

---

[37] Daniel 3:16–18 (emphasis added)
[38] John 14:15 (emphasis added)
[39] Deuteronomy 6:5, 6 (emphasis added)
[40] Exodus 20:3 (emphasis added)

showing mercy to thousands, to those who *love Me and keep My commandments.*[41]

A loving faith relationship with God and obedience to His commandments go hand in hand. In fact, it is only through a loving faith relationship that true obedience from the heart is possible. Anything else is hypocrisy—a fake love—a mask hiding the ugliness inside. In the book of Revelation, we find God calling His end-time people into that type of loving faith relationship: "Here is the patience of the saints; here are those who *keep the commandments of God* and the *faith of Jesus.*"[42]

Shadrach, Meshach, and Abed-Nego gained their strength to face death through "the faith of Jesus." Daniel 3 and 4 illustrate the truth so clearly proclaimed in both the Old and New Testaments: salvation comes by faith ALONE![43]

> For by *grace* you have been saved *through faith*, and that not of yourselves; it is the gift of God, *not of works*, lest anyone should *boast*. For we are *His workmanship, created in Christ Jesus for good works*, which God prepared beforehand that we should walk in them.[44]

Let us contemplate this passage of Scripture for a few moments. God's grace is truly amazing, as the well-known song "Amazing Grace" reminds us. It was by grace that God pursued a relationship with the pagan king. He had initiated the relationship and relentlessly pursued it, even though Nebuchadnezzar kept rebelling against Him and sliding back into his old patterns of life.

God takes us just as we are. He does not ask us to change before we come to Him. Instead, He invites us to come to Him just as we are, sinful and rebellious though we may be. He did not require Nebuchadnezzar to repent of his paganism before He pursued a relationship with him.

We are saved by grace through faith—not by works. If we were saved by works, we would have something about which to boast. And if that were the case, Nebuchadnezzar would not have needed a change of heart. All he would need to do was intellectually acknowledge that the God of heaven is the true God.

---

[41] Exodus 20:4–6 (emphasis added)
[42] Revelation 14:12 (emphasis added)
[43] See Romans 4; Hebrews 11
[44] Ephesians 2:8–10 (emphasis added)

The Conflict and the Safety Net 29

However, this is something he had already done at the end of Daniel 2, but it did not change his heart. He was experiencing the same difficulty of which the apostle Paul spoke:

> For we know that the law is spiritual, but I am carnal, sold under sin. For what I am doing, I do not understand. *For what I will to do, that I do not practice; but what I hate, that I do*. If, then, I do what I will not to do, I agree with the law that it is good. But now, it is no longer I who do it, but sin that dwells in me. For I know that in me (that is, in my flesh) nothing good dwells; *for to will is present with me, but how to perform what is good I do not find*. For the good that I will to do, I do not do; but the evil I will not to do, that I practice.[45]

Have you ever found yourself doing things you had determined not to do? New Year's resolutions rarely last a year. Paul goes on a few verses later to make his point even clearer: "Because the carnal mind is enmity against God; for it is not subject to the law of God, nor indeed can be."[46]

The "carnal mind" is the proud, self-centered way of thinking with which we are all born. Nebuchadnezzar found this to be his experience. He intellectually acknowledged God's existence and power, but his heart was not changed. Obviously, he did not yet have a loving faith relationship. You might say he had the same type of faith the devil has. "You believe that there is one God. You do well. Even the *demons believe—and tremble!*"[47]

Let us return to Shadrach, Meshach, and Abed-Nego facing the fiery furnace. When these three young Hebrews defied Nebuchadnezzar's command, he became furious and ordered the furnace to be heated seven times hotter than normal, and they were thrown, bound hand and foot, into the furnace by strong soldiers. Because of the intense heat, the men who threw them in died instantly. However, Shadrach, Meshach and Abed-Nego stood up in the flames and walked freely about. Nebuchadnezzar was astonished!

> "Did we not cast three men bound into the midst of the fire?" They answered and said to the king, "True, O king." "Look!" he answered, "I see *four men loose, walking in the midst of the fire;*

---

[45] Romans 7:14–19 (emphasis added)
[46] Romans 8:7
[47] James 2:19 (emphasis added)

and they are not hurt, and the form of the fourth is like the *Son of God*."[48]

Jesus, the "Son of God," was their only hope of salvation. He was Nebuchadnezzar's only hope as well, just as He is our only hope. The apostle Peter made it clear: "Nor is there salvation in any other, for there is no other name under heaven given among men by which we must be saved."[49]

Before Jesus came to this earth and died for our sins, God's people were saved by faith in the *promise* of His coming and dying for our sins, as illustrated by the animal sacrifices pointing to the Lamb of God. However, after His death, animal sacrifices were no longer needed. The true Lamb of God has been sacrificed for us. Today we have faith in the *fulfillment* of God's promise. Talking of Jesus, Peter wrote, "Who Himself *bore our sins* in His own body on the tree, that we, having died to sins, might *live for righteousness*—by whose stripes you were *healed*."[50]

Righteousness is right-doing (as well as right-being), and that is something none of us can claim for ourselves. There is only one thing we as humans deserve, and that is death. However, we have a God who is so full of self-sacrificing love that He took our sins and died in our place so we can go free and have a chance to learn to love and obey Him in response. "For the wages of sin is death, but the *gift of God* is eternal life in Christ Jesus our Lord."[51]

For a gift to be a gift, it cannot be worked for or deserved in any way. The gift of God is an incredible exchange: your life record of moral corruption, hate, anger, pride, selfishness, sin, and rebellion are exchanged for the record of Christ's life of perfect obedience, righteousness, holiness, loyalty, selflessness, humility, and love. There is no one on planet earth who deserves that exchange, yet it is offered as a free gift to us all—the undeserving, including Nebuchadnezzar.

Jesus was treated as we deserve so we can be treated as He deserves. When we accept this wonderful gift, we are covered with the perfect righteousness of Jesus! And when God looks at us, He does not see our sinfulness but instead only the perfect, holy, sinless life of Jesus!

---

[48] Daniel 3:24, 25 (emphasis added)
[49] Acts 4:12 (emphasis added)
[50] 1 Peter 2:24 (emphasis added)
[51] Romans 6:23 (emphasis added)

"For *all have sinned* and fall short of the glory of God, being *justified freely* by His *grace* through the redemption that is in Christ Jesus,"[52] The best way to remember what the word "justified" means is to accept the fact God treats me (each of you can apply it personally) "just [as] if I" never sinned.

"For He made Him *who knew no sin* to be sin for us, that we might become the *righteousness of God in Him*."[53] He takes our life of wrongdoing and, in its place, gives us His life of right-doing. What an incredible exchange! This is what humbles our rebellious hearts, subdues our arrogant pride, and changes the focus of our lives, causing us to love right-doing, which we used to despise, and hate wrongdoing and selfishness, which we used to love. Jesus called this "being born again" to a new life: "Most assuredly, I say to you, unless one is *born again*, he cannot see the kingdom of God."[54]

The kingdom of God is in stark contrast to the kingdoms/nations of this world, which are in a freefall of chaos, crime, bigotry, injustice, immorality, and every conceivable form of evil, vice, and darkness. The apostle Paul was given a picture of our society today:

> But know this, that *in the last days perilous times will come*: For men will be lovers of themselves, lovers of money, boasters, proud, blasphemers, disobedient to parents, unthankful, unholy, unloving, unforgiving, slanderers, without self-control, brutal, despisers of good, traitors, headstrong, haughty, lovers of pleasure rather than lovers of God, *having a form of godliness but denying its power*. And from such people turn away![55]

God has the power to change the corruption and darkness every one of us finds lurking in our own hearts. His power will not just modify our old lives, but it will create us brand new—completely and radically different from what we were before. The Bible tells us what characteristics He will create in us: "But the fruit of the Spirit is *love*, joy, peace, longsuffering, kindness, goodness, faithfulness, gentleness, self-control. Against such there is no law. And those who are Christ's have *crucified the flesh with its passions and desires*."[56]

---

[52] Romans 3:23, 24 (emphasis added)
[53] 2 Corinthians 5:21 (emphasis added)
[54] John 3:3 (emphasis added)
[55] 2 Timothy 3:1–5 (emphasis added)
[56] Galatians 5:22–24 (emphasis added)

The power of the love displayed by the death of Jesus on the cross for our sins will break our stubborn hearts and mold our characters into the same likeness of His lovely character. When we accept Jesus into our hearts, He will do what we are incapable of doing. We cannot change our hearts,[57] but if we let Jesus in, He will do it in us. "For it is *God who works in you* both to *will* and to *do* for His good pleasure."[58]

Jesus made it clear that we cannot change our hearts by our own willpower. We are dependent upon Him for even the desire to do what is right. He said, "Without Me you can do *nothing*."[59] Sometimes we have a hard time understanding the word "nothing." We cannot even come to Him or repent on our own![60] It is God's amazing grace that empowers us to repent. "Or do you despise the riches of His goodness, forbearance, and longsuffering, not knowing that the *goodness of God leads you to repentance?*"[61]

This is exactly what Nebuchadnezzar was experiencing. The goodness of God was slowly reaching his proud, selfish, sinful, pagan heart. When he saw Jesus walking and talking with Shadrach, Meshach, and Abed-Nego in the fiery furnace, he again acknowledged the God of heaven as supreme and proclaimed this wonderful truth to the world leaders.

> Then Nebuchadnezzar went near the mouth of the burning fiery furnace and spoke, saying, "Shadrach, Meshach, and Abed-Nego, *servants of the Most High God*, come out, and come here." Then Shadrach, Meshach, and Abed-Nego came from the midst of the fire. And the *satraps, administrators, governors, and the king's counselors gathered together*, and they saw these men on whose bodies the fire had no power; the hair of their head was not singed nor were their garments affected, and the smell of fire was not on them.[62]

The God of heaven was beginning to make an impact on Nebuchadnezzar's life. Clearly, He was in pursuit of a love/faith relationship with the king and, through the king, trying to reach the world leaders. This story shows how God can take very negative events and turn them into very positive outcomes—for those who allow Him to do so. It illustrates the truth about which the apostle Paul spoke. "And we know that *all*

---

[57] See Job 14:4; Jeremiah 13:23
[58] Philippians 2:13 (emphasis added)
[59] John 15:5 (emphasis added)
[60] See Acts 5:31
[61] Romans 2:4 (emphasis added)
[62] Daniel 3:26, 27 (emphasis added)

things work together for *good* to those who love God, to those who are the called according to His purpose."[63]

After proclaiming God's supremacy, Nebuchadnezzar made a decree affecting religious affairs in his kingdom. He was making progress, but he had much more to learn.

> Nebuchadnezzar spoke, saying, "*Blessed be the God of Shadrach, Meshach, and Abed-Nego*, who sent His Angel and delivered His servants who trusted in Him, and they have frustrated the king's word, and yielded their bodies, that they should not serve nor worship any god except their own God! *Therefore I make a decree* that any people, nation, or language which *speaks anything amiss against the God* of Shadrach, Meshach, and Abed-Nego *shall be cut in pieces*, and their houses shall be made an ash heap; because there is no other God who can deliver like this." Then the king promoted Shadrach, Meshach, and Abed-Nego in the province of Babylon.[64]

Even though Nebuchadnezzar had come to recognize and publicly acknowledge the supremacy of the true God, he still had not surrendered himself to Him or understood the character of the kingdom of heaven. God does not use force! He does not turn to the governments of this world to enforce His principles of righteousness, the Ten Commandments. Instead, He shows His goodness, which leads us to repentance.

Now, it is true that the last six commandments form the foundation for most of the laws of the nations of the world, and that is appropriate. However, the first four commandments, dealing with our relationship with God, should never be addressed by human governmental laws.[65] This was a lesson Nebuchadnezzar had yet to learn, and it is a subject that will surface at the end of time.

> **God does not use force! He does not turn to the governments of this world to enforce His principles of righteousness, the Ten Commandments. Instead, He shows His goodness, which leads us to repentance.**

---

63   Romans 8:28 (emphasis added)
64   Daniel 3:28–30 (emphasis added)
65   See Acts 4:18–20; 5:29

Let us now go to Daniel 4, which is a very unique passage of Scripture. It was not written by Daniel. It was written by King Nebuchadnezzar himself. It is his personal conversion testimony. What is fascinating is that he wrote his testimony and then sent it to the world. It has been said that as soon as one is born again through the Holy Spirit, there is instilled within that person a desire to tell the world about the wonderful love and freedom he or she has found in Jesus. This was the king's experience.

> Nebuchadnezzar the king, *To all peoples, nations, and languages that dwell in all the earth*: Peace be multiplied to you. I thought it good *to declare* the signs and wonders that *the Most High God has worked for me*. How great are His signs, And how mighty His wonders! *His kingdom* is an everlasting kingdom, And *His dominion* is from generation to generation.[66]

You can read how his conversion took place in Daniel 4. God gave him another disturbing dream, and because his wise men again could not interpret it, Daniel was called. After hearing the dream, Daniel stood stunned and speechless.

> Then Daniel, whose name was Belteshazzar, was astonished for a time, and his thoughts troubled him. So the king spoke, and said, "Belteshazzar, do not let the dream or its interpretation trouble you." Belteshazzar answered and said, "My lord, *may the dream concern those who hate you*, and its interpretation concern your enemies!"[67]

The interpretation of the dream revealed that because of Nebuchadnezzar's pride, he would have a serious mental illness that would cause him to live like an animal for seven years. He would dwell in the fields and eat grass like a cow. Therefore, Daniel appealed to the king to change his ways and repent of his wrongdoing. "Therefore, O king, let my advice be acceptable to you; *break off your sins by being righteous, and your iniquities by showing mercy to the poor*. Perhaps there may be a lengthening of your prosperity."[68]

Unfortunately, Nebuchadnezzar refused to humble his proud heart and accept Daniel's godly advice. Therefore, he suffered the consequences.

---

[66] Daniel 4:1–3 (emphasis added)
[67] Daniel 4:19 (emphasis added)
[68] Daniel 4:27 (emphasis added)

All this came upon King Nebuchadnezzar. At the end of the twelve months he was walking about the royal palace of Babylon. The king spoke, saying, "Is not this great Babylon, *that I have built for a royal dwelling by my mighty power* and for *the honor of my majesty*?" While the word was still in the king's mouth, a voice fell from heaven: "King Nebuchadnezzar, to you it is spoken: the kingdom has departed from you! And they shall drive you from men, and your dwelling shall be with the beasts of the field. They shall make you eat grass like oxen; and seven times shall pass over you, until you know that the Most High rules in the kingdom of men, and gives it to whomever He chooses." *That very hour the word was fulfilled concerning Nebuchadnezzar*; he was driven from men and ate grass like oxen; his body was wet with the dew of heaven till his hair had grown like eagles' feathers and his nails like birds' claws.[69]

Fortunately, this was not the end of the story. At the end of seven years, God healed Nebuchadnezzar's mind, and he became king again. Even though the Bible does not state it, I cannot help but think Daniel was the one who preserved the rulership of the kingdom for Nebuchadnezzar, since he knew the interpretation of the dream. Nebuchadnezzar finally surrendered his all to God and gave Him all the glory.

At the same time my reason returned to me, and for the glory of my kingdom, my honor and splendor returned to me. My counselors and nobles resorted to me, I was restored to my kingdom, and excellent majesty was added to me. *Now I, Nebuchadnezzar, praise and extol and honor the King of heaven*, all of whose works are *truth*, and His ways *justice*. And *those who walk in pride He is able to put down*.[70]

God hates pride because it is the root of all sin.[71] Pride was Satan's sin when he rebelled against God in heaven. The name "Satan" means "adversary." He was originally called "Lucifer," which means "light bearer." In other words, God created a wonderful and powerful angel and gave him the highest position in heaven, next to His throne. His work was to bear the truth (light) about God to the universe. However, he eventually began to think too highly of himself and rebelled against God and His laws. He

---

[69] Daniel 4:28–33 (emphasis added)
[70] Daniel 4:36–37 (emphasis added)
[71] See Proverbs 8:13

thought he was smarter than God and had better plans, so he became "Satan," God's adversary. The prophets Isaiah and Ezekiel describe his prideful fall into rebellious sin.

> How you are fallen from heaven, O *Lucifer*, son of the morning! How you are cut down to the ground, You who weakened the nations! For you have said in your *heart*: "*I will* ascend into heaven, *I will* exalt my throne above the stars of God; *I will* also sit on the mount of the congregation On the farthest sides of the north; *I will* ascend above the heights of the clouds, *I will* be like the Most High." [72]
>
> Thus says the Lord GOD: "*You were the seal of perfection*, Full of wisdom and perfect in beauty. You were in Eden, the garden of God; Every precious stone was your covering: The sardius, topaz, and diamond, Beryl, onyx, and jasper, Sapphire, turquoise, and emerald with gold. The workmanship of your timbrels and pipes Was prepared for you on *the day you were created*. You were the *anointed cherub who covers*; I established you; You were on the holy mountain of God; You walked back and forth in the midst of fiery stones. *You were perfect* in your ways from the day you were created, *Till iniquity was found in you.* By the abundance of your trading You became filled with *violence within, And you sinned*; Therefore *I cast you as a profane thing out of the mountain of God*; And I destroyed you, O covering cherub, From the midst of the fiery stones. Your *heart was lifted up because of your beauty*; You corrupted your wisdom for the sake of your splendor;"[73]

Here we see a glimpse of the battle we all face in our own hearts: the battle of pride—a battle that Nebuchadnezzar eventually won. Because of sin in our hearts, we are naturally proud and want to live our lives our way, not God's way. Another form of pride is that we want to work our way into God's favor instead of accepting Christ's righteousness as a free gift, which hurts our pride. We want to feel deserving of His love, or maybe we think our definition of right-doing is all that matters. We resist accepting God's definition as revealed in the Bible. That is too humbling.

However, like Nebuchadnezzar, when we realize our proud hearts only lead to death and humbly submit ourselves to God, all boasting comes to

---

[72] Isaiah 14:12–14 (emphasis added)
[73] Ezekiel 28:12–17 (emphasis added)

an end. We realize we are nothing and Jesus is everything! Therefore, the apostle Paul stated:

> Now we know that whatever the law says, it says to those who are under the law, that every mouth may be stopped, and all the world may become guilty before God. Therefore by the deeds of the law no flesh will be justified in His sight, for by the law *is* the knowledge of sin.[74]

The battle over pride and selfishness is the battle that rages in the heart of every human being. This is the source of all violence, crime, wars, and everything evil and destructive.[75] As you continue reading this book, you will see how pride has played out in history and how it is the cause of our society's freefall today.

There is a solution in the free gift of Jesus, but how many will accept Him? Jesus made it clear that only a few will walk that humbling path. The humility required to accept the gift will be too difficult for most to swallow. "Enter by the *narrow gate*; for wide is the gate and broad is the way that leads to destruction, and there are many who go in by it. Because narrow is the gate and difficult is the way which leads to life, and there are *few who find it*."[76]

Will you be part of those who find it? It is my prayer that you will. You can do so right now by opening your heart to Jesus and accepting His love, which will lead you to repentance, free and full forgiveness, and cleansing from all sin. "If we confess our sins, He is faithful and just to *forgive us our sins* and to cleanse us from all unrighteousness."[77]

The book of Revelation gives a word picture of those who accept the gift of God's righteousness at the end of time, and again it does not appear to be a large group. It is described as the "remnant," which indicates a small number.[78] However, there is room for one more—YOU! Will you accept His gift today?

---

[74] Romans 3:19, 20
[75] See James 1:14, 15
[76] Matthew 7:13, 14 (emphasis added)
[77] 1 John 1:9 (emphasis added)
[78] See Revelation 12:17 (KJV)

Chapter 3

The Conflict Turned Global

In Daniel 7, the end-time antichrist power is identified. However, before we jump into that, let me briefly state that chapter 5 records the fall of ancient Babylon, and Revelation uses this to illustrate significant end-time events. We will deal with this later, but to whet your appetite, I will just quote one passage from Revelation: "And another angel followed, saying, *'Babylon is fallen, is fallen, that great city*, because she has made all nations drink of the wine of the wrath of her fornication.'"[79]

Daniel 6 tells the well-known story of Daniel in the lion's den, but it is far more than an interesting story to tell children. In chapter 3, we saw *false* worship being forced on pain of death, and now, in chapter 6, we see *true* worship being forbidden on pain of death. When we come to Revelation, we will find that both of these death decrees are instructive to us at the end of time.

In Daniel 7, the conflict described in Nebuchadnezzar's experience turns global in nature, with the antichrist power at the center. Nebuchadnezzar's personal conflict is an illustration of this global conflict.

The God of heaven gave Daniel himself, rather than Nebuchadnezzar, a vision. He used different symbols to convey His message to Daniel: strange beasts, horns, wings, wind, etc. We could try to guess what they mean, but that would be an exercise in futility, so we will let the Bible interpret itself. Apocalyptic Bible prophecy is given in code language, and the only way to accurately break the code is with the Bible itself. These messages are significant to us, and we must study carefully to understand them correctly.

God is very compassionate and reveals the events coming upon this planet ahead of time so we can be prepared and not be taken by surprise. "Surely the Lord GOD does *nothing*, Unless He reveals His secret to His servants the *prophets*."[80]

The information in this chapter and the next chapter was believed and preached by Martin Luther, John Calvin, John Wesley, John Knox, and many other reformers; it's what gave strength to the Protestant

---

[79] Revelation 14:8 (emphasis added)
[80] Amos 3:7 (emphasis added)

The Conflict Turned Global

Reformation. I want to emphatically state that God has true followers in every Christian denomination and fellowship that exists today. The prophecy is not pointing a finger at individuals, but at institutions, powers, and systems of belief that affect our relationship with Him. Our salvation is dependent upon our relationship with God. That is why Satan wants to interfere with and destroy it.

Daniel starts relating the prophetic vision by saying, "I saw in my vision by night, and behold, the *four winds* of heaven were stirring up the *Great Sea*. And *four great beasts* came up from the sea, each different from the other."[81] Here we find three symbols: winds, sea, and beasts. Let us allow the Bible to break the symbolic code for us. Four winds are often used in the Bible to describe warfare and strife among nations. Here is one example:

> "Against Elam I will bring the *four winds from the four quarters of heaven*, and scatter them toward all those winds; There shall be no nations where the outcasts of Elam will not go. For I will cause Elam to be dismayed before their enemies and before those who seek their life. I will bring disaster upon them, My fierce anger," says the LORD; "And I will send the sword after them until I have consumed them."[82]

The "Great Sea" was a term used to describe the Mediterranean Sea.[83] This indicates the strife and warfare being described would center on those countries in the Mediterranean region of the world. "Sea" or "waters" is used in the Bible to mean a multitude of people and nations living in the same region and speaking different languages.[84] This is true of the Mediterranean section of the world. The following passage is an example of the sea and waters representing a multitude of people and nations:

> Woe to the *multitude of many people* Who make a noise like the *roar of the seas*, And to the rushing of *nations* That make a rushing like the rushing of *mighty waters*! The *nations* will rush like the rushing of *many waters*; But God will rebuke them and they will flee far away, And be chased like the chaff of the mountains before the wind, Like a rolling thing before the whirlwind.[85]

---

[81] Daniel 7:2, 3 (emphasis added)
[82] Jeremiah 49:36, 37 (emphasis added)
[83] See Numbers 34:6, 7; Joshua 1:4; 9:1; 15:12, 47
[84] See Revelation 17:15
[85] Isaiah 17:12, 13 (emphasis added)

What about the "four great beasts" that came up from the sea? From what we have seen so far, whatever these beasts represent, they came up in a territory close to the Mediterranean Sea. Notwithstanding, the Bible does not leave us without the identity of these "four great beasts." Daniel was given the meaning: "*Those great beasts*, which are four, are *four kings*."[86]

Kings rule over kingdoms, of course. Daniel is given further clarification that these "four great beasts" do not just represent four kings, but, more broadly, four kingdoms, just as we found in chapter 2. "Thus he said: 'The *fourth beast* shall be a *fourth kingdom* on earth, Which shall be different from all other kingdoms, And shall devour the *whole earth*, Trample it and break it in pieces.'"[87]

If the fourth beast is a fourth kingdom, then the first, second, and third beasts are also kingdoms. These are not small and insignificant kingdoms either; they are world-ruling kingdoms. These four, successive beasts represent the same four successive kingdoms outlined in Daniel 2. That prophecy sets a pattern that is followed by the rest of the prophecies of Daniel as well as Revelation, every succeeding prophecy giving increased detail and insight into the issues we are facing today and will be facing soon.

Even though we saw the identity of the four successive kingdoms in Daniel 2, let us not take anything for granted. Let us allow the Bible to make it clear. The first beast in Daniel 7 is described this way: "The first was like a *lion*, and had *eagle's wings*. I watched till its wings were plucked off; and it was lifted up from the earth and made to stand on two feet like a man, and *a man's heart was given to it*."[88]

This is obviously symbolic. There is no such creature on earth. A lion with an eagle's wings is a fit description of the kingdom of Babylon in Daniel's

---

[86] Daniel 7:17 (emphasis added)
[87] Daniel 7:23 (emphasis added)
[88] Daniel 7:4 (emphasis added)

time. If you remember our study of Daniel 2, lions with an eagle's wings were carved on the walls of Babylon, but that is archeological evidence, not biblical evidence. Does the Bible give us the answer to this symbol?

In describing Babylon's army coming to destroy Jerusalem and the surrounding cities and nations, Jeremiah, who was also a prophet during Daniel's time, said:

> The *lion* has come up from his thicket, And the *destroyer of nations* is on his way. He has gone forth from his place To make your land desolate. Your cities will be laid waste, Without inhabitant.... Behold, he shall come up like clouds, And his chariots like a whirlwind. His horses are *swifter than eagles*. Woe to us, for we are plundered![89]

A very interesting detail about this lion with an eagle's wings is that "a man's heart was given to it." Man's ways are not God's ways. The wisest man who ever lived, King Solomon, wrote, "There is a way that *seems right to a man*, But its end is the way of *death*."[90]

Additionally, Isaiah quoted God as saying, "For *My thoughts* are *not your thoughts*, Nor are your ways My ways,' says the LORD. 'For as the heavens are higher than the earth, So are My ways higher than your ways, *And My thoughts than your thoughts*.'"[91]

God's thoughts and ways are of "love, joy, peace, longsuffering, kindness, goodness, faithfulness, gentleness, self-control."[92] These were just the opposite of the thoughts and ways of Nebuchadnezzar's grandson, Belshazzar, the last king of Babylon. They are also opposite from the thoughts and ways of most people in our world today. This is why our society is in freefall.

What we need is the mind of Christ! We need new thought patterns—not just modified, but new. The apostle Paul urges us:

> Let *this mind* be in you which was also in *Christ Jesus*, who, being in the form of God, did not consider it robbery to be equal with God, but *made Himself of no reputation*, taking the form of a bondservant, and coming in the likeness of men. And being found in

---

[89] Jeremiah 4:7, 13 (emphasis added; see also Jeremiah 49:19–22; Deuteronomy 28:49)
[90] Proverbs 14:12 (emphasis added)
[91] Isaiah 55:8, 9 (emphasis added)
[92] Galatians 5:22, 23

appearance as a man, He *humbled Himself* and became obedient to the point of death, even the *death of the cross*.[93]

Christ's way of thinking is opposed to Satan's way of thinking. As we have already seen, Satan's way of thinking is self-aggrandizement, but Christ's way of thinking is self-subjugation. Jesus came to serve, but Satan wants to rule, and his rule is by force, as we have seen so far in the book of Daniel. It is interesting that, when Nebuchadnezzar became a converted man, he no longer resorted to force to promote his beliefs. Instead, he praised the God of heaven who rules by love.[94]

The global conflict in which we are all involved is the battle over our minds. Whose mindset will we adopt? The more our society indulges Satan's mindset, the faster the freefall will be.

The apostle Paul tells us on what we should allow our minds to dwell:

> *Rejoice in the Lord always.* Again I will say, rejoice! Let your gentleness be known to all men. The Lord is at hand. *Be anxious for nothing*, but in everything by prayer and supplication, with thanksgiving, let your requests be made known to God; and *the peace of God, which surpasses all understanding, will guard your hearts and minds through Christ Jesus.* Finally, brethren, whatever things are *true*, whatever things are *noble*, whatever things are *just*, whatever things are *pure*, whatever things are *lovely*, whatever things are *of good report*, if there is any *virtue* and if there is anything *praiseworthy—meditate on these things*."[95]

That is the healthy way to think, but how to do it is another question. Paul expressed the conflict over his mind this way: "For the *good* that I will to do, *I do not do*; but the *evil* I will not to do, *that I practice*."[96]

Christ, when He had been arrested on false charges, condemned by false witnesses, whipped, beaten, mocked, and sentenced to death unjustly, raised not a word of protest or self-defense. As He was being nailed to the cross, instead of railing against His persecutors, He merely raised His voice in prayer, saying, *"Father, forgive them,* for *they do not know what they do."*[97] He not only asked that His persecutors be forgiven, but He recognized they were struggling with the same conflict with which

---

[93] Philippians 2:5–8 (emphasis added)
[94] See Daniel 4:37
[95] Philippians 4:4–8 (emphasis added)
[96] Romans 7:19 (emphasis added)
[97] Luke 23:34 (emphasis added)

we all struggle and of which Paul spoke ("the evil I will not to do, that I practice"). Such self-sacrificing love is the mindset of Christ.

God has given us mighty weapons with which to win this war—weapons capable of bringing our thoughts into harmony with the mind of Christ.

> For though we walk in the flesh, we do not *war* according to the flesh. For the *weapons of our warfare* are not carnal but *mighty in God* for *pulling down strongholds*, casting down *arguments* and every high thing that exalts itself against the knowledge of God, *bringing every thought into captivity to the obedience of Christ*.[98]

When our every thought reflects the mind of Christ, our feelings, words, and actions will also reflect His character. We will be freed from the slavery of sin (wrong doing) and become the servants of righteousness (right doing). We will become totally new people—transformed into Christ's likeness! "And do not be conformed to this world, but be *transformed* by the *renewing of your mind*, that you may prove what is that *good and acceptable and perfect will of God*."[99]

The word "transformed" is the Greek word μεταμορφόω (*metamorphoō*), from which we get the word "metamorphosis," the process of an ugly caterpillar turning into a beautiful monarch butterfly, a tadpole turning into a frog, etc. They become totally different creatures, not just modifications of the old. It is like being created all over again. The apostle Paul repeatedly wrote about this. "And be renewed in

> *Christ, when He had been arrested on false charges, condemned by false witnesses, whipped, beaten, mocked, and sentenced to death unjustly, raised not a word of protest or self-defense. As He was being nailed to the cross, instead of railing against His persecutors, He merely raised His voice in prayer, saying, "Father, forgive them, for they do not know what they do."*

---

[98] 2 Corinthians 10:3–5 (emphasis added)
[99] Romans 12:2 (emphasis added)

the spirit of your *mind*, and that you put on the *new man* which was *created according to God, in true righteousness and holiness*."[100]

When we get into the book of Revelation, we will see this conflict between having the mind of either Christ or Satan is the focus of end-time events. It is the cause of the freefall. Revelation succinctly summarizes this warfare: "And the *dragon* was wroth with the *woman*, and went to *make* war with the remnant of her seed, which *keep the commandments of God*, and *have the testimony of Jesus Christ*."[101]

Let us return to Daniel 7. The lion with an eagle's wings clearly represents the kingdom of Babylon, which ruled from 605–539 BC. The second beast is described this way: "And suddenly *another beast*, a second, like a *bear*. It was *raised up on one side*, and had *three ribs in its mouth* between its teeth. And they said thus to it: 'Arise, devour much flesh!'"[102] The identity of this bear-like creature is without a doubt the Medo-Persian kingdom.[103]

According to Daniel 5, as well as secular history, Medo-Persia conquered Babylon, as we noted in our study of chapter 2. The fact that this bear is raised up on one side is a very fit description of the Medo-Persian Empire because the Persians became stronger and more dominant than the Medes were. The three ribs in its mouth are likewise descriptive because they not only conquered the kingdom of Babylon, but also Lydia and Egypt. The territory of the Medo-Persian Empire extended far beyond what Babylon had controlled, so it is true that they did "devour much flesh!" Medo-Persia ruled from 539–331 BC and was followed by the third world-ruling kingdom.

"After this I looked, and there was another, like a *leopard*, which had on its *back four wings of a bird*. The beast also had *four heads*, and

---

[100] Ephesians 4:23, 24 (emphasis added)
[101] Revelation 12:17 (KJV, emphasis added)
[102] Daniel 7:5 (emphasis added)
[103] See Isaiah 13:17–19

dominion was given to it."[104] The identity of this third beast, the leopard, is beyond doubt the kingdom of Greece, which ruled from 331–168 BC.

Daniel 8, which covers the same history chapter 7 does, pointedly tells us this, but by using different symbols. After describing the symbol of a ram which was destroyed by the symbol of a goat,[105] the angel Gabriel told Daniel, "The *ram* which you saw, having the two horns—they are the kings of *Media and Persia*. And the male *goat* is the kingdom of *Greece*. The large horn that is between its eyes is the first king."[106]

Alexander the Great, the first king of Greece, died shortly after he conquered the Medo-Persian Empire, and his four generals (Cassander, Lysimachus, Ptolemy, and Seleucus) eventually divided the empire into four parts. This is clearly represented by the four wings and four heads of the leopard. Again, God's word is incredibly accurate!

Let us review the first three beasts:

1. The lion represents Babylon, which ruled from 605–539 BC
2. The bear represents Medo-Persia, which ruled from 539–331 BC
3. The leopard represents Greece, which ruled from 331–168 BC

It is interesting that each succeeding kingdom expanded the territory they occupied further to the west. The fourth beast expands his territory to the west even more.

So far, this prophecy has been accurate in every detail. That gives us confidence in the description of the fourth beast's activities being accurate as well. The pattern has been set. One world-ruling kingdom has followed the next throughout the centuries. With that said, what world-ruling kingdom does the fourth beast represent?

---

[104] Daniel 7:6 (emphasis added)
[105] See Daniel 8:3–8
[106] Daniel 8:20, 21 (emphasis added)

After this I saw in the night visions, and behold, a *fourth beast*, *dreadful* and *terrible*, *exceedingly strong*. It had *huge iron teeth*; it was devouring, breaking in pieces, and trampling the residue with its feet. It was different from all the beasts that were before it, and *it had ten horns*.[107]

The question is, What kingdom conquered the splintered Grecian Empire? The very next world-ruling empire mentioned in the Bible is the pagan Roman Empire, which was in power when Jesus was born, lived, and died on the cross, as well as during the first centuries of the early Christian church.[108]

Rome was "exceedingly strong" and cruel in the treatment of the kingdoms they conquered. This is why the Jews of Christ's day hated them so intensely. That is the background behind His words regarding the abuse rendered by Roman soldiers: "And whoever compels you to go one mile, go with him two."[109] Love and self-sacrificing service were powers Rome did not know how to handle. The "huge iron teeth" are also linked to the iron legs of the statue in Daniel 2, which we discovered represents the kingdom of Rome.

Nevertheless, what are the ten horns? We will find there were three phases to this fourth beast, which represents Rome. The first phase was the dreadful, terrible, exceedingly strong beast with huge iron teeth, the pagan Roman Empire, which conquered Greece in 168 BC and ruled until AD 476.

Daniel wanted to know more about this fourth kingdom, and he was given the following explanation: "Thus he said: 'The *fourth beast* shall be A *fourth kingdom* on earth, Which shall be different from all other kingdoms, And shall *devour the whole earth*, Trample it and

---

[107] Daniel 7:7 (emphasis added)
[108] See Acts 2:10; 18:2; 19:21; 23:11; 28:14, 16; Romans 1:7, 15; 2 Timothy 1:17
[109] Matthew 5:41

break it in pieces. The *ten horns* are *ten kings* Who shall *arise from this kingdom.*'"[110]

As we have already seen, kings rule kingdoms. These ten kings ruled ten kingdoms that would "arise from this kingdom." That is exactly what happened to Rome after it conquered all of western Europe. It was not a world-ruling power that conquered Rome. Instead, it fell apart from internal corruption and, by AD 476, was divided into the ten nations of Europe (of that day).

Therefore, the first phase of the fourth beast was the pagan Roman Empire. The second phase was the divided ten kingdoms of Europe, in direct parallel to the image of Daniel 2, which had feet and ten toes of iron and clay that were divided, never to be united again. The ten kingdoms were as follows:

- Anglo-Saxons—English
- Franks—French
- Alamanni—Germans
- Lombards—Italians
- Burgundians—Swiss
- Visigoths—Spanish
- Suevi—Portuguese
- Heruli—extinct
- Ostrogoths—extinct
- Vandals—extinct

I am a visual learner and know many others are as well, so I included the following chart to review what we have learned so far from Daniel 7:

The third phase of Rome, which is also the antichrist phase, is the subject of the next chapter of this volume. I hope you recognize the Word of God is powerful, accurate to detail, and trustworthy. In this world of fake

---

[110] Daniel 7:23, 24 (emphasis added)

news and rewritten history, we can turn to the Bible in confidence. That is why King David, the great psalmist, wrote:

> Your word I have hidden in my heart, That I might not sin against You.[111]
> Forever, O LORD, Your word is settled in heaven.[112]
> Your word is a lamp to my feet And a light to my path.[113]
> You are my hiding place and my shield; I hope in Your word.[114]
> Your word is very pure; Therefore Your servant loves it.[115]
> The entirety of Your word is truth, And every one of Your righteous judgments endures forever.[116]
> I rejoice at Your word As one who finds great treasure.[117]
> My tongue shall speak of Your word, For all Your commandments are righteousness.[118]

As we move into the next chapter, we can do so with confidence that God's entire Word is true and trustworthy, but just recognizing that fact is not enough. It is by *accepting* God's Word into our hearts by faith that the new birth takes place.

> Since you have purified your souls in *obeying the truth through the Spirit* in sincere love of the brethren, love one another fervently with a pure heart, having been *born again*, not of corruptible seed but incorruptible, *through the word of God* which lives and abides forever, because "All flesh is as grass, and all the glory of man as the flower of the grass. the grass withers, and its flower falls away, but *the word of the LORD endures forever.*"[119]

As we study the third phase of Rome, there will likely be truths that will cut deeply into your heart, but that is exactly what the Word of God is designed to do. If we take hold of it by faith, the Word of God will remove from us the mind of Satan and give us the mind of Christ. "For the *word of God* is *living* and *powerful*, and *sharper than any two-edged sword*, piercing

---

[111] Psalm 119:11
[112] Psalm 119:89
[113] Psalm 119:105
[114] Psalm 119:114
[115] Psalm 119:140
[116] Psalm 119:160
[117] Psalm 119:162
[118] Psalm 119:172
[119] 1 Peter 1:22–25 (emphasis added)

even to the division of soul and spirit, and of joints and marrow, and is a *discerner of the thoughts and intents of the heart.*"[120]

As we continue this study, I invite you to open your heart to the Word and will of God!

---

[120] Hebrews 4:12 (emphasis added)

Chapter 4

The Attack of the Antichrist

The third phase of Rome is one of the most significant parts of the prophecy of Daniel 7. Revelation speaks of this phase of Rome when describing the final events just before Jesus returns. It tells us this phase of Rome is one of the major players in end-time events. It is extremely crucial for us to accurately identify and thoroughly understand the principles of its operation.

We will look at ten identifying points. Statistically, if all ten points of the prophecy are fulfilled by one power, we can know for sure we have identified the correct power. Let us see how Daniel 7 describes this power:

I was considering the horns, and there was *another horn*, a *little one*, coming up *among them*, before whom *three of the first horns were plucked out by the roots*. And there, in this horn, were *eyes like the eyes of a man*, and a *mouth speaking pompous words*.[121]

Then I wished to know the truth about the fourth beast, which was different from all the others, exceedingly dreadful, with its teeth of iron and its nails of bronze, which devoured, broke in pieces, and trampled the residue with its feet; and the ten horns that were on its head, and the other horn which came up, *before which three fell*, namely, that horn which had *eyes* and a *mouth which spoke pompous words*, whose *appearance was greater than his fellows*. I was watching; and the same horn was *making war against the saints*, and prevailing against them.[122]

---

[121] Daniel 7:8 (emphasis added)
[122] Daniel 7:19–21 (emphasis added)

The *ten horns* are *ten kings who shall arise from this kingdom*. And *another shall rise after them*; He shall be *different from the first ones*, And shall *subdue three kings*. He shall *speak pompous words against the Most High*, Shall *persecute the saints of the Most High*, And shall *intend to change times and law*. Then the saints shall be given into his hand for *a time and times and half a time*.[123]

This little horn power is none other than the antichrist power, which is further described in Revelation 13. Let us list the ten identifying points as we find them in the passages above:

1. The little-horn power comes up "among" the ten horns, which we identified in the last chapter as the nations of Europe in Rome's second phase.[124] Therefore, this power arises somewhere in Europe.
2. It comes up "after" Rome divided into the ten nations of Europe.[125] This means it came up after AD 476, since Rome was divided by that year.
3. "He shall subdue" ("plucked out by the roots"; "before which three fell") three of the ten nations of Europe.[126]
4. It has "eyes like the eyes of a man."[127] In the Bible, a prophet is called a "seer" because he or she sees with God's eyes.[128] Having eyes like the eyes of a man would indicate a power using human wisdom instead of God's wisdom—a religious system based on mankind's teachings.
5. It speaks "pompous words* against the most High"[129] (*"great things," according to the marginal reading).[130]

    A. Revelation speaks of this same power: "And he was given a *mouth* speaking *great things* and *blasphemies*, and he was given authority to continue for forty-two months. Then he opened his mouth in *blasphemy against God*, to blaspheme His *name*, His *tabernacle*, and those who *dwell in heaven*."[131]

---

[123] Daniel 7:24, 25 (emphasis added)
[124] Daniel 7:8
[125] Daniel 7:24
[126] Daniel 7:24 (emphasis added; see also vs. 8, 20)
[127] Daniel 7:8 (see also v. 20)
[128] See 1 Samuel 9:9; Psalm 32:8
[129] Daniel 7:25
[130] See also Daniel 7:8, 20
[131] Revelation 13:5, 6 (emphasis added)

B. One of the prime definitions of blasphemy in the Bible is when a human professes to take upon oneself the prerogatives that belong to God alone. Let me give you two examples of this:

   I. "Why doth this Man speak *blasphemies like this? Who can forgive sins but God only?*"[132] Jesus was accused of blasphemy because He forgave a man of his sins. If He was a mere human, He would have been blaspheming; but Jesus was (and still is) 100% God as well as 100% man. Therefore, He was not blaspheming. However, a mere human claiming the power to forgive sins is blaspheming—speaking great things against the Most High.

   II. Another example of blasphemy is when a person claims to be God on earth. "'I and My Father are one.' Then the Jews took up stones again to stone Him. Jesus answered them, 'Many good works I have shown you from My Father. For which of those works do you stone Me?' The Jews answered Him, saying, 'For a good work we do not stone You, but for *blasphemy*, and because *You, being a Man, make Yourself God.*'"[133]

   Again, Jesus was accused of blasphemy, but He was not blaspheming because He is God.[134]

6. It was a "little horn"[135] "whose appearance was greater than his fellows."[136] This was a small kingdom among the nations of Europe, but it had a disproportionate amount of power. It exercised control over the other European nations.
7. This power would "persecute the saints of the Most High."[137]
8. This little horn would "intend to change times and law."[138]

   A. Even though it would intend to change God's "times" and "law," in reality, it does not have the ability to do so. However, it will appear it has done so.

---

[132] Mark 2:7 (emphasis added; see also Luke 5:20, 21)
[133] John 10:30–33 (emphasis added)
[134] See Matthew 1:23; John 1:1–14
[135] Daniel 7:8
[136] Daniel 7:20
[137] Daniel 7:25 (see also v. 21)
[138] Daniel 7:25

B. The word "times" here indicates the idea of "prophetic times." Therefore, it will try to change God's prophecies, just as King Nebuchadnezzar tried to do in Daniel 3.
   C. In the context, the word "law" can only refer to God's holy, moral law. Therefore, it will intend to change His Ten Commandments.
9. It will be "different from the first ones."[139] As we have seen, this kingdom not only has a political nature like the other kingdoms of Europe have, but it also has a religious nature because it claims to have powers that only belong to God. We found this characteristic in the feet and toes of the Daniel 2 image: they were composed of iron and clay, which indicate a church/state combination.
10. "Then the saints shall be given into his hand for a time and times and half a time."[140] Just like the beasts and horns are symbolic, so this timeframe is symbolic. A length of time is only symbolic when it is found in a passage of apocalyptic prophecy.
   A. "A time" refers to one year. In the Bible/Hebrew context, a year had 360 days.
   B. "Times" being plural without a number in front of it (e.g., five times) refers to two years, which would equal 720 days.
   C. "Half a time" would refer to half a year or 180 days.
   D. If you add those numbers together (360 + 720 + 180), you come up with 1,260 days. As we will see clearly in a later chapter, a day in symbolic Bible prophecy represents a literal year.[141]
   E. Therefore, this power would last for 1,260 years. This timeframe is mentioned seven times in Daniel and Revelation.[142] Seven is a significant number in the Bible. Do you think God is telling us to pay special attention to this period of time? The events during the 1,260 years are very significant for us living at the end of time. It identifies one of the major players in end-time events.

---

[139] Daniel 7:24
[140] Daniel 7:25
[141] See Numbers 14:34 and Ezekiel 4:6 for examples of the day-year principle
[142] See Daniel 7:25; 12:7; Revelation 11:2, 3; 12:6, 14; 13:5. Forty-two months times thirty days in a biblical/Hebrew month equals 1,260 days.

Now, let us list the ten identifying points of the little-horn power succinctly:

1. It comes up among the ten nations of Europe
2. It comes up after Rome divides into the ten nations of Europe
3. It destroys three of the ten nations of Europe
4. It has a religious system based on human teachings
5. It claims powers that belong to God alone
6. It is a small kingdom that exercises control over the other European nations
7. It persecuted the true followers of God
8. It is intent on changing God's prophecies and the Ten Commandments
9. It is different from the other nations of Europe in that it is a politico-religious power
10. It retained power over Europe for 1,260 years

There is only one power that matches all ten of these characteristics. However, before we identify this antichrist power, I want to state again that the information in this chapter was believed and preached by Martin Luther, John Calvin, John Wesley, John Knox, and many others. This is what gave strength to the Protestant Reformation. I want to emphatically state that God has true followers in every Christian denomination and fellowship that exists today. This prophecy is not pointing a finger at individuals, but at institutions, powers, and systems of belief that affect our relationship with God. This relationship is the most important thing at stake!

The purpose of this prophecy is not to condemn, but to save those who will heed the warning. Jesus is the living Word of God,[143] and the writings of the prophets are considered the "testimony" of Jesus.[144] Jesus clearly declared His intentions: "For God so *loved* the world that He gave His only begotten Son, that whoever believes in Him *should not perish* but have *everlasting life*. For God *did not* send His Son into the world to *condemn* the world, but that the world through Him *might be saved*."[145]

God does not reveal these truths to condemn anyone. He wants to save everyone. God demonstrated the fact that He would rather die than see even one person lost. That is what the cross of Christ is all about! "The Lord is not slack concerning His promise, as some count slackness,

---

[143] See John 1:1–3, 14
[144] See Isaiah 8:20; Luke 24:25–27; John 5:39; 1 Corinthians 1:4–7; Revelation 1:1–3; 19:10)
[145] John 3:16, 17 (emphasis added)

but is *longsuffering toward us*, not willing that *any should perish* but that *all* should come to *repentance*."[146]

If you have been running away from God, repentance is turning around and running toward Him. Repentance from sin includes sorrow for sin *and* turning away from it. Our hearts are prone to wander from God. We need to continually seek a closer relationship with Him.

Let us take each of these ten identifying characteristics and see how they match with history:

1. It comes up among the ten nations of Europe

    During the first few centuries after the death of Christ, a center of religious power and authority began to develop in the city of Rome. The bishop of Rome slowly began to extend his control over an increasing percentage of Christianity. His decisions as well as the decisions of church councils over which he presided gradually became more authoritative than the Bible. The apostle Paul repeatedly warned about this development:

> *I want to emphatically state that God has true followers in every Christian denomination and fellowship that exists today. This prophecy is not pointing a finger at individuals, but at institutions, powers, and systems of belief that affect our relationship with God.*

> For I know this, that *after my departure* savage wolves will come in among you, not sparing the flock. Also from among yourselves men will rise up, *speaking perverse things*, to draw away the disciples after themselves.... So now, brethren, *I commend you to God and to the word of His grace*, which is able to *build you up* and give you an *inheritance* among all those who are sanctified.[147]

And again, he wrote about the development of this system of religion:

> For the *time will come* when they will *not endure sound doctrine*, but according to their *own desires*, because they have

---
[146] 2 Peter 3:9 (emphasis added)
[147] Acts 20:29–32 (emphasis added)

itching ears, they will heap up for themselves teachers; and they will turn their ears *away from the truth*, and be turned aside to *fables*.[148]

The apostle John stated the antichrist power had already begun developing toward the close of his life. Even though the full power of antichrist was not manifest, the "spirit" or attitude (disposition, principles) was rearing its ugly head. The full manifestation was yet to come, but of this power he clearly stated, "And this is the *spirit* of the *Antichrist*, which you have heard was coming, and is *now already in the world*."[149]

2. It comes up after Rome divides into the ten nations of Europe

Rome divided into the ten nations of Europe by AD 476. It took five hundred years after the death and resurrection of Christ for the bishop of Rome to gain controlling power over all of Europe. It was in AD 538 that the bishop of Rome, who by that time had taken the title of "pope," solidified his power to control the minds and consciences of western Christians. The only ones who did not submit to his power were the ones who maintained the Bible as the supreme authority.

By AD 538, the city of Rome lay largely in ruins, and the population had diminished to about 20,000 residents. Five years earlier, Emperor Justinian had elevated the pope to be the supreme leader of Christianity, but now he made Vigilius not only the new pope but also gave him the emperor's throne, authority, and royal titles like "Pontifex Maximus." Therefore, the Holy Roman Empire was established. Revelation predicted this event.[150] "The dragon gave him his *power*, his *throne*, and *great authority*."[151]

3. It destroys three of the ten nations of Europe

By the early AD 500s, virtually all of Europe had embraced the Christian faith. However, not all were in harmony with the pope of Rome. The churches in three countries (Heruli, Vandals, and Ostrogoths) embraced a theology called Arianism, which denied

---

[148] 2 Timothy 4:3, 4 (emphasis added)
[149] 1 John 4:3 (emphasis added)
[150] See Keum Young Ahn et al., "538 A.D. and the Transition from Pagan Roman Empire to Holy Roman Empire: Justinian's Metamorphosis from Chief of Staffs to Theologian," International Journal of Humanities and Social Science 7 (2017).
[151] Revelation 13:2 (emphasis added)

the Catholic teaching of the Trinity. Therefore, the pope orchestrated their destruction. This signaled the end of the second phase of Rome and the beginning of the third phase in 538.

Historian Robert Browning wrote in great detail of how the Heruli, Vandals, and the Ostrogoths were uprooted by the church's effort to establish authority. He described the conquest of the Heruli and their king Odoacer, then went on to give an account of Justinian's final battle with the Vandals in AD 534.

After describing this battle, Browning stated, "The Vandal force no longer existed. Indeed, the Vandals as a people vanished from the face of the earth." He then described the retaking of Rome from the Ostrogoths in the spring of AD 538 and stated that shortly thereafter, "the Ostrogothic kingdom had ceased to exist."[152]

4. It has a religious system based on mankind's teachings

The Roman Catholic Church makes some very high claims regarding its authority to change the Word of God and sets the decrees of its church councils equal with or above the authority of the Bible. They boldly declare:

> The *Pope* is of so great *authority* and power that he can *modify*, explain, or interpret even divine laws.[153]

The Council of Trent took decisive action in regard to the authority of Scripture and tradition:

> The first decision dealt with the matter of *authority*. The Council decreed that both *Scripture* and *tradition* were to be of *equal authority*. This was a denial of the position known as sola scriptura or the Bible alone possessing the supreme authority in the Church.... The Council of Trent also reiterated the *Church's sole authority* to *interpret the Scriptures*. This reinforced the position of the Magisterium or the teaching office of the Church. The *exclusive right of the Church* to *interpret Scripture* was one of the positions that Luther had attacked in

---

[152] See Robert Browning, Justinian and Theodora (New York: Thames and Hudson, 1987), pp. 24, 25, 98, 111, 114

[153] Lucius Ferraris, "Papa," art. 2, Prompta Bibliotheca, Vol. VI, (Venice: Gaspar Storti, 1772), p. 29 (emphasis added)

his tract, An Address to the Christian Nobility of the German Nation.[154]

The Catholic Catechism states:

> *Sacred Tradition* and *Sacred Scripture* make up a single sacred deposit of the *Word of God*.[155]

However, Jesus makes it clear that the Bible—not the church—is our only source of truth. He trusted His word to common people like fishermen and tax collectors instead of to scholars and religious leaders. This clearly indicates, through the working of the Holy Spirit, the common believer can read and understand the Bible correctly. Praying about His humble disciples, Jesus said, "*Sanctify* them by Your truth. *Your word is truth.*"[156]

It is impossible to hold the Bible, church tradition, and decrees of church councils as having equal authority because they contradict each other repeatedly. You have to take one as having greater authority, and in practice, the Church of Rome takes tradition and the decrees of church councils over the Bible.

By elevating church tradition to be of equal authority with Scripture and restricting biblical interpretation to the Catholic clergy, the papacy has effectively put the words of mankind where only the Word of God belongs. This destroys the sanctifying power of the Bible. Paul, writing to young Timothy, stated an interesting fact regarding salvation:

> And that from childhood you have known the *Holy Scriptures*, which are able to make you wise for *salvation through faith which is in Christ Jesus*. *All Scripture* is given by inspiration of God, and is profitable for *doctrine*, for reproof, for correction, for instruction in righteousness, that the *man of God* may be complete, thoroughly equipped for every good work.[157]

The Bible is for every believer to read, study, and understand—not just scholars and church leaders. The real danger of

---

[154] Dr. Herbert Samworth, "The Council of Trent," Grace Sola Foundation, Inc., https://1ref.us/1o3 (accessed February 3, 2021) (emphasis added)
[155] Peter Geiermann, The Convert's Catechism of Catholic Doctrine (St. Louis, MO: B. Herder Book Co., 1957) (emphasis added)
[156] John 17:17 (emphasis added)
[157] 2 Timothy 3:15–17 (emphasis added)

restricting the interpretation of the Bible to clergy is that it limits a person's ability to understand the true plan of salvation. It hinders our relationship with God. This is Satan's goal. He wants you to  be lost with him. As we go through these characteristics, it will become clear why this little-horn power is called antichrist.

5. It claims powers that belong to God alone

> Note the claims of the Roman Church:
>
> Seek where you will, through heaven and earth, and you will find one created being who *can forgive the sinner*, who can *free him from the chains of hell*. That extraordinary being is the priest, the *Roman Catholic priest*.[158]
>
> *The official powers of the priest*: The *official powers of the priest* are intimately connected with the sacramental character, indelibly imprinted on his *soul*. Together with this character is conferred, not only the power of offering up the *Sacrifice of the Mass* and the (virtual) *power of forgiving sins*, but also authority to administer extreme unction and, as the regular minister, solemn *baptism*.[159]
>
> Pope John Paul II declared, "Confronted with the *Pope*, one must make a choice. The leader of the Catholic Church is defined by the faith as the *Vicar of Jesus Christ* (and is accepted as such by believers). The Pope is considered the *man on earth who represents the Son of God*, who 'takes the place' of the Second Person of the omnipotent God of the Trinity."[160]

---

[158] Michael Muller, CSSR, The Catholic Priest (Baltimore, MD: Kreuzer Brothers, 1872), pp. 78, 79 (emphasis added)

[159] *Catholic Encyclopedia,* Priesthood: https://1ref.us/1o5 (accessed February 3, 2021) (emphasis added)

[160] Pope John Paul II, Crossing the Threshold of Hope (New York: Alfred A. Knopf, Inc., 1994), p. 3.

These are blasphemous statements that directly contradict the Bible. Notice what the Bible says:

> For there is one God and *one Mediator* between God and men, the Man *Christ Jesus*.[161]
>
> If we confess our sins, He is *faithful* and *just* to *forgive us our sins* and to cleanse us from all unrighteousness.[162]

Church traditions and decrees of popes and councils contradict the Bible. Ultimately, one has to take one over the other. Regarding this same antichrist power, we read:

> He even *exalted himself* as high as the *Prince of the host*; and by him the daily sacrifices were taken away, and the place of His sanctuary was cast down. Because of transgression, an army was given over to the horn to oppose the daily sacrifices; and *he cast truth down to the ground*. He did all this and prospered.[163]

The apostle Paul also spoke of this power:

> Let no one deceive you by any means; for that Day will not come unless the *falling away comes first*, and the *man of sin* is revealed, the son of perdition, who opposes and *exalts himself above all that is called God* or that is worshiped, so that he *sits as God* in the *temple of God*, showing himself that *he is God*.[164]

Some people think the "temple of God" spoken of here is a rebuilt Jewish temple in Jerusalem. If the Jewish temple is ever rebuilt, they will be offering animal sacrifices just like they did before Christ died for our sins on the cross. That will be the clearest sign that it is not the "temple of God." Jesus, the true Lamb of God, has given His life for us.[165] Restarting animal sacrifices would be a rejection of Jesus!

In the New Testament, the church (true believers in Jesus) is described as the temple of God.

---

[161] 1 Timothy 2:5 (emphasis added)
[162] 1 John 1:9 (emphasis added)
[163] Daniel 8:11, 12 (emphasis added)
[164] 2 Thessalonians 2:3, 4 (emphasis added)
[165] See John 1:29; 1 Corinthians 5:7

If anyone defiles the *temple of God*, God will destroy him. For the *temple of God* is holy, *which temple you are*.[166]

Now, therefore, you are no longer strangers and foreigners, but fellow citizens with the saints and *members of the household of God*, having been built on the foundation of the *apostles* and *prophets, Jesus Christ Himself being the chief cornerstone*, in whom the whole building, being fitted together, grows into a *holy temple* in the Lord, in whom you also are being built together for a *dwelling place of God in the Spirit*.[167]

And what agreement has the *temple of God* with idols? For *you are the temple of the living God*. As God has said: "*I will dwell in them* and walk among them. I will be their God, and they shall by my people."[168]

Paul's prediction in 2 Thessalonians 2 was fulfilled by the pope of Rome exerting his power over the Christian church, the temple of God. He claims to have powers that belong to God alone.

Much more could be said about this identifying point, but I want to remind you that God did not give this prophecy for the purpose of condemnation. He gave it for the purpose of salvation for those outside *and inside* the Catholic Church. The critical issue is salvation. When a mere human is placed where only God belongs, the gospel loses its saving power. Likewise, when the words of mankind are believed over and above the Word of God, the creative power of the Word is lost, and the believer is left to battle with the host of darkness without the armor of God.[169]

> **Much more could be said about this identifying point, but I want to remind you that God did not give this prophecy for the purpose of condemnation. He gave it for the purpose of salvation for those outside and inside the Catholic Church.**

---

[166] 1 Corinthians 3:17 (emphasis added)
[167] Ephesians 2:19–22 (emphasis added)
[168] 2 Corinthians 6:16 (emphasis added)
[169] See Ephesians 6:10–18

Christ's access to the heart is blocked by human wisdom, and therefore society loses its only safety net against the freefall into wrongdoing. God's armor provides us with only one offensive weapon with which to defeat the forces of evil, and that is the "sword of the Spirit which is the *Word of God*."[170]

6. It is a small kingdom that exercised control over the other European nations

Even though Vatican City occupies only 109 acres of land, it has exercised a disproportionate amount of political and religious control throughout the centuries and still does today. The papacy has never had an army of their own, but they have been able to persuade the nations around them to fight their wars.

Notice the following regarding Vatican City:

> The Holy See, often referred to as Vatican City or simply the Vatican, is the seat of the Roman Catholic Church and its ruler, the Supreme Pontiff or Pope. The Holy See is not only the world's smallest independent state, but the workings of its government and financial affairs are unique, as are its non-commercially based economic structures, which do not conform to any conventional pattern.[171]

> The Holy See has diplomatic relations with one hundred and eighty-one countries! What other church has that global political power today? None![172]

7. It persecuted the true followers of God

British Historian William Edward Lecky wrote, "That the *Church of Rome* has *shed more innocent blood* than any other institution that has ever existed among mankind, will be questioned by no Protestant who has a *competent knowledge of history*."[173]

The Church of Rome tried for centuries to annihilate other Christian groups, such as the Waldenses, Huguenots, Albigenses, Protestants, Lollards, and others who kept the Bible as their sole

---

[170] Ephesians 6:17 (emphasis added)
[171] https://1ref.us/1o6 (accessed February 4, 2021)
[172] See https://1ref.us/1o7 (accessed February 17, 2021)
[173] William Lecky, The History of the Rise and Influence of the Spirit of Rationalism in Europe, Vol. 2 (London: Longmans, Green, & Co., 1872), p. 32 (emphasis added)

authority. It is conservatively estimated that at least 50 million Christians were tortured and killed by the Church of Rome, and their only crime was they believed the Bible should be their highest religious authority.

All one needs to do is study into the Catholic Church's use of the Inquisition to see how they forced people to accept their doctrines and control. Millions were burned at the stake, but that was merciful in comparison to their other methods of torture and death. I have been to museums of the Inquisition in Europe and know what I am saying. I will not dwell on this point further because it is so dark.

8. It intends to change God's prophecies and the Ten Commandments

The Church of Rome has largely been effective in accomplishing both goals for most of Christianity. However, they can never really do either. "For I am the LORD, *I do not change*; Therefore you are not consumed, O sons of Jacob."[174]

Let us first deal with their intent to change God's prophecies. This came as a result of their attempt to change the Protestant method of interpreting Bible prophecy. The Protestant reformers were the first to label the pope as antichrist:

> Wycliffe, Tyndale, Luther, Calvin, Cranmer; in the seventeenth century, Bunyan, the translators of the King James Bible and the men who published the Westminster and Baptist Confessions of Faith; Sir Isaac Newton, John Wesley, Whitfield, Jonathan Edwards; and more recently, Spurgeon, Bishop J.C. Ryle and Dr. Martyn Lloyd-Jones; these men among countless others, *all saw the office of the Papacy as the antichrist....* The Reformers and their heirs were great scholars and knew the Word of God and the Holy Spirit as a living teacher.[175]
>
> Many of the great Christians of Reformation and post-Reformation times shared this view of prophetic truth and *identified antichrist with the Roman Papacy...* Among Adherents of this interpretation were the Waldenses, the Hussites, Wycliffe,

---

[174] Malachi 3:6 (emphasis added)
[175] Michael De Semlyen, All Roads Lead to Rome (Gerrards Cross, England: Dorchester House, 2010), pp. 205, 206 (emphasis added)

Luther, Calvin, Zwingli, Melanchthon, Tyndale, Latimer, and Ridley.[176]

Leaders such as Luther, Calvin, Knox, and Cranmer, pointed to Daniel 7 and Revelation 17, *identifying the great apostasy with headquarters in Rome*. The Scriptural message of Revelation 18:4 formed the basis of many of their sermons, "Come out of her, my people, that ye be not partakers of her sins."[177]

Because the reformers were having such great success in drawing people away from the Catholic Church by teaching Bible prophecy, the pope commissioned two Jesuit priests to find alternative ways to interpret prophecy that would alleviate the stigma of antichrist from the pope. Those two Jesuit priests were Luis de Alcazar (AD 1554–1613) and Francisco Ribera (AD 1537–1591). A renowned Protestant scholar wrote about Ribera's futurist theory:

> It will probably come as a shock to many modern futurists to be told that the first scholar in relatively modern times who returned to the patristic futuristic interpretation was a *Spanish Jesuit named Ribera*. In *1590* Ribera published a commentary on the Revelation as a *counter-interpretation* to the prevailing view among Protestants which identified the papacy with the Antichrist. *Ribera applied all of Revelation but the earliest chapters to the end time rather than to the history of the Church. Antichrist would be a single evil person who would be received by the Jews and would rebuild Jerusalem, abolish Christianity, deny Christ, persecute the Church and rule the world for three and a half years.*[178]

Therefore, with this reinterpretation, the little-horn power of Daniel 7 and the beast power of Revelation 13 and 17 could not refer to the papacy. Ribera was successful in developing an interpretation that relieved the pope of the label "antichrist." This theory remained within the Catholic Church for approximately two hundred years. In the 1800s, a few Protestant scholars began

---

[176] George Eldon Ladd, The Blessed Hope (Grand Rapids, MI: Eerdman's, 1972), p. 33 (emphasis added)

[177] R. A. Anderson, Unfolding Daniel's Prophecies (Mountain View, CA: Pacifica Press Publishing Association, 1974), p. 92 (emphasis added)

[178] Ladd, The Blessed Hope, p. 37 (emphasis added).

to embrace it, and in the 1900s, it became popular within the Evangelical community. This is the theory that the "Left Behind" books and videos have made popular in recent years.

Luis de Alcazar, the other Jesuit priest, developed a very different theory than Ribera did. Alcazar promoted the idea that the little horn of Daniel 7 was fulfilled by Antiochus Epiphanies, a Seleucid king of the Hellenistic Syrian kingdom who reigned from 175–164 BC.[179] He also proposed the beast power of Revelation was fulfilled by Nero, the Roman *emperor*, who ruled from AD 54–68. It was Nero who had the apostle Paul beheaded.

This theory proposes the prophecies of Daniel and Revelation were fulfilled long before the papacy came into existence, so these prophecies could in no way refer to the pope. Today, many Protestants have embraced this view of prophecy. Therefore, the papacy has been largely successful in changing God's prophetic times. He has been able to do to almost all of Christianity what Nebuchadnezzar tried to do with the golden image in Daniel 3.

Continuing on, what about the little horn's intent to change God's law? Has the Catholic Church tried to do that? And if they have, how successful have they been throughout Christendom? To answer these questions, I will quote from their own sources:

> The Church, after *changing the day of rest* from the Jewish *Sabbath of the seventh day of the week*, made the third Commandment refer to *Sunday as the day to be kept as the Lord's day*.[180]

Of course it is not the Sabbath of the Jews. It was given to all of mankind at creation.[181]

> Perhaps the boldest thing, the most revolutionary *change the Church ever did* happened in the first century. The holy day, *the Sabbath, was changed from Saturday to Sunday*… not from any directions noted in the Scriptures, but from the Church's sense of its own power… People who think that the *Scriptures*

---

[179] See Appendix A for further study into this false theory
[180] *The Catholic Encyclopedia*, Vol. 4, An International Work of Reference on the Constitution, Doctrine, Discipline, and History of the Catholic Church (Classic Reprint) (London: Forgotten Books, 2017), p. 153 (emphasis added)
[181] See Genesis 2:1–3; Mark 2:27, 28

should be the sole authority, should logically become Seventh-day Adventists, and *keep Saturday holy*.[182]

It was actually during the second and third centuries that this change took place, but the point is that the Roman Church claims to have made the change. The Archbishop of Baltimore made the following statement:

> You may read the Bible from *Genesis to Revelation*, and you will *not find a single line authorizing the sanctification of Sunday*.[183]

The Convert's Catechism of Catholic Doctrine, written by the Archbishop of St. Louis, states the following regarding the Sabbath commandment. It is in question-and-answer format. You will notice they number their commandments differently. The reason they do this will become clear.

Q. What is the Third Commandment?
A. The Third Commandment is: *Remember that thou keep holy the Sabbath day*.

Q. Which is the Sabbath day?
A. *Saturday is the Sabbath day*.

Q. Why do we observe Sunday instead of Saturday?
A. We observe Sunday instead of Saturday because *the Catholic Church transferred the solemnity from Saturday to Sunday*.

Q. Why did the Catholic Church substitute Sunday for Saturday?
A. The Church substituted Sunday for Saturday, because Christ rose from the dead on a Sunday, and the Holy Ghost descended upon the Apostles on a Sunday.

Q. By what authority did the Church substitute Sunday for Saturday?

---

[182] *Saint Catherine Catholic Church Sentinel*, Vol. 50, Number 22, Algonac, MI, May 21, 1995 (emphasis added)
[183] James Gibbons, The Faith of Our Fathers (London: John Murphy & Co., 1898), pp. 111, 112 (emphasis added)

A. The *Church substituted Sunday for Saturday by the plenitude of that divine power which Jesus Christ bestowed upon her.*[184]

That is what the church says, but what did God say and write with His own finger on tables of stone and promise to write on our hearts if we allow Him? The Sabbath commandment of the Bible reads as follows:

> *Remember the Sabbath day, to keep it holy.* Six days you shall labor and do all your work, but *the seventh day is the Sabbath* of the LORD your God. In it you shall do no work: you, nor your son, nor your daughter, nor your male servant, nor your female servant, nor your cattle, nor your stranger who is within your gates. For in six days the LORD made the heavens and the earth, the sea, and all that is in them, and *rested the seventh day*. Therefore the *LORD blessed the Sabbath day and hallowed it.*[185]

The commandment is clear. It says, "the seventh day is the Sabbath," not "a seventh day." Jesus, our Creator,[186] made the seventh day of creation week His holy day. The Catholic Church not only changed the Sabbath to Sunday (from the seventh day to the first day) without any authorization from Jesus, our Creator, but they also deleted the second commandment, which deals with idols. This is why they number their commandments differently. The second commandment is:

> You shall not make for yourself a *carved image*—any likeness of anything that is in heaven above, or that is in the earth beneath, or that is in the water under the earth; *you shall not bow down to them* nor serve them. For I, the LORD your God, am a jealous God, visiting the iniquity of the fathers upon the children to the third and fourth generations of those who hate Me, but showing mercy to thousands, to those who *love Me and keep My commandments.*[187]

---

[184] Peter Geiermann, The Convert's Catechism of Catholic Doctrine (St. Louis, MO: B. Herder Book Co., 1957).
[185] Exodus 20:8–11 (emphasis added)
[186] See John 1:1–3, 14; Colossians 1:16; Hebrews 1:1, 2
[187] Exodus 20:4–6 (emphasis added)

It is obvious why the Catholic Church wanted to minimize the second commandment. They have statues of Mary, the apostles, and others all over their churches, and they pray to them, especially to Mary.

The Bible makes it clear what God thinks of any attempt to change His law or Word in any way.

> My covenant I will not break, *Nor alter the word that has gone out of My lips*.[188]
>
> *Do not think* that I came to *destroy the Law* or the Prophets. *I did not come to destroy but to fulfill*. For assuredly, I say to you, till heaven and earth pass away, *one jot or one tittle will by no means pass from the law till all is fulfilled*.[189]
>
> You shall *not add to the word which I command* you, *nor take from it*, that you may *keep the commandments of the LORD* your God which I command you.[190]
>
> Whatever I command you, be careful to observe it; *you shall not add to it nor take away from it*.[191]
>
> For I testify to everyone who hears the words of the prophecy of this book: If anyone *adds to these things*, God will add to him the plagues that are written in this book; and if anyone *takes away from the words* of the book of this prophecy, God shall take away his part from the Book of Life, from the holy city, and from the things which are written in this book.[192]
>
> Hypocrites! Well did Isaiah prophesy about you, saying: "These people draw near to Me with their mouth, And honor Me with their lips, But their heart is far from Me. And in vain they worship Me, Teaching as doctrines the commandments of men."[193]

Trying to change God's Word is clearly a sin; but Jesus came to save us from sin.[194] There are two biblical definitions of sin, and they are inseparably related.

---

[188] Psalm 89:34 (emphasis added)
[189] Matthew 5:17, 18 (emphasis added)
[190] Deuteronomy 4:2 (emphasis added)
[191] Deuteronomy 12:32 (emphasis added)
[192] Revelation 22:18, 19 (emphasis added)
[193] Matthew 15:7–9
[194] See Matthew 1:21

- "Whosoever commits sin transgresses also the law: for *sin is the transgression of the law*."[195]
- "For whatever is *not from faith* is *sin*."[196]

The example of Eve illustrates the relationship between these two definitions of sin. God told Adam and Eve not to eat the fruit of the forbidden tree in the Garden of Eden. If they did, they would die.[197] This was the only thing God commanded them not to do. However, Satan, using the medium of the serpent,[198] enticed Eve to eat it, saying, "You will not surely die."[199] He directly contradicted God. Eve believed Satan's lie and doubted God's word of truth, and her lack of faith led her to transgress God's commandment.

True obedience follows faith in God's Word. Disobedience follows doubt or ignorance of God's Word. The issue boils down to faith.

In order to maintain ten commandments, after dropping the second one, the Roman Church divided the tenth commandment into two. Therefore, they have effectively changed God's law in two ways, and most of Christianity has gone along with their substitution of Sunday for Sabbath. The majority of Christianity believes the pope's word and doubts God's Word.

> *True obedience follows faith in God's Word. Disobedience follows doubt or ignorance of God's Word. The issue boils down to faith.*

The issue is far more than just one day versus another day. The issue is faith. Who do you believe? Whose word do you accept? If you compromise here, what will keep you from compromising in other areas? In a future study, we will see how important this Sabbath/Sunday issue really is. We will see true Sabbath keeping is the sign of our faith relationship with

---

[195] 1 John 3:4 (KJV; emphasis added)
[196] Romans 14:23 (emphasis added)
[197] See Genesis 2:16, 17
[198] See Revelation 12:7–9
[199] Genesis 3:4

God—not a works relationship! We will also find there is a vast difference between true Sabbath keeping and mere Saturday keeping.

9. It is different from the other nations of Europe in that it is a politico-religious power

   This characteristic needs little explanation, but I will quote one historian's analysis of the Papal power: "Out of the chaos of the great Northern migrations, and the ruins of the Roman Empire, there gradually arose a new order of states, whose central point was the Papal See. Therefrom inevitably resulted a position not only new, but very different from the former."[200]

10. It retained power over Europe for 1,260 years

    The Papacy gained its power in AD 538. The question is, Did anything significant happen to the papacy 1,260 years later, in 1798? The answer is, Yes, something very significant.

    Napoleon was the king of France at that time, and the French Revolution (May 5, 1789–November 9, 1799) was in full sway. Belief in God and the Bible had been thrown out, and the goddess of reason was set up in their place. In 1798, an incident took place in Rome that gave Napoleon the excuse for which he was looking to send General Berthier into Rome, arrest the pope, and remove his civil powers.

    "Berthier entered Rome on 10th February 1798, and proclaimed a Republic. The aged Pontiff refused to violate his oath by recognizing it, and was hurried from prison to prison into France. Broken with fatigue and sorrow, he died . . . [in] August 1799, in the French fortress of Valence, aged 82 years. No wonder that half Europe thought Napoleon's veto would be obeyed, and that with the Pope the Papacy was dead."[201]

    Even though a new pope was elected, he did not have the civil authority the papacy had exercised for the previous 1,260 years.

---

[200] J.J. Ignatious Von Dollinger, The Church and the Churches (London: Hurst and Blackett Publishing, 1862), p. 42 (emphasis added)

[201] Joseph Rickaby, "The Modern Papacy," in *Lectures on the History of Religions,* Vol. 3, [lecture 24, p. 1] (London: Catholic Truth Society, 1910).

This ended the third phase of Rome. The world rejoiced, thinking the papacy would never regain its power, but oh, how wrong they were! The book of Revelation predicted this blow to the papal power, calling it a "deadly wound." However, it also indicated the wound would be healed.

"And I saw one of his heads as if it had been *mortally wounded*, and his *deadly wound was healed*. And *all* the world *marveled* and *followed* the beast."[202] We will look at that prophecy in Revelation in greater detail in a future chapter. You will see the wound is now in the process of being healed.

Here is a chart of the three phases of Rome:

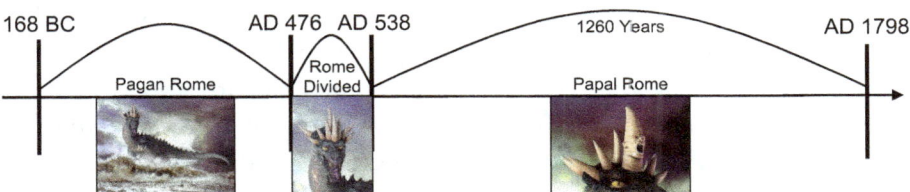

We live in a battlefield that affects us not only spiritually, but physically, mentally, and socially. Before Jesus came to this world, Satan had been successful in leading God's people, the Jewish nation, into apostasy and open rebellion against God.[203] When Jesus was born in Bethlehem over 2,000 years ago, the world had fallen into deep darkness. Sickness and misery were everywhere.

That is why Jesus spent so much of His time healing those in need. He demonstrated that God is compassionate and cares for our wellbeing. Suffering and sickness are not caused by God but by His adversary, the devil. "And Jesus went about all Galilee, *teaching* in their synagogues, *preaching* the gospel of the kingdom, and *healing* all kinds of *sickness* and all kinds of *disease* among the people."[204]

Just as Satan was successful in leading Israel into apostasy, so he has been successful in leading God's people, His church, into apostasy ("the falling away"). Jesus clearly revealed Satan's objective in contrast to His. "The thief does not come except to *steal*, and to *kill*, and to *destroy*. I have come that they may have *life*, and that they may have it *more abundantly*."[205]

---

[202] Revelation 13:3 (emphasis added)
[203] See 2 Chronicles 36:11–16
[204] Matthew 4:23 (emphasis added)
[205] John 10:10 (emphasis added)

Again, our society is being plunged into physical, mental, spiritual, and social chaos, and Satan is doing all he can to remove the only remedy—the only safety net. However, Jesus offers complete restoration and His perfect righteousness; He offers peace amid the storm.

This battle between the forces of righteousness (right doing) and the forces of evil (wrong doing) started in heaven before this world was created. What we are experiencing is the continuation of that war. Our victory in the battle is through "the blood of the Lamb," Jesus Christ. He is our safety net.

> And *war* broke out in heaven: Michael and his angels *fought* with the dragon; and the dragon and his angels *fought*, but they did not prevail, nor was a place found for them in heaven any longer. So the great dragon was cast out, that *serpent of old*, called the *Devil* and *Satan*, who *deceives the whole world*; he was cast to the earth, and his angels were cast out with him. Then I heard a loud voice saying in heaven, *"Now salvation, and strength, and the kingdom of our God, and the power of His Christ have come,* for the accuser of our brethren, who accused them before our God day and night, has been cast down. And *they overcame him by the blood of the Lamb and by the word of their testimony,* and they did not love their lives to the death."[206]

In this battle with Satan and his forces, Jesus is our only hope. The prophecies of Daniel make this clear. There are two parts to the prophecy of Daniel 7. One part is bad news and the other is good news. So far, we have covered the bad news with the rise of the little-horn power. Now we will look at the good news, so keep reading.

---

[206] Revelation 12:7–11 (emphasis added)

Chapter 5

God's Counterattack

According to Daniel 7, after the papacy received its deadly wound in 1798 (as we saw in the previous chapter), a special event transpired in heaven. That event affects us today! Most Christians have a good idea of what Jesus did for us when He walked on this earth 2,000 years ago, but few are aware of what Jesus is doing for us in heaven now. The last part of the prophecy of Daniel 7, along with the prophecies of chapters 8 and 9, pulls back the curtain and reveals Christ's work for us today. By now, I hope you recognize Bible prophecy is all about Jesus and His work to defend us from Satan's attacks in this war in which we all find ourselves.

There is good news! We can read the end of the story. Satan's forces will not win. Daniel assures us of this: "I watched then because of the sound of the *pompous words which the horn was speaking*; I watched till the *beast was slain*, and its body destroyed and given to the burning flame."[207]

Instead of the little horn on the beast being victorious, Jesus will win the war and give the kingdom of heaven to His faithful followers. This good news is repeated several times in Daniel 7, which is God's way of emphasizing its importance. Notice how this assurance is repeated:

> *By now, I hope you recognize Bible prophecy is all about Jesus and His work to defend us from Satan's attacks in this war in which we all find ourselves.*

> Then to Him [Son of Man] was given *dominion* and *glory* and a *kingdom*, that *all* peoples, nations, and languages should *serve Him*. His dominion is an *everlasting dominion*, which shall *not pass away*, and His kingdom the one Which shall *not be destroyed*.[208]

> But the *saints of the Most High* shall *receive the kingdom*, and *possess the kingdom* forever, even *forever and ever*.[209]

---

[207] Daniel 7:11 (emphasis added)
[208] Daniel 7:14 (emphasis added)
[209] Daniel 7:18 (emphasis added)

> *Judgment* was made in *favor of the saints of the Most High*, and the *time came* for the *saints to possess the kingdom.*[210]
>
> Then the *kingdom* and *dominion*, and the greatness of the kingdoms under the whole heaven, shall be *given to the people, the saints of the Most High*. His kingdom is an *everlasting kingdom*, and *all* dominions shall *serve and obey Him*.[211]

Wow! The entire world will be in harmony with God! Could the news get any better than that? Jesus described the characteristics of those who will be part of the kingdom of heaven in His famous sermon on the mount, in which He spoke the beatitudes:

> Blessed are the *poor in spirit*, for theirs is the kingdom of heaven.
> Blessed are those who *mourn*, for they shall be comforted.
> Blessed are the *meek*, for they shall inherit the earth.
> Blessed are those who *hunger and thirst for righteousness*, for they shall be filled.
> Blessed are the *merciful*, for they shall obtain mercy.
> Blessed are the *pure in heart*, for they shall see God.
> Blessed are the *peacemakers*, for they shall be called sons of God.
> Blessed are those who are *persecuted for righteousness' sake*, for theirs is the kingdom of heaven.[212]

Unfortunately, not everyone who claims to be a follower of Jesus displays those characteristics. Jesus mentioned this later in the sermon:

> *Not everyone* who says to Me, "*Lord, Lord,*" shall enter the *kingdom of heaven*, but he who *does the will of My Father* in heaven. Many will say to Me in that day, "Lord, Lord, have we not *prophesied* in Your name, *cast out demons* in Your name, and *done many wonders* in Your name?" And then I will declare to them, "*I never knew you*; depart from Me, you who practice *lawlessness!*"[213]

Therefore, the question is, How does God plan to solidify His kingdom and give it to His true followers? According to Daniel 7, that is the next event to take place after 1798. The answer is found in an unexpected solution: the judgment. Daniel explains:

---

[210] Daniel 7:22 (emphasis added)
[211] Daniel 7:27 (emphasis added)
[212] Matthew 5:3–10 (emphasis added)
[213] Matthew 7:21–23 (emphasis added)

> I watched till thrones were put in place, and the *Ancient of Days* was seated; His garment was white as snow, and the hair of His head was like pure wool. His throne was a fiery flame, its wheels a burning fire; A fiery stream issued and came forth from before Him. A thousand thousands ministered to Him; *Ten thousand times ten thousand* stood before Him. *The court was seated, And the books were opened*.[214]

The Ancient of Days is none other than God the Father, the first Person of the Godhead. This scene is the most important and exciting event taking place in heaven. The heavenly host are all gathered around God's throne to view the judgment process. The King James Version translates the last sentence this way: "The judgment was set, and the books were opened."

What is this judgment all about? Is it something of which to be afraid, or is it something to which to look forward? It is in the judgment that the kingdom of heaven is solidified and given to God's people; it is in the judgment that Satan and his forces are defeated; it is in the judgment that God and His people are vindicated and the verdict is rendered in their favor. In other words, the judgment is good news to those who put their faith in Jesus.

Daniel predicts when and where the judgment takes place, and Revelation describes it in more detail. In the heart of Revelation, we find three angels proclaiming three significant messages to the entire world. The first of these three messages is as follows:

> Then I saw another angel flying in the midst of heaven, having the *everlasting gospel* to preach to those who dwell on the earth—to *every nation, tribe, tongue,* and *people*—saying with a loud voice, "Fear God and give glory to Him, *for the hour of His judgment has come*; and worship Him who made heaven and earth, the sea and springs of water."[215]

This is a pronouncement that the judgment is no longer in the future, but in the present. In the next couple chapters, we will see the judgment is in process now, but first, we need to understand what this judgment is all about.

What about the books that are being opened in the judgment? What do these books contain? Why does God need books anyway?

---

[214] Daniel 7:9, 10 (emphasis added)
[215] Revelation 14:6, 7 (emphasis added)

> And behold, I am coming quickly, and My *reward* is with Me, to *give* to every one *according* to his *work*.[216]

We are judged according to our deeds, and God keeps a record of our deeds in His record system in heaven.

> And *books* were *opened*. And another book was opened, which is the *Book of Life*. And the dead were *judged* according to their *works*, by the *things* which were *written* in the *books*.[217]

We are not given our reward at the point of death, but at the glorious second coming of Jesus. Therefore, the judgment takes place before He returns.

> For the *Son of Man* will *come* in the glory of His Father with His angels, and *then* He will *reward* each *according* to his *works*.[218]

Therefore, in the judgment, our lives will be evaluated according to the way we live, speak, and behave. For those who do not have a love-faith relationship with Jesus, this truly is a frightening reality.

However, there is good news—wonderfully good news! Even though we are judged by our works (behavior), we are saved by God's grace through faith in Jesus Christ. "For by *grace* you have been *saved through faith*; and that not of yourselves: it is the *gift* of God: *Not of works*, lest anyone should *boast*."[219]

If we are saved by grace, you may ask, Why are we judged by what we do? The answer is simple: Words are cheap. The old saying is true: "Actions speak louder than words." Genuine faith in Jesus is a power that changes the way you live. Others around you will see the evidence by how you live your life. The Bible says, "Faith without works is dead."[220] This is especially important for us living in the time of the judgment. This is the reason Jesus asked a very penetrating question: "Nevertheless, when the *Son of Man comes*, will He *really find faith* on the earth?"[221]

"A thousand thousands ministered to Him; *Ten thousand times ten thousand stood before Him*. The court was seated, and the books were opened."[222] In assessing Daniel's description of the judgment, the atten-

---

[216] Revelation 22:12 (emphasis added)
[217] Revelation 20:12 (emphasis added)
[218] Matthew 16:27 (emphasis added)
[219] Ephesians 2:8, 9 (emphasis added)
[220] James 2:26
[221] Luke 18:8 (emphasis added)
[222] Daniel 7:10 (emphasis added)

tion of the heavenly host is riveted on the process. The host is composed of created beings, the heavenly angels who remained loyal to God when Satan and his angels rebelled and were eventually cast out of heaven.[223] These angels cannot read our minds as God can. The only way they can know if our faith is genuine is by the life we live.

Do you think the loyal angels want to know we will not start the rebellion all over again if we are brought to heaven? The evidence of our faith empowering a changed life is all they can examine. God is respectful of their concerns, so He judges us according to our works to see if they are produced by faith or not. We will return to that thought in a bit.

Daniel 8 talks about the judgment, using symbols from the Hebrew sanctuary services. "And he said to me, 'For *two thousand three hundred days*; then *the sanctuary shall be cleansed.*'"[224]

There are two parts to this verse: the time period and the event. We will deal with the time period in the next two chapters, but here, we will study the event: the cleansing of the sanctuary—symbolic language describing the judgment. When we understand the cleansing of the sanctuary, we will understand the significance and workings of the judgment.

Everything about the Hebrew sanctuary symbolizes Jesus and His work of saving us from our sins. Everything about it points to Jesus, our Savior. God's plan of salvation is revealed in the sanctuary. "*Your way*, O God, *is in the sanctuary*; Who is so great a God as our God?"[225]

God longs to be with us. However, sin separates us from Him.[226] It drives a wedge between us. The first thing Adam and Eve did when they sinned was hide from God. The problem is not on His part, but on ours. We are embarrassed and afraid to open our hearts to Him. Sin causes distrust and fear.

God's purpose for the Hebrew sanctuary was to draw near to His people and have fellowship and a loving relationship with them. Therefore, He instructed Moses to build the sanctuary. "And let them make Me a sanctuary, *that I may dwell among them.*"[227]

God wants to dwell in our hearts and lives. How this is to take place is the lesson the earthly sanctuary teaches. The earthly sanctuary was patterned after God's sanctuary in heaven.[228] It is to lead us to an intimate

---

[223] See Revelation 12:7–9
[224] Daniel 8:14 (emphasis added)
[225] Psalm 77:13 (emphasis added)
[226] See Isaiah 59:1, 2
[227] Exodus 25:8 (emphasis added)
[228] See Exodus 25:40; Hebrews 8:5

relationship with Jesus—a faith relationship—a "Christ in you" relationship. The apostle Paul wrote eloquently about this intimate relationship God wants with each of us:

> To them God willed to make known what are the riches of the glory of this mystery among the Gentiles: which is *Christ in you*, the *hope of glory*.[229]
>
> That He would grant you, according to the riches of His glory, to be *strengthened* with *might* through *His Spirit* in the *inner man*, that *Christ may dwell in your hearts through faith*.[230]

The sanctuary is a complete and balanced description of God's plan to save us from sin. However, we no longer need to practice the ceremonies (animal sacrifices, etc.) because Jesus, the true Lamb of God, has been slain for us. Still, we need to study the sanctuary carefully because, in so doing, it will keep us from overlooking vital parts of God's plan of salvation. It will also keep us from becoming unbalanced in our relationship with Jesus.

You will notice there was a courtyard surrounding the tabernacle (see chart on page 80). The fence around that courtyard was made of pure white linen. As soon as a sinner stepped through the open door into the courtyard, he (or she) was instantly surrounded by white, symbolizing the gift of Christ's righteousness (right doing), even before the sacrifice was made.

The person who sinned by breaking the Ten Commandments[231] would bring a lamb (or other specified animal) into the courtyard, place his hands on the head of the lamb, and confess his sin, thereby symbolically transferring the guilt of his sin onto the lamb.[232] He was then required to kill the lamb with his own hands. This all pointed forward to the promise that Jesus would die for our sins—not His, for He had no sin.[233]

The lamb's body was burned on the altar of sacrifice, which was the first piece of furniture you would approach when you walked into the courtyard. This represented the cross of Christ. However, some of the blood of the lamb was caught in a bowl, and the priest would sprinkle a few drops of that blood on the horns of the altar of incense, which was in

---

[229] Colossians 1:27 (emphasis added; see also Exodus 29:43–46)
[230] Ephesians 3:16, 17 (emphasis added)
[231] See 1 John 3:4 for the biblical definition of sin
[232] See Leviticus 1:4
[233] See 1 John 3:5

front of the curtain separating the Holy Place from the Most Holy Place of the tabernacle.[234] Thus, a record was made of the sin that had been confessed and forgiven through the blood of the lamb, which symbolized the true "Lamb of God who takes away the sin of the world!"[235]

That service and others like it were conducted daily in the sanctuary, showing us we need to open our hearts to God daily, seeking His mercy, grace, and cleansing power. Every day, we need to spend time in Bible study and prayer, connecting our hearts with God and lifting our thoughts in contemplation of His love and purity. Daily, our prayer should be, "Create in me a clean heart, O God, and renew a steadfast spirit within me."[236] Daily, we should claim God's promises, such as, "If we *confess* our sins, He is *faithful* and *just* to *forgive* us our sins and to *cleanse* us from *all unrighteousness*."[237]

The Hebrew sanctuary was only an illustration of the true sanctuary in heaven, where Jesus ministers for us as our true High Priest. The real sanctuary to which we need to pay attention is the one in heaven. "Now this is the main point of the things we are saying: We have such a *High Priest*, who is seated at the right hand of the throne of the Majesty in the *heavens*, a Minister of the *sanctuary* and of the *true tabernacle* which the Lord *erected*, and *not man*."[238]

Therefore, when we confess our sins and claim the death of Jesus to take the place of our death as a consequence for our sins ("for the wages of sin is death"[239]), those sins are recorded as forgiven in the record books of the heavenly sanctuary. They are removed from us—"As far as the east is from the west, So far has He removed our transgressions from us."[240] This record serves as evidence in our defense against Satan's accusations in the judgment.[241]

The sanctuary describes how God permanently removes our sins from us. And the judgment is the final phase of that removal process. The following is a simple diagram of the Hebrew sanctuary—a miniature replica of the sanctuary in heaven:

---

[234] See Leviticus 1:4–9
[235] John 1:29
[236] Psalm 51:10
[237] 1 John 1:9 (emphasis added)
[238] Hebrews 8:1, 2 (emphasis added)
[239] Romans 6:23
[240] Psalm 103:12 (see also Micah 7:19; Isaiah 43:25; Jeremiah 31:34; 50:20; 1 John 1:7)
[241] See Zechariah 3:1–5

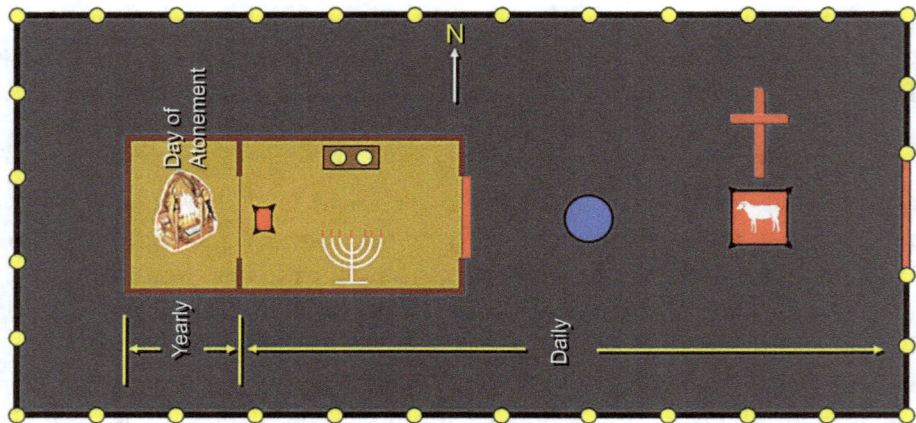

There was only one way to enter the courtyard and the tabernacle: through the door on the east side. Jesus said, regarding Himself as the Good Shepherd, "*I am the door*. If anyone *enters by Me*, he will be *saved*, and will go in and out and find pasture."[242]

In the courtyard, there were two items other than the tabernacle. The altar of sacrifice represented the cross of Christ. The large bowl of water the priests used for washing in the courtyard, called the laver, represented baptism—being washed clean from sin.

The tabernacle contained two compartments: the Holy Place and the Most Holy Place. The Holy Place contained three articles of furniture: a table with bread on it, a seven-branched candlestick, and an altar with burning incense. These all represented Jesus and the daily relationship He wants with us.

The table with bread on it represented Jesus as the Bread of Life.[243] Jesus is the Living Word of God.[244] The seven-branched candlestick represented Jesus as the Light of the world.[245] And the altar with burning incense on it represented Jesus as our Mediator, Intercessor, High Priest, and Righteousness.[246]

The Most Holy Place contained only one piece of furniture, with multiple parts. It was called the ark of the covenant.[247] It was forty-five inches long, twenty-seven inches wide, and twenty-seven inches tall, made of

---

[242] John 10:9 (emphasis added)
[243] See John 6:35
[244] See John 1:1, 14
[245] See John 8:12
[246] See Titus 2:5; Hebrews 4:14–16; 1 John 2:1, 2; Revelation 8:3, 4
[247] See Hebrews 9:3–5)

acacia wood and covered with gold inside and out. The lid was made of solid gold and called the "mercy seat." The glorious presence of God, called the Shekinah glory, was above the mercy seat—God's throne in the Most Holy Place. Therefore, the Bible encourages us to "come boldly to the *throne of grace*, that we may obtain *mercy* and find *grace* to *help in time of need*."[248]

Angels of solid gold were standing with outstretched wings on either side of the ark, with their faces looking toward the mercy seat, where the Shekinah Glory shown. Inside the ark were the two tables of stone on which God had written the Ten Commandments with His own finger.

> Then you came near and stood at the foot of the mountain, and *the mountain burned with fire* to the midst of heaven, with darkness, cloud, and thick darkness. And *the LORD spoke* to you out of the midst of the fire. You heard the sound of the words, but saw no form; you only heard a voice. So He declared to you *His covenant* which He commanded you to perform, the *Ten Commandments*; and *He wrote* them on *two tablets of stone*.[249]
>
> And Moses turned and went down from the mountain, and the *two tablets of the Testimony* were in his hand. The tablets were written on both sides; on the one side and on the other they were written. Now the tablets were *the work of God*, and the writing was *the writing of God engraved on the tablets*.[250]
>
> And you shall put *into the ark* the *Testimony which I will give you*.[251]

This "Testimony" (the tables of stone on which were written the Ten Commandments) were placed inside the ark. These commandments were to be distinguished from all the other laws that God told Moses to write in a book (scroll) and place on the outside of the ark.

> So it was, when *Moses* had *completed writing the words of this law in a book*, when they were finished, that Moses commanded the Levites, who bore the ark of the covenant of the LORD, saying: "Take this *Book of the Law*, and put it *beside the ark of the covenant*

---

[248] Hebrews 4:16 (emphasis added)
[249] Deuteronomy 4:11–13 (emphasis added)
[250] Exodus 32:15, 16 (emphasis added)
[251] Exodus 25:16 (emphasis added)

of the LORD your God, that it may be there as a witness against you;"[252]

The "book of the law" was written by Moses, but the Ten Commandments were written by the finger of God on stone. We will see the significance of this later.

It has been stated that the earthly sanctuary is a sandbox illustration of God's plan of salvation—His plan to remove our sins from us and give us His righteousness in exchange. Believe it or not, there is even greater news than the forgiveness of our sins. There will come a time when God will remove even the record of our forgiven sins from the sanctuary; they will be gone forever.

> **Believe it or not, there is even greater news than the forgiveness of our sins. There will come a time when God will remove even the record of our forgiven sins from the sanctuary; they will be gone forever.**

This is part of what happens in the heavenly judgment, which is taking place right now. The earthly sanctuary service that illustrated this final cleansing of the record of our forgiven sins was called the Day of Atonement—the day of judgment. When Daniel speaks of the judgment beginning and the books being opened in chapter 7,[253] he is speaking of the heavenly judgment to which the earthly Day of Atonement pointed forward.

This was a special day for cleansing the people of Israel and the sanctuary of all record of forgiven sins. The word "atonement" comes from the Hebrew word רפכ (*kaw-far'*), which means "to cover, cancel, cleanse, forgive, be merciful, reconcile."[254] The Day of Atonement was held at the conclusion of the Jewish ceremonial year; it was a very sacred and holy day of fasting and prayer. The people were to make sure all their sins were confessed and forgiven, or they would be cut off from the community of God. The word "atonement" can easily be understood by breaking it into three words: "at-one-ment." God wants to be "at one" with us. He wants to dwell in us. "Christ in you" is our only source of strength to conquer the evil that lurks in our own hearts and the world surrounding us.

---

[252] Deuteronomy 31:24–26 (emphasis added)
[253] See v. 10
[254] See Strong's Hebrew and Greek Dictionaries

God's Counterattack

Once a year, on The Day of Atonement, the high priest would go alone into the Holy Place as well as the Most Holy Place and perform the ministry of cleansing the sanctuary from the record of forgiven sin.

> For on that day the priest shall make *atonement* for you, to *cleanse you*, that you may be *clean from all your sins* before the LORD.[255]
>
> So he shall make *atonement* for the *Holy Place*, because of the *uncleanness of the children of Israel*, and because of their *transgressions*, for *all their sins*.[256]

The high priest's work on The Day of Atonement symbolized the work Jesus, our Great High Priest, is doing for us now, just before He returns to take us to be with Him. This work has often been called the "investigative judgment" and is described throughout Scripture:

> Let us hear the conclusion of the whole matter: *Fear God and keep His commandments*, for this is man's all. For *God will bring every work into judgment*, Including every *secret thing*, whether *good or evil*.[257]
>
> Rejoice, O young man, in your youth, and let your heart cheer you in the days of your youth; Walk in the ways of your heart, and in the sight of your eyes; but know that for all these *God will bring you into judgment*.[258]

Jesus said, "But I say to you that for every *idle word* men may speak, they will *give account of it in the day of judgment*. For by your *words* you will be *justified*, and by your *words* you will be *condemned*."[259] Have you ever wished you could erase words you have spoken? You can! Jesus will do it in the judgment if you let Him take it from you now and give you His righteousness in exchange.

One of the most important questions to be answered is, By what standards or criteria are we judged?

> For whoever shall keep the *whole law*, and yet *stumble in one point*, he is *guilty of all*. For He who said, "do not commit adultery," also said, "do not murder." Now if you do not commit adultery,

---

[255] Leviticus 16:30 (emphasis added)
[256] Leviticus 16:16 (emphasis added)
[257] Ecclesiastes 12:13, 14 (emphasis added)
[258] Ecclesiastes 11:9 (emphasis added)
[259] Matthew 12:36, 37 (emphasis added)

but you do murder, you have become a transgressor of the law. So speak and so do as those who will be *judged by the law of liberty*.[260]

This "law of liberty" is none other than the Ten Commandments, which were kept inside the ark of the covenant. This is the law by which we are judged. This is evident because two of the Ten Commandments are quoted in this very passage. Nevertheless, with that being true, what chance does anyone have in the judgment? We have all broken God's law and fallen short of the mark repeatedly.[261]

No one has the righteousness (right doing) the law requires…[262] that is, no one except Jesus Christ. And the good news is He offers that righteousness (right doing) as a gift to everyone who will receive it.

Clothing is symbolic of righteousness in the Bible. Our own "righteousnesses are like filthy rags,"[263] but Christ's righteousness is depicted as a white robe. John the Revelator was given a vision of the redeemed in heaven symbolically clothed in white robes.

> Then one of the elders answered, saying to me, "Who are these arrayed in *white robes*, and where did they come from?" And I said to him, "Sir, you know." So he said to me, "These are the ones who come out of the great tribulation, and *washed their robes* and *made them white in the blood of the Lamb*."[264]

Our only source of righteousness is not from within us, but from our loving and wonderful God who has provided it for us because He knows we have no righteousness of our own.[265] And He will give it to you if you ask Him and believe His promise to do so.

"'No weapon formed against you shall prosper, and *every tongue which rises against you in judgment You shall condemn*. This is the heritage of the servants of the LORD, and *their righteousness is from Me*,' Says the LORD."[266] If we tried to stand alone before the law in the judgment, we would not stand a chance. However, God's righteousness, displayed in Jesus, is exactly what the law requires. Do you want it? It is a gift!

---

[260] James 2:10–12 (emphasis added)
[261] See Romans 3:10–18, 23
[262] See Galatians 3:22
[263] Isaiah 64:6
[264] Revelation 7:13, 14 (emphasis added)
[265] See Matthew 22:1–14
[266] Isaiah 54:17 (emphasis added)

The righteousness of Christ comes in two forms that are distinct from each other but cannot be separated. The Bible labels them "justification" and "sanctification." We need to understand these two terms.

"Justification" is translated from the Greek word δικαιοσύνη (*dikaiosunē*), but it comes from the same root word that is translated "righteousness." Justification is the righteousness of Christ that is credited (imputed) to you when you confess your sins and accept God's forgiveness. In other words, the very instant you lay hold of Christ's forgiveness, God looks at you *just as if* you had never sinned. The record of your life of sin and failure is exchanged for Christ's perfect life of right doing. When God looks at you, He does not see your past, but He sees Jesus. The apostle Paul put it this way:

> But to him who *does not work* but *believes* on Him who *justifies the ungodly*, his *faith* is *accounted for righteousness*, just as David also describes the blessedness of the man to whom God *imputes righteousness* apart from works: "Blessed are those whose lawless deeds are forgiven, And whose sins are covered; Blessed is the man to whom the Lord shall not impute sin."[267]

Please note it is the ungodly that God justifies, not based on our works (right-doing), but on faith—believing it is so because He said so. When you believe the promise of God, it is that faith that "is accounted for righteousness." Christ's right doing is credited to you in the record books of heaven. At that moment, you have the type of righteousness the law requires—the type of righteousness that will pass the judgment. "For *all have sinned* and fall short of the glory of God, being *justified freely* by His *grace* through the redemption that is in Christ Jesus."[268]

Justification is the type of righteousness that is provided through the courtyard ministry of the sanctuary. On the other hand, sanctification is the type of righteousness that is provided through the Holy Place/Most Holy Place ministry of Christ. The word "sanctified" means "holy" or "set aside for holy purposes only."

Justification is given the instant you believe. Sanctification is a lifelong process of growing ever more into the likeness of Christ's character by letting Him live out His life in you by faith. The apostle Paul testified of how this happens: "I have been crucified with Christ; *it is no longer I who live,*

---

[267] Romans 4:5–8 (emphasis added)
[268] Romans 3:23, 24 (emphasis added)

but *Christ lives in me*; and *the life which I now live* in the flesh *I live by faith in the Son of God*, who loved me and gave Himself for me."[269]

In the Holy Place of the tabernacle, we find three key elements that enable Jesus to live His life in us by faith. The first is the table of showbread. This bread represents Jesus, who is "the Bread of Life."[270] It also represents the Word of God. "It is written, 'Man shall not live by bread alone, but by every word that proceeds from the mouth of God.'"[271]

It is just as essential to spend time daily reading and studying the Bible for spiritual life and growth as it is to eat food daily for physical life and growth. It is through incorporating the Word of God into your life that Jesus lives His life in you. The Bible testifies of this fact.

> For this reason we also thank God without ceasing, because when you *received the word of God* which you heard from us, you welcomed it *not as the word of men*, but as it is *in truth, the word of God*, which also *effectively works in you who believe*.[272]
>
> For the *word of God* is *living* and *powerful*, and *sharper than any two-edged sword*, piercing even to the division of soul and spirit, and of joints and marrow, and is *a discerner of the thoughts and intents of the heart*.[273]
>
> "I have written to you, young men, because you are strong, and the *word of God abides in you*, And you have *overcome the wicked one*."[274]

Another piece of furniture in the Holy Place was the altar of incense. A fire was kept burning on that altar continuously, and fresh incense was placed on the fire daily. This is symbolic of our prayers of faith laying hold of Christ's intercessory work for us. The only thing that recommends our prayers to God is the righteousness of Christ.

> Then another angel, having a golden censer, came and stood at the *altar*. He was given much *incense*, that he should *offer it with the prayers of all the saints* upon the golden altar which was before the throne. And the *smoke of the incense*, with the *prayers of the saints*, ascended before God from the angel's hand.[275]

---

[269] Galatians 2:20 (emphasis added)
[270] John 6:35
[271] Matthew 4:4 (emphasis added; see also Deuteronomy 8:3; Luke 4:4)
[272] 1 Thessalonians 2:13 (emphasis added)
[273] Hebrews 4:12 (emphasis added)
[274] 1 John 2:14 (emphasis added)
[275] Revelation 8:3, 4 (emphasis added; see also Revelation 5:8; Psalm 141:2)

Prayer in the hand of faith is what unlocks all of God's blessings. Prayer is not for the purpose of bringing God down to us, but for lifting us out of the atmosphere of this evil generation into the pure atmosphere of heaven. Prayer and Bible study need to go together. Every time you open the Bible to read, you need to ask God to send His Holy Spirit to open your mind to the truths it contains because spiritual things are spiritually discerned.[276] We cannot understand the Bible by strength of intellect, but by the Holy Spirit enlightening our minds.

It is through prayer that we lay hold of and accept the promises of the Bible and have access to the power of God (His divine nature) in our lives to overcome sin and live a righteous (sanctified) life in the midst of this corrupt society. The apostle Peter opened his second epistle with these significant words:

> *It is just as essential to spend time daily reading and studying the Bible for spiritual life and growth as it is to eat food daily for physical life and growth. It is through incorporating the Word of God into your life that Jesus lives His life in you.*

> Grace and peace be multiplied to you in the knowledge of God and of Jesus our Lord, as *His divine power has given to us all things that pertain to life and godliness*, through the knowledge of Him who called us by glory and virtue, by which have been given to us *exceedingly great and precious promises*, that *through these you may be partakers of the divine nature,* having *escaped the corruption that is in the world* through lust.[277]

The third piece of furniture in the Holy Place of the tabernacle was the seven-branched candlestick, which was kept burning continuously. The light this candlestick emitted represents Jesus, who is the "Light of the World."[278] However, in talking about those who have faith in Him, He said, "*You* are the *light* of the *world*."[279] We are like the moon, which has no light in itself. The only light it has is what it reflects from the sun. We

---

[276] See 1 Corinthians 2:14
[277] 2 Peter 1:2–4 (emphasis added)
[278] John 8:12 (see also John 9:5)
[279] Matthew 5:14 (emphasis added)

have no light in us, but if Jesus is truly living His life in us, His character will shine out and be seen.

He indicated this by saying, "Let *your light so shine* before men, that they may see your good works *and glorify your Father in heaven.*"[280] Ministering to the needs of others is one of God's most powerful tools to keep faith growing strong in our hearts.

The reason our "good works" glorify God is because it is only by Jesus dwelling in our hearts through faith that He can live out His life of righteousness (right doing) within us. All the glory goes to God!

Thus, the three pieces of furniture in the Holy Place of the tabernacle describe the way in which sanctification takes place—the way in which Jesus can live out His life in us. However, there is another compartment in the tabernacle: The Most Holy Place.

The Most Holy Place contained the ark of the covenant, which held the Ten Commandments written by the finger of God on tables of stone. However, God doesn't want His law to remain on stone. His intent all along has been for His law to be inscribed on our hearts. When He first gave His law from Mount Sinai, He instructed, "And these words which I command you today shall be *in your heart.*"[281]

This is also what God stated was the goal of the new covenant: "For this is the covenant that I will make with the house of Israel after those days, says the Lord: *I will put My laws in their mind and write them on their hearts*; and I will be their God, and they shall be My people."[282]

God doesn't just want the letter of the law written on our hearts, but also the spirit of the law as well. Every principle of righteousness found in the Bible is summarized in the Ten Commandments. God's law is the foundation of His government—the description of His character. The

---

[280] Matthew 5:16 (emphasis added)
[281] Deuteronomy 6:6 (emphasis added)
[282] Hebrews 8:10 (emphasis added)

spiritual implications of the law of God are inexhaustible because He is infinite.

The Most Holy Place was the most sacred spot on earth. It represented the throne room of God in the judgment. There is good news about the judgment:

- Jesus is our judge[283]
- Jesus is our defense attorney[284]
- Jesus is our righteousness[285]

Jesus is everything we need in the judgment. The judgment is stacked in your favor. If you have Jesus abiding in your heart, you cannot lose! The message of the judgment shows the importance of maintaining a daily love-faith relationship with Jesus. We have no need to be afraid of the judgment.

> *Love* has been perfected among us in this: that we may have *boldness in the day of judgment*; because *as He is, so are we* in this world. There is *no fear in love*; but *perfect love casts out fear*, because fear involves torment. But he who fears has not been made perfect in love. *We love Him because He first loved us*.[286]

The judgment does tell us there is a day of reckoning coming. Nobody will be given an exemption. "We must all appear before the judgment seat of Christ."[287] "Each of us shall give account of himself to God."[288]

The issue at stake is our faith. Will our faith be shown to be genuine? Will our faith endure through hard trials like Daniel and his friends endured, or will it give way to popular demand? Will our faith be like the faith Jesus had when He lived on earth, or will it be like the Pharisees? Will our faith produce a life of obedience to the Ten Commandments, or will we indulge in excuses? Will our faith produce the character of Jesus within us, or will it produce the character of the adversary? Will our faith be mere words, or will it tap into the life-changing power of God? Will our faith be real faith or fake faith?

Some people are content to enter the courtyard of the sanctuary experience and receive the gift of justification by faith in Jesus. However, they

---

[283] See John 5:22
[284] See 1 John 2:1, 2
[285] See Jeremiah 23:6; 33:16
[286] 1 John 4:17–19 (emphasis added)
[287] 2 Corinthians 5:10
[288] Romans 14:12

are unwilling to enter the Holy and Most Holy Places of the tabernacle. Others are willing to partake of Christ's ministry in the Holy Place and begin the process of sanctification by faith in Jesus. This is a great step forward, but what God wants is for us to go all the way with Him into the Most Holy Place and let Him write His law on our hearts, making His principles of righteousness our delight. King David, whom Paul used as one of his prime examples of righteousness by faith, declared, "I *delight* to do *Your will*, O my God, and *Your law* is *within my heart*."[289]

Will you let Him take you all the way to the ark of the covenant in the Most Holy Place? By doing this, you will be ready when your name comes up in the investigative judgment in heaven.

Now that we know what the judgment is about, we are ready to discover when it begins. Daniel 8 and 9 tell us when the judgment begins, as well as other significant information. This is what we will study in the next two chapters, so keep reading.

---

[289] Psalm 40:8 (emphasis added)

Chapter 6

The Vision of Truth's Fall and Rise Again

Our world is used to the term "fake news." Truth has fallen in the streets. Justice is seemingly nowhere to be found. Equality is only a mirage. Oppression and revolt occupy our cities. We look for light but find none. The way of peace eludes us. The innocent suffer and die without hope. Anxiety rules our thoughts and emotions. Violence and destruction rule our streets. Empty words, lies, and false accusations are the norm. The one who shuns evil becomes prey.[290]

Our society is truly in freefall! King Solomon instructed, "Buy the truth, and *sell it not*."[291] However, we have sold it. The Bible prophesied this long ago. Daniel paints another picture of the decline of our society, when truth is cast "to the ground,"[292] and points to the judgment at the end of time as the ultimate solution—our only real hope. In chapters 8 and 9, we will discover the date of the beginning of Christ's final phase of ministry in the heavenly sanctuary: the judgment.

With that said, let us begin with Daniel 8. Daniel was given a vision of a ram and a goat. These animals are of a different nature than were the ones in chapter 7. The conglomerate beasts in 7 are beasts of prey. However, the animals in Daniel 8 are animals that were used for sacrifices in the Hebrew sanctuary. This prophecy is saturated with sanctuary imagery and language. In fact, beginning with chapter 8, the language in which Daniel originally wrote this book changes from Aramaic to Hebrew—the language of the sanctuary. The only way to understand this prophecy is to study the Hebrew sanctuary, and that is why we spent so much time doing just that in the previous chapter.

The vision began by describing the ram and his activities.

> Then I lifted my eyes and saw, and there, standing beside the river, was a *ram* which had *two horns*, and the two horns were high; but *one was higher than the other*, and the *higher one came up last*. I

---

[290] See Isaiah 59:1–15
[291] Proverbs 23:23 (emphasis added)
[292] Daniel 8:12

saw the ram pushing westward, northward, and southward, so that no animal could withstand him; nor was there any that could deliver from his hand, but he did according to his will and *became great*.[293]

This description is similar to that of the bear in Daniel 7, which was higher on one side. We discovered the bear represented the Medo-Persian Empire, and again, we are not left to guess what this ram represents. The angel Gabriel gave Daniel the interpretation: "And he said, 'Look, I am making known to you what shall happen in the *latter time of the indignation*; for at the *appointed time the end shall be*. The *ram* which you saw, having the two horns—they are the kings of *Media and Persia*.'"[294]

Gabriel made it clear that this prophecy began in Daniel's day and extended to the very time of the end—a time God had appointed. He also made it clear that the ram represented the Medo-Persian Empire, which conquered Babylon in 539 BC and ruled until 331 BC, as we have previously seen in chapters 2 and 7.

Daniel then described the goat:

And as I was considering, suddenly a *male goat* came from the *west*, across the surface of the whole earth, without touching the ground; and the goat had a *notable horn* between his eyes. Then he came to the ram that had two horns, which I had seen standing beside the river, and ran at him with furious power. And I saw him confronting the ram; he was moved with rage against him, *attacked the ram, and broke his two horns*. There was no power in the ram to withstand him, but he cast him down to the ground and trampled him; and there was no one that could deliver the ram from his hand. Therefore the *male goat grew very great*; but

---

[293] Daniel 8:3, 4 (emphasis added)
[294] Daniel 8:19, 20 (emphasis added)

when he became strong, *the large horn was broken*, and in place of it *four notable ones came up* toward the four winds of heaven.²⁹⁵

Some of the features of this goat parallel the four-headed, four-winged leopard of Daniel 7. This goat grows four notable horns after the large horn is broken. Again, we are not left to guess. Gabriel continued with his explanation: "And the *male goat* is the *kingdom of Greece*. The *large horn* that is between its eyes is the *first king*. As for the broken horn and the four that stood up in its place, *four kingdoms shall arise out of that nation*, but not with its power."²⁹⁶

This is exactly what happened, according to the records of history. Alexander the Great was the first king of the world-ruling Grecian Empire, but he died within a few years of conquering the world. His four generals (Cassander, Lysimachus, Ptolemy, and Seleucus) warred among themselves, dividing the kingdom into four parts. Eventually, they consolidated into two kingdoms who continued to war against each other.

So far, this vision prophesied the same succession of kingdoms as did the visions of Daniel 2 and 7. The next event follows the same pattern. "And out of one of them came a little horn which grew exceedingly great toward the south, toward the east, and toward the Glorious Land."²⁹⁷

Just as in Daniel 2 and 7, Babylon was followed by Medo-Persia, which was followed by Greece, which was followed by Rome; so we see the same sequence here in Daniel 8. Rome, small at first, grew into a contending power. Linguistically, the phrase "out of one of them," according to Hebrew grammar, can only refer to the "four winds of heaven" describing the four points of the compass (north, south, east, west).

At times, the road to the Colosseum was lighted on both sides by Christians being burned at the stake so the emperor could find his way in the dark.

Rome arose from the west and conquered toward the south and east, including Palestine (the Glorious Land).

Whereas the prophecy predicted Greece, the goat, would grow "very great," it says Rome, in the little-horn phase, would grow "exceedingly great."²⁹⁸ This is in direct harmony with the description of Rome in Daniel

---

²⁹⁵ Daniel 8:5–8 (emphasis added)
²⁹⁶ Daniel 8:21, 22 (emphasis added)
²⁹⁷ Daniel 8:9 (emphasis added)
²⁹⁸ See "Appendix A" regarding the theory of Antiochus Epiphanes fulfilling this prophecy

7, which says it was to be "exceedingly strong."[299] It is also in harmony with the description of Rome in Daniel 2, which says "the fourth kingdom shall be as strong as iron."[300]

The Pagan Roman Empire was ruthless. The history of how they tried to stamp out Christianity will turn the stomach of anyone who studies into it very deeply. There was wave after wave of persecution over a period of more than 200 years. At times, the road to the Colosseum was lighted on both sides by Christians being burned at the stake so the emperor could find his way in the dark.

However, the blood of the martyrs was the seed of the gospel. The more the Christians ("the host of heaven") were persecuted, the more those who observed it accepted Jesus as their Savior. Because they learned to love Jesus supremely, they found Him to be so worthy, they would die for Him. Daniel 8 described Rome's persecution of the church this way: "And it grew up to the *host of heaven*; and it *cast down* some of the *host* and some of the *stars* to the *ground*, and *trampled them*."[301]

> **However, the blood of the martyrs was the seed of the gospel.**

Just as in Daniel 2, we saw that Rome transitioned from the legs of pure iron to the feet and toes "partly of iron and partly of clay" (church and state combined); and as we saw in Daniel 7, the fourth beast had three phases (the dragon-like beast, the ten horns, and then the little horn); so, in Daniel 8, we find that Rome transitions from a political power to a politico-religious power (the Roman Church). What was true about the pagan Roman Empire persecuting the church at large was also true about the papacy persecuting portions of the church that refused to fall under her authority and control. Therefore, this verse signals the transition from pagan Rome to papal Rome.

Again, I want to make it very clear that even though Bible prophecy reveals papal Rome is the antichrist (Greek *antichristos*— "in the place of Christ") power, the members of the Catholic Church are not antichrist. The prophecy is pointing out a religious system that obscures Jesus and puts mankind where only God belongs. However, that does not mean there are not true-hearted followers of Christ in the Catholic communion. There are true followers of Christ in every denomination, including the

---

[299] Daniel 7:7 (emphasis added)
[300] Daniel 2:40 (emphasis added)
[301] Daniel 8:10 (emphasis added)

Roman Catholic Church. God is pointing out the errors promoted by the antichrist so we may have the strength of faith needed to escape its deceptions and go through the trials into which this world is being plunged and be guarded against Satan's traps.

The Roman Church phase is described like this:

> He even *exalted himself* as *high* as the *Prince of the host*; and by him the *daily sacrifices* were taken away, and the *place of His sanctuary was cast down*. Because of *transgression*, an *army* was given over to the horn *to oppose the daily sacrifices*; and he *cast truth down to the ground*. He did all this and *prospered*.[302]

There is a lot in this passage that needs to be unpacked. We will take it phrase by phrase:

"He even exalted himself as high as the Prince of the host."

This is exactly what Lucifer did in heaven when he rebelled against the law of God. He said, "*I will ascend* into heaven, *I will exalt my throne* above the stars of God: I will also sit on the mount of the congregation on the farthest sides of the north; *I will ascend* above the heights of the clouds; *I will be like the most High*."[303]

This is the same pit into which Satan has led the papacy, as we saw in Daniel 7.[304] The pope claims power and authority that belongs to God alone. The apostle Paul predicted this apostasy:

> Let no one deceive you by any means; for that Day will not come unless the *falling away comes first*, and the *man of sin* is revealed, the son of perdition, who opposes and *exalts himself* above all that is called God or that is worshiped, so that he sits as God in the temple of God, *showing himself that he is God*.[305]

The term "man of sin" is rendered "man of lawlessness" in some old manuscripts.[306] A few verses later, Paul goes on to describe the papacy as the "lawless one" because it has done everything it can to change God's holy law, written with His own finger on tables of stone.

---

[302] Daniel 8:11, 12 (emphasis added)
[303] Isaiah 14:13, 14 (emphasis added)
[304] See comments on verse 25
[305] 2 Thessalonians 2:3, 4 (emphasis added)
[306] Nestle-Aland Greek New Testament

> And then the *lawless one* will be revealed, whom the Lord will consume with the breath of His mouth and destroy with the brightness of His coming. The coming of the *lawless one* is *according to the working of Satan*, with all power, signs, and lying wonders, and with all *unrighteous deception* among those who perish, because they *did not receive the love of the truth*, that they might be saved.[307]

It is not an intellectual knowledge of the truth alone that protects us from Satan's deceptions. It is a love of the truth. We will look at this more in a minute, but the prophecy continues.

> "By him the daily sacrifices were taken away, and the place of His sanctuary was cast down"

The word "sacrifices" is not found in the original Hebrew text. It was added by the translators because they thought that was the best explanation of the word "daily." It is not a bad explanation because the sacrifices were done daily in the courtyard of the sanctuary. However, that was not the only thing done daily (or "continually") in the sanctuary. The candlesticks were kept burning daily; the incense was burned daily; bread was on the table daily; the priests ministered daily; etc. Therefore, a fuller understanding of the term "daily" would include everything done in the sanctuary every day. A better term might be "daily ministration," which would represent all of Christ's daily ministries in the heavenly sanctuary on our behalf.

The Roman Church has truly taken Christ's daily ministry in the heavenly sanctuary away and cast down the truth taught by the earthly sanctuary services and articles of furniture. We looked at some of those services and articles of furniture in our last chapter and saw they represent Jesus and what He has done for us and is doing for us now. By putting human ideas, mediators, and laws where only God and His Word, intercession, and commandments belong, the Roman Church has effectively cast the truth of Christ's ministration in the heavenly sanctuary down. They have put fallible humans in the place of Jesus. Let us continue with the prophecy.

> "Because of transgression, an army was given over to the horn to oppose the daily sacrifices"[308]

The history of the Dark Ages, when the papacy outlawed the Bible and warred against groups of Christians who preserved the sacred Scriptures,

---

[307] 2 Thessalonians 2:8–10 (emphasis added)
[308] Daniel 8:12 (emphasis added)

The Vision of Truth's Fall and Rise Again

clearly fulfills this prediction. In order to raise armies to war against these groups (Waldenses, Albigenses, Lollards, Hussites, Protestants, etc.), the pope often resorted to false promises. He promised to give full and free forgiveness of any immoral crime committed by those who would join his army. Therefore, he used "transgression" as the motive for recruiting soldiers.

The next specification of the prophecy needs special attention.

> "And he cast truth down to the ground. He did all this and prospered"[309]

We have already seen how the papacy cast down the truth of the sanctuary, which is all about Jesus and His plan to save sinners. In this verse, we again find truth being cast to the ground. Repetition is one of God's ways of emphasizing the point being discussed.

Truth is found in Jesus, who said, "I am the *way*, the *truth*, and the *life*. No one comes to the Father *except through Me*."[310] Jesus, not any human or church, is the only way to heaven. He is the source of truth about God. And it is His life lived in us by faith that gives us eternity. Jesus lives His life in us through the indwelling of the Holy Spirit, who is called the "Spirit of *truth*" and will guide us "into all *truth*."[311]

When King David confessed his sin of adultery, he acknowledged, "Behold, You desire *truth* in the *inward parts*, and in the *hidden part* You will make me to know *wisdom*."[312] God does not want us to merely, intellectually acknowledge truth. He wants His truth to take up residence in our hearts. This is exactly where God's law is to be written.[313] David also said God's "*law is truth*."[314] We accept truth as the operating principle of our lives and base everything we do and say upon it. When a person is converted to Christ, loyalty to God's truth replaces the attitude of compromise and rebellion.

The truth of God's Word is what sets us free from Satan's control and the dominion of sin in our lives. Jesus said, "And you shall know the *truth*, and the *truth shall make you free*."[315] God's truth will expel the bondage of Satan's lies. The apostle Paul described the spiritual warfare in which we are involved against Satan and his hosts of evil angels, then showed

---

[309] Daniel 8:12 (emphasis added)
[310] John 14:6 (emphasis added)
[311] John 16:13 (emphasis added)
[312] Psalm 51:6 (emphasis added)
[313] See Jeremiah 31:31–34; Hebrews 8:10
[314] Psalm 119:142
[315] John 8:32 (emphasis added)

how God has supplied us with spiritual armor in order to withstand his attacks.[316] The first piece of God's armor is the belt of truth.[317] Satan led Adam and Eve into sin by telling a lie.[318] This is why God starts his spiritual armor with truth. Truth removes the deception from lies.

The deceptiveness of lies has been Satan's tactic throughout his warfare with God, beginning with his attack in heaven.

> And *war* broke out in *heaven*: Michael and his angels *fought* with the *dragon*; and the dragon and his angels *fought*, but they did not prevail, nor was a place found for them in heaven any longer. So the great dragon was cast out, that serpent of old, called the *Devil* and *Satan*, who *deceives the whole world*; he was cast to the earth, and his angels were cast out with him.[319]

Not only did Satan begin his warfare against God by using deceptive lies, but that is still his tactic now at the end of time. "Then the beast was captured, and with him the false prophet who worked signs in his presence, by which he *deceived* those who received the mark of the beast and those who worshiped his image."[320]

A lie must attach itself to truth in order to be deceptive enough to be accepted as truth. In the Bible, light is used as a symbol of truth.[321] Therefore, Satan and his agents on earth pretend to be messengers of truth (light). Notice how the apostle Paul described this:

> For such are *false apostles*, *deceitful workers*, transforming themselves into *apostles of Christ*. And no wonder! For *Satan* himself transforms himself into an *angel of light*. Therefore it is no great thing if *his ministers* also transform themselves into *ministers of righteousness*, whose end will be according to their works.[322]

Lies attached to truth are Satan's mode of operation, especially now in the end of time!

> But *evil men* and *impostors* will grow *worse and worse, deceiving and being deceived*.[323]

---

[316] See Ephesians 6:10–18
[317] See Ephesians 6:14
[318] See Genesis 3:1–6
[319] Revelation 12:7–9 (emphasis added)
[320] Revelation 19:20 (emphasis added)
[321] See Psalm 119:105
[322] 2 Corinthians 11:13–15 (emphasis added)
[323] 2 Timothy 3:13 (emphasis added)

The Vision of Truth's Fall and Rise Again

The list of deceptions promoted by the papacy is long. Many books have been written about them, but that is not the purpose of this book. The intent is not to condemn, but to direct people away from the human and deceptive to the divine and true. This is what the apostle Paul instructed young Timothy to do.

> I charge you therefore before God and the Lord Jesus Christ, who will judge the living and the dead at His appearing and His kingdom: *Preach the word!* Be ready in season and out of season. Convince, rebuke, exhort, with all longsuffering and teaching. For *the time will come when they will not endure sound doctrine*, but according to their own desires, because they have itching ears, they will heap up for themselves teachers; and *they will turn their ears away from the truth*, and be turned aside to *fables*.[324]

The Roman Church has turned multitudes away from the truth as it is in Jesus. It is interesting that Daniel foretold that "He did all this and *prospered.*"[325] The Catholic Church boasts over 1 billion members worldwide. They are likely the richest institution in the world; the pope is the most popular person in the world and has gained great political power over the last number of years. Yes, they have prospered.

The next thing Daniel records of his vision is a conversation between two heavenly beings and himself:

> Then I heard a holy one speaking; and another holy one said to that certain one who was speaking, *"How long* will the *vision be*, concerning the *daily* sacrifices and the *transgression of desolation*, the giving of both the *sanctuary* and the *host* to be *trampled underfoot?*"[326]

These heavenly beings are anxious for us to know the antichrist power will not win in the end.[327] As this world's history is winding down, God will make sure the truth of Christ's sanctuary ministry in heaven will be restored and His people will finally be delivered from oppression. Thus, the heavenly being asks the "How long" question. Have you ever asked the "How long" question?

According to the Hebrew language, this question should be phrased "Until when...." The emphasis is not on the duration, but the ending

---

[324] 2 Timothy 4:1–4 (emphasis added)
[325] Daniel 8:12 (emphasis added)
[326] Daniel 8:13 (emphasis added)
[327] See Daniel 8:24, 25

point. And the answer comes back: "And he said to me, 'For *two thousand three hundred days*; then the *sanctuary shall be cleansed.*'"[328]

In the previous chapter, we saw the cleansing of the sanctuary was done on the Day of Atonement, which symbolized the investigative-judgment ministry of Jesus in the heavenly sanctuary. Therefore, we now know the essence of the cleansing of the sanctuary, but the part about the 2,300 days still needs to be understood.

The word "days" in this passage is translated from the Hebrew phrase "evening and morning" in the original text. The translators chose to translate it "days" here, but a few verses later, as Gabriel explains this part of the vision, they literally translated it "evenings and mornings."[329]

"And the vision of the *evenings and mornings* which was told is *true*; therefore *seal up the vision*, for *it refers to many days in the future.*"[330] Gabriel does not reveal to Daniel the meaning of the 2,300 days. The only information he gives is that it extends far into the future. Taken literally, 2,300 days is only a little over six years. This would not extend "to many days in the future." When a time factor is given in the context of a symbolic prophecy, that time factor is symbolic as well (a day represents a year[331]).

Again, in chapter 12, Daniel is instructed by a heavenly being, "Go your way, Daniel, for *the words are closed up* and *sealed* till the *time of the end.*"[332] The part of the book that was closed up and sealed was the part concerning the 2,300 days. He was told several times to seal this part of the prophecy. "But you, Daniel, *shut up the words*, and *seal the book* until the *time of the end*; many shall run to and fro, and *knowledge shall increase.*"[333]

This indicates the prophecy is for the time of the end, and it is at the time of the end that the prophecy will be unsealed and knowledge about its fulfillment will spread widely throughout the world. Revelation predicted this as well, but that is a study for another book.[334]

Obviously, God wants us to know that at the end of this 2,300-day prophecy, a major event was to take place in heaven. And whenever major events take place in heaven that affect the plan of salvation on earth, there are corresponding events that take place here. The event to take place is

---

[328] Daniel 8:14 (emphasis added)
[329] See Strong's Greek and Hebrew and Dictionary
[330] Daniel 8:26 (emphasis added; see Appendix B for a careful study of the words translated "vision")
[331] See Numbers 14:34; Ezekiel 4:6
[332] Daniel 12:9 (emphasis added)
[333] Daniel 12:4
[334] See Revelation 10:1–11

"the sanctuary shall be cleansed." The word "cleansed" comes from the Hebrew word "צדק" (*tsaw-dak'*), which means "to be made right, cleanse, clear self, be just, do justice, be righteous, or turn to righteousness."[335] In other words, the truth of the sanctuary will be made right or restored from where it has been cast down.

Let us briefly review that casting down, and then we will look at how God has brought restoration:

- The **altar of sacrifice** in the courtyard of the sanctuary represented Christ's one-time sacrifice for our sins ("Christ was *offered once* to bear the sins of many"[336]). However, the Roman Church claims the literal body and blood of Jesus is sacrificed every time they have the Eucharist at Mass.
- The **laver**, which was a large container of water in the courtyard, represented the cleansing symbolized by being immersed in water at baptism. Jesus was baptized by immersion at the age of thirty.[337] However, the Roman Church says sprinkling is good enough and administered to adults as well as infants, who have no choice in the matter.
- The **table of showbread** in the Holy Place of the tabernacle represented the Word of God.[338] The Roman Church claims the common people cannot understand the Bible for themselves; they must let the church tell them what truth is. The words of humans take precedence over the Word of God.
- The **altar of incense** in the Holy Place represented the intercessory ministry of Jesus that we receive through prayer. Jesus is our mediator.[339] However, the Roman Church directs people to pray to dead "saints," especially Mary, the mother of Jesus. They also require believers to confess their sins to priests instead of directly to God. The implication is that God and Jesus need to be persuaded to give us grace.
- The **candlestick** in the Holy Place represented Jesus as the "The Light of the World."[340] Jesus also said His followers are the "light of the world."[341] Every believer in Jesus is a minister (witness) of the good news about Him. The Roman Church limited ministry to the

---

[335] See Strong's Greek and Hebrew Dictionary
[336] Hebrews 9:28 (emphasis added)
[337] See Matthew 3:16
[338] See Matthew 4:4
[339] See 1 Timothy 2:5
[340] John 9:5
[341] Matthew 5:14

clergy, so Jesus was obscured, and the world was plunged into what we call the "Dark Ages."

- The **ark of the covenant** in the Most Holy Place contained the Ten Commandments, and as we have seen, the Roman Church claims they changed God's law. They deleted the second commandment, changed the Sabbath commandment to refer to Sunday, and split the tenth commandment.

> *Every believer in Jesus is a minister (witness) of the good news about Him. The Roman Church limited ministry to the clergy, so Jesus was obscured, and the world was plunged into what we call the "Dark Ages."*

They did all this and prospered, but God said He would restore His truth and there would be a cleansing of the sanctuary. It is interesting to note that over a period of about 500 years, God restored all the truths of the sanctuary in preparation for the cleansing to take place:

- In the 1300s, God raised up John Wycliffe to translate the Bible into the English language for the first time. Thus, he restored the table of showbread (the Word of God). The Roman Church wanted the Bible to be kept in Latin so the priests would be the only ones who could read it. Others followed Wycliffe by translating the Bible into more languages. After his death, the Roman Church dug up his remains and burned them because they hated him so much. Today, the Bible is translated into over 600 languages.
- In the 1500s, God used Martin Luther to proclaim the truth of justification by faith—not by works. He taught that the death of Jesus was adequate to provide forgiveness for our sins. He restored the altar of sacrifice. Those who followed his teachings formed the Lutheran Church. The Roman Catholic Church tried to kill him, but God protected him.
- In the 1500s, John Calvin, a Protestant reformer, strongly emphasized prayer. He taught that we need not go to a priest to have our sins forgiven, but we can go directly to God in prayer. He restored the altar of incense. He founded the Presbyterian Church, and the Roman Catholic Church persecuted them and treated them as a cult.

The Vision of Truth's Fall and Rise Again

- In the 1600s, John Smyth discovered the Bible truth about baptism. He restored the laver. He taught that baptism should be by immersion, and the person being baptized should be old enough to make an intelligent decision to accept Jesus as one's personal Savior. This excluded infant baptism. He founded the Baptist Church, but they were treated as a cult as well.
- In the 1700s, God raised up John Wesley, who strongly emphasized witnessing. He insisted that ministry belonged to every believer. He restored the candlestick and founded the Methodist Church. They were also treated as a cult.
- In the 1800s, God raised up a movement of believers from a wide range of church backgrounds who intensely studied the Bible and the Bible only. They recovered the truth of the Ten Commandments in the ark of the covenant. Would they also be treated as a cult? The answer is obvious: Yes.

Thus, the truths of the sanctuary were restored, and the judgment, symbolized by the Day of Atonement services, could begin. Gabriel did not give Daniel the beginning or ending dates of the 2,300 days, so Daniel became sick because he did not understand that part of the vision. "And I, Daniel, *fainted* and was *sick* for days; afterward I arose and went about the king's business. I was *astonished by the vision*, but *no one understood it*."[342]

Two thousand, three hundred literal days equals about six-and-one-third years. That certainly does not extend to the end of time. However, as we saw when we studied the prophecy of Daniel 7, a day in prophetic time represents a literal year. Now, that makes a big difference! Two thousand, three hundred years from Daniel's time would extend a long way toward the end of time. However, Daniel was not given a beginning date, so we still are left without the ending date—the date of the beginning of Christ's judgment ministry in the heavenly sanctuary.

Gabriel came back to Daniel in chapter 9 and revealed to him the beginning date, and he did so in a way that makes the date solid.[343] The prophecy of Daniel 9 is the most exciting prophecy in the Bible. We will study that in our next chapter, so keep reading.

---

[342] Daniel 8:27 (emphasis added)
[343] See Appendix B for more information about the connection between Daniel 8 and 9

Chapter 7

The Most Exciting Prophecy

If there is one prophecy in the entire Bible that I enjoy the most, it is the prophecy of Daniel 9. It is a time prophecy connected with the yearly Passover service that is so exact that it pinpoints not only the year, but also the month, day, and very hour of the most important event this world has ever witnessed! With that said, let us get into it.

As we ended Daniel 8, the prophet was in great distress over the 2,300-day time period. He was afraid it may be indicating an extension of the seventy-year captivity of Israel, prophesied by Jeremiah. Therefore, he spent time fasting and praying about what God had revealed through Jeremiah; he then described this experience:

> In the *first year* of Darius the son of Ahasuerus, of the lineage of the *Medes*, who was made king over the realm of the Chaldeans—in the first year of his reign I, Daniel, *understood by the books* the *number of the years specified by the word of the LORD through Jeremiah the prophet*, that He would accomplish *seventy years* in the desolations of Jerusalem. Then *I set my face toward the Lord God* to make *request by prayer and supplications*, with fasting, sackcloth, and ashes.[344]

The prophecy Daniel was studying in the book of Jeremiah is as follows:

> Therefore thus says the LORD of hosts: *"Because you have not heard My words, behold*, I will send and take all the families of the north," says the LORD, "and *Nebuchadnezzar* the king of Babylon, My servant, and will bring them against this land, against its inhabitants, and against these nations all around, and will *utterly destroy them*, and make them an astonishment, a hissing, and perpetual desolations...." And this whole land shall be a desolation and an astonishment, and these nations shall *serve the king of Babylon seventy years*. "Then it will come to pass, when *seventy years are completed*, that I will punish the king of Babylon and that nation, the

---

[344] Daniel 9:1–3 (emphasis added)

land of the Chaldeans, for their iniquity," says the LORD; "and I will make it a perpetual desolation."[345]

Jeremiah also prophesied that after the seventy-year captivity, the Jews would be freed to return to their homeland

"For behold, the days are coming," says the LORD, "that *I will bring back from captivity My people Israel and Judah*," says the LORD. "And I will *cause them to return* to the land that I gave to their fathers, and they shall possess it."[346]

Daniel's prayer is one of the greatest prayers recorded in the Bible. His relationship with God was characterized not only by Bible study, but by earnest prayer three times a day throughout his life.[347] It was his intimate relationship with God that made Daniel who he was.

It would be hard to overestimate the influence Daniel's life has had in history. He was the top governmental official in two world-ruling empires (Babylon and Media-Persia).[348] His reputation and influence were known and felt throughout the world.[349] His fidelity to God was publicly proclaimed by three kings (Nebuchadnezzar, Belshazzar, Darius). Even though Jesus encouraged reading and studying all the books of the Old Testament, the only book He specifically instructed His followers to read and understand was the book of Daniel.[350]

> ***It was his intimate relationship with God that made Daniel who he was.***

Besides all that, the book of Revelation is based on the book of Daniel to the point that the only way to correctly understand Revelation's prophecies is to understand Daniel's prophecies first. Therefore, the book of Daniel plays a significant role in the lives of God's people clear to the end of time.

Even in his prayer, Daniel demonstrated the merciful character of our loving God. Put yourself in his shoes. He had been taken captive to Babylon because of the sins of his people, Israel. He was made a eunuch,

---

[345] Jeremiah 25:8–12 (emphasis added)
[346] Jeremiah 30:3 (emphasis added)
[347] See Daniel 6:10
[348] See Daniel 2:48; 5:29; 6:1–3
[349] See Daniel 4:1–37; 6:25–27
[350] See Matthew 24:15; Mark 13:14

never to marry and have children. He was exiled from home, never to see his homeland or family again. Would you be bitter?

Not Daniel! In his prayer, he did not speak condemning words against Israel. Instead, he included himself in the guilt of the sins that caused Jerusalem's destruction. His prayer is a prayer that deserves our careful attention because it is filled not only with godly confession but also confident assurance in God's love, mercy, and forgiveness.

> And I *prayed* to the LORD my God, and made *confession*, and said, "O Lord, great and awesome God, who *keeps His covenant and mercy* with those who *love Him*, and with those who *keep His commandments*, *we* have sinned and committed iniquity, *we* have done wickedly and rebelled, even by departing from Your precepts and Your judgments. Neither have *we* heeded Your servants the prophets, who spoke in Your name to our kings and our princes, to our fathers and all the people of the land."[351]

Notice Daniel's use of "we" in his confessions. Also notice he was praying directly to God, not confessing to a human priest. "To the *Lord our God* belong *mercy* and *forgiveness*, though *we* have rebelled against Him. *We* have not obeyed the voice of the LORD our God, to walk in His laws, which He set before us by His servants the prophets."[352]

Daniel concluded his prayer by pleading with God not to extend the seventy years of Babylonian captivity. What he had in mind was clearly the 2,300-day prophecy of chapter 8. "O Lord, *hear*! O Lord, *forgive*! O Lord, *listen* and *act*! *Do not delay* for *Your own sake*, my God, for *Your city* and *Your people* are called by *Your name*."[353]

While he was still in prayer, the angel Gabriel was sent from heaven to answer Daniel's prayer and give him understanding in regard to the vision he had received earlier (especially the part about the 2,300 days).[354]

What Gabriel told Daniel is quite typical of the way God answers our prayers. God's answers are often very different from what we expect, but His answers are always far better than what we have in mind. The apostle Paul mentioned this in His prayer. "Now to Him who is able to do *exceedingly abundantly* above all that we *ask* or *think*, according to the power that

---

[351] Daniel 9:4–6 (emphasis added)
[352] Daniel 9:9, 10 (emphasis added)
[353] Daniel 9:19 (emphasis added)
[354] See Daniel 9:21–23

The Most Exciting Prophecy

works in us, to Him be glory in the church by Christ Jesus to all generations, forever and ever. Amen."[355]

Gabriel's explanation not only gave the beginning date of the 2,300 days, but it connected this beginning date to another time prophecy that is so accurate, it pinpoints not only the year, but the month, day, and hour of Christ's death on Calvary, the most significant event to ever happen on planet earth. By connecting these two time prophecies, Gabriel showed the significance of both. The two are inseparably connected.

Have you ever wondered what Paul meant when he said, "When the *fullness of the time* had come, God sent forth His Son"?[356] Or to what Jesus was referring when He said, "The *time is fulfilled*, and the kingdom of God is at hand"?[357] To what prophecy were they referring that would pinpoint the date of Christ's life and death on this earth? There is only one prophecy in the entire Bible that does that: Daniel 9.

Gabriel began his explanation by saying, "*Seventy weeks* are *determined* for *your people* and for *your holy city*, To finish the transgression, To make an end of sins, To make reconciliation for iniquity, To bring in everlasting righteousness, To seal up vision and prophecy, And to anoint the Most Holy."[358]

Seventy weeks is 490 days (7 x 70), which is about one-and-one-third years. This prophecy would not make sense if the time factor was to be taken literally. However, by applying the biblical principle that a prophetic day represents a literal year, this prophecy becomes amazing.[359] Let us see what happens when we take the 70 weeks to represent 490 literal years.

Israel, as a nation, would be given 490 years of probationary time to do the following six things:

1. Finish the transgression (אלכ עשפ)
2. Make an end of sins (םתח האטח תאטח)
3. Make reconciliation for iniquity (רפכ ןוע ןווע)
4. Bring in everlasting righteousness (אוב םלוע םלע)
5. Seal up vision and prophecy (וזח םתח איבנ)
6. Anoint the Most Holy (חשמ שדק שדק)

---

[355] Ephesians 3:20, 21 (emphasis added)
[356] Galatians 4:4 (emphasis added)
[357] Mark 1:15 (emphasis added)
[358] Daniel 9:24 (emphasis added)
[359] See Numbers 14:34; Ezekiel 4:6

An interesting pattern is established with these six requirements for Israel and Jerusalem. The first three are goals that could only be accomplished through faith in Jesus. Jesus came to take away our sins.[360] Notice these three consist of two Hebrew words. On the other hand, the last three contain three Hebrew words. Outlining it may help clarify the pattern:

your people	your holy city
to—	to—
-finish transgression	-bring everlasting righteousness
-end sins	-seal vision prophecy
-reconcile iniquity	-anoint holy sanctuary

We find this same pattern in the next three verses (25–27), so there are two parts to each verse. We will soon see why this is important to understand. The first part refers to what Jesus will do for His people, and the last part deals with the city of Jerusalem in one way or another.

Gabriel began to tell Daniel what will take place during those 490 years. "Know therefore and understand, That from the *going forth of the command* To *restore and build Jerusalem until Messiah the Prince*, There shall be *seven weeks and sixty-two weeks*; The *street* shall be *built again*, and the *wall*, Even in troublesome times."[361]

First, there would be a "command" or decree to restore and build Jerusalem, and the streets and walls would be built again during troublesome times. The biblical books of Ezra and Nehemiah reveal this happened exactly as Gabriel foretold. The city was rebuilt under strong opposition from the surrounding people.[362] There were three decrees given by Medo-Persian kings regarding the rebuilding of Jerusalem. However, it was the third one that was finally successful.

> This is a copy of the letter that *King Artaxerxes* gave Ezra the priest, the scribe, expert in the words of the commandments of the LORD, and of His statutes to Israel: Artaxerxes, king of kings, To Ezra the priest, a scribe of the Law of the God of heaven: Perfect peace, and so forth. *I issue a decree* that all those of the people of Israel and the priests and Levites in my realm, who volunteer to go up to Jerusalem, may go with you.[363]

---

[360] See Matthew 1:21
[361] Daniel 9:25 (emphasis added)
[362] See Nehemiah 4:1–23; 6:1–19
[363] Ezra 7:11–13 (emphasis added)

The Most Exciting Prophecy

What is interesting about this decree is that it also gave the Jews the authority to make Jerusalem the capital city of that region of the Medo-Persian Empire. They were given permission to appoint government officials and judges, which implied the building of facilities in which these leaders would function.[364]

The date of this decree is one of the most firmly fixed dates in antiquity. We not only know it was issued in the year 457 BC, but we also know it was issued in the fall of that year.[365] Therefore, the beginning date of the 490-year prophecy is the autumn of 457 BC. Gabriel now began to break these 490 years into four sections. The first two are "seven weeks and sixty-two weeks" "until Messiah the Prince." Seven weeks (7 x 7) is forty-nine days, or forty-nine years in this case. This was the timeframe for the reestablishment of Jerusalem under Ezra and Nehemiah's leadership.

Sixty-two weeks (7 x 62) comes to 434 years. By adding 49 years (7 weeks) to 434 years (62 weeks), we have 483 years (69 weeks). Therefore, beginning at 457 BC and going forward 483 years, we should come to Messiah the Prince, according to this prophecy.

Gabriel explained that from the decree to rebuild Jerusalem "until Messiah the Prince" would be 483 years (49 years + 434 years). When you calculate a length of years that starts in the BC era and extends to the AD era, you must add a year because there was no year zero. Therefore, 483 years from the starting date of 457 BC comes to the year AD 27 (instead of AD 26). The following chart will help explain what we have discovered so far regarding this seventy-week prophecy.

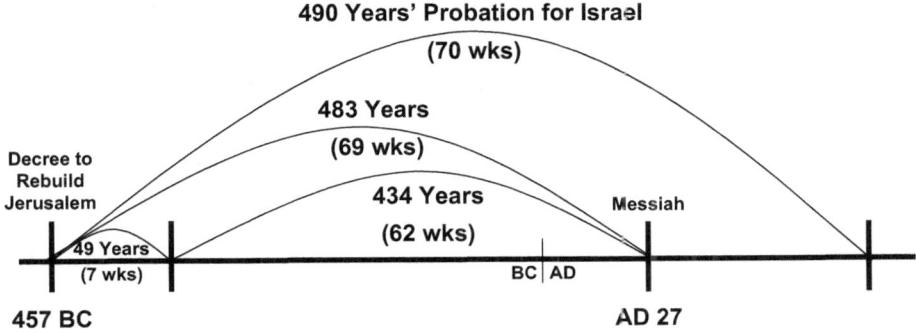

---

[364] Read the entire decree in Ezra 7:12–26
[365] See C. Mervyn Maxwell, God Cares, vol. 1, (Boise, ID: Pacific Press Publishing Association, 1981), pp. 251–253

The question is, What happened in AD 27? And who is Messiah the Prince? The word "Messiah" in Hebrew means "the Anointed One," and the word "Christ" is the Greek equivalent. With that said, was Jesus anointed in AD 27? Yes, at His baptism.

> The word which God sent to the children of Israel, preaching peace through Jesus Christ—*He is Lord of all*—that word you know, which was proclaimed throughout all Judea, and *began from Galilee after the baptism* which John preached: how *God anointed Jesus of Nazareth with the Holy Spirit and with power*, who went about doing good and healing all who were oppressed by the devil, for God was with Him.[366]

Christ's anointing by the Holy Spirit at His baptism signaled the beginning of His public ministry, where He demonstrated the power of God in healing, teaching, and preaching. Luke, a physician, records this in his gospel:

> When all the people were baptized, it came to pass that *Jesus also was baptized*; and while He prayed, the heaven was opened. And the *Holy Spirit descended in bodily form like a dove upon Him*, and a voice came from heaven which said, "You are My beloved Son; in You I am well pleased." Now *Jesus Himself began His ministry* at about thirty years of age.[367]

Luke tells us the year in which Jesus was baptized and anointed by the Holy Spirit:

> Now in the *fifteenth year of the reign of Tiberius Caesar*, Pontius Pilate being governor of Judea, Herod being tetrarch of Galilee,

---

[366] Acts 10:36–38 (emphasis added)
[367] Luke 3:21–23 (emphasis added)

his brother Philip tetrarch of Iturea and the region of Trachonitis, and Lysanias tetrarch of Abilene, while Annas and Caiaphas were high priests, the word of God came to John the son of Zacharias in the wilderness. And he went into all the region around the Jordan, preaching a *baptism of repentance* for the remission of sins."[368]

In talking about His baptism, Jesus quoted Isaiah's prophecy about His anointing. "The *Spirit of the Lord is upon Me*, because *He has anointed Me* to *preach* the gospel to the poor; He has sent Me to *heal* the brokenhearted."[369]

Luke gives us plenty of historical information so we can know for certain when the "fifteenth year of the reign of Tiberius Caesar" was. By our method of dating, it was AD 27, and Jesus was baptized in the fall of that year. God's prophecies are amazingly precise!

That brings us to the end of the 69th week (483 years), but there is still 1 week (7 years) left of the 70. What happened then? Gabriel continued his explanation: "And *after the sixty-two weeks Messiah shall be cut off*, but *not for Himself*; And the people of the prince who is to come Shall *destroy the city and the sanctuary*. The end of it shall be with a flood, And till the end of the war desolations are determined."[370]

Gabriel explained that sometime after AD 27—after the 62 weeks—"Messiah shall be cut off." Gabriel is clearly announcing that Jesus would be crucified sometime after AD 27. This is where it really begins to get exciting, because the crucifixion of Christ is the most significant event to ever happen on this

planet. This prophecy pinpoints when salvation was accomplished for our sinful world. It would happen sometime in the final seven years (one week) of this prophecy. Gabriel made it clear that Jesus would not die for His own sins, but for yours and mine.

---

[368] Luke 3:1–3 (emphasis added)
[369] Luke 4:18 (emphasis added)
[370] Daniel 9:26 (emphasis added)

The prophet Isaiah confers with that: *"He was cut off from the land of the living; For the transgressions of My people He was stricken."*[371] In talking about Christ's death, Peter stated, "Who *Himself bore our sins* in His own body on the tree, that we, having died to sins, might live for righteousness—*by whose stripes you were healed."*[372]

Considering all these things, what about the part that says, "the people of the prince who is to come shall destroy the city and the sanctuary"? The prophecy specified that sometime after AD 27, the city and sanctuary would be destroyed. In fulfillment of this prophecy, the Roman general Titus attacked Jerusalem and burned it and the sanctuary to the ground in AD 70. Jesus had also predicted the destruction of Jerusalem by the Romans: "But when you see *Jerusalem surrounded by armies*, then know that its desolation is near. Then let those who are in Judea *flee to the mountains."*[373]

Matthew also records Christ's prophecy. Notice how both Luke and Matthew record Jesus saying, "flee to the mountains." The surrounding of Jerusalem by armies is a fulfillment of Daniel's prophecy. "'Therefore when you see the *"abomination of desolation," spoken of by Daniel* the prophet, standing in the holy place' (whoever reads, let him understand), 'then let those who are in Judea *flee to the mountains.'"*[374]

Jesus predicted the destruction of Jerusalem in several other places. He told a parable about a king who threw a party for his son's wedding, but the people who were invited to the feast killed his servants who gave the invitation. Jesus was referring to the Jewish nation. Then He described the king's reaction: "But when the king heard about it, he was furious. And he *sent out his armies*, destroyed those murderers, and *burned up their city."*[375]

Jesus made other startling predictions about the fate of Jerusalem:

> Then Jesus went out and departed from the temple, and His disciples came up to show Him the buildings of the *temple*. And Jesus said to them, "Do you not see all these things? Assuredly, I say to you, *not one stone shall be left here upon another, that shall not be thrown down."*[376]

---

[371] Isaiah 53:8 (emphasis added)
[372] 1 Peter 2:24 (emphasis added)
[373] Luke 21:20, 21 (emphasis added)
[374] Matthew 24:15, 16 (emphasis added)
[375] Mathew 22:7 (emphasis added)
[376] Matthew 24:1, 2 (emphasis added)

Now as He drew near, He saw the city and *wept over it*, saying, "If you had known, even you, especially in this your day, the things that make for your peace! But now they are hidden from your eyes. For days will come upon you when your *enemies will build an embankment around you, surround you and close you in on every side, and level you*, and your children within you, to the ground; and they will not leave in you one stone upon another, because you did not know the time of your visitation."[377]

Each of these verses adds more details so we can know with certainty the significance of the events being predicted. Gabriel made it clear that it was not the Roman emperor who would come with his army to destroy Jerusalem, but it was the "people of the prince who is to come" who would destroy the city and temple. It was not Emperor Vespasian who led the Roman army that destroyed Jerusalem; it was his son, Titus.

Gabriel concluded his explanation with these words:

> Then *he* shall *confirm a covenant* with many for *one week*; But in the *middle of the week* He shall *bring an end to sacrifice and offering*. And on the wing of abominations shall be one who makes desolate, Even until the consummation, which is determined, Is *poured out on the desolate* [margin, "desolator"].[378]

The first question that comes to mind when we read this verse is, To whom does the pronoun "he" refer? This is answered in the previous verse, but there seems to be two options: one being the "Messiah" and the other being the "people of the prince who is to come." However, for two reasons, the only possible answer is the Messiah:

1. Linguistically, the "he" being singular matches the Messiah, who is singular. On the other hand, the "people of the prince" is plural and therefore does not match. Gabriel worded this very specifically to clarify to whom he was referring.
2. As we noted earlier, there is a pattern Gabriel used as he was talking to Daniel. The first half of verses 25 and 26 talked about the Messiah, and this sets the pattern for the first half of verse 27. Let us take each phrase of the verse and see how this plays out:

---

[377] Luke 19:41–44 (emphasis added)
[378] Daniel 9:27 (emphasis added)

"Then he shall confirm a covenant with many": The word "confirm" (רבג *gaw-bar'*) means "strengthen." Jesus strengthened the covenant. The old covenant was confirmed by the blood of animals, but the blood of animals could not atone for sin. The animal sacrifices could only point forward to the Messiah, who would shed His blood for our sins. Jesus ratified the covenant. The New Testament makes this clear.

> For it is *not possible* that the *blood* of bulls and goats could *take away sins*.[379]
> So *Christ was offered* once to *bear the sins* of many.[380]

When Jesus instituted the Lord's Supper, He referred to His death as that which confirmed the new covenant.

> And as they were eating, Jesus took bread, blessed and broke it, and gave it to the disciples and said, "Take, eat; *this is My body*." Then He took the cup, and gave thanks, and gave it to them, saying, "Drink from it, all of you. For *this is My blood of the new covenant*, which is shed for many *for the remission of sins*."[381]

Prophesying about the coming Messiah, Isaiah quoted the Lord as saying He would be given as a covenant.

> I, the LORD, have called You in righteousness, And will hold Your hand; I will keep You and *give You as a covenant to the people*, As a light to the Gentiles, To open blind eyes, To bring out prisoners from the prison, Those who sit in darkness from the prison house.[382]

"He shall confirm a covenant with many for one week." Jesus not only confirmed the new covenant with His blood, but He also confirmed His covenant with the nation of Israel for those last seven years. The covenant with the nation of Israel would end one week (seven years) from the time of Christ's baptism. At that time, probation for the nation of Israel as God's chosen people would come to an end, and the gospel would go to the Gentiles. The Christian church would become the new chosen people—the new Israel.

---

[379] Hebrews 10:4 (emphasis added)
[380] Hebrews 9:28 (emphasis added)
[381] Matthew 26:26–28 (emphasis added)
[382] Isaiah 42:6, 7 (emphasis added)

Jews could still be saved as individuals, but the nation would no longer be God's chosen instrument to take His message of love and truth to the world. Jesus plainly predicted this: "Therefore I say to you, the *kingdom of God will be taken from you* and *given to a nation bearing the fruits of it*."[383] The church would be the new Israel.

> For he is *not a Jew* who is one *outwardly*, nor is circumcision that which is outward in the *flesh*; but *he is a Jew* who is one *inwardly*; and circumcision is that of the **heart**, in the **Spirit**, not in the letter; whose praise is not from men but from God.[384]
>
> And *if you are Christ's*, then you are *Abraham's seed*, and *heirs according to the promise*.[385]

The book of Acts records this transition from physical Israel to spiritual Israel. Three-and-a-half years after the cross, the Jewish leaders began killing church leaders, beginning with the stoning of Steven, one of the seven deacons. They had already killed the Messiah, and now by killing His followers, there was nothing more God could do to reach their hearts. Their probation had come to an end. After Steven was stoned, Saul, who later became converted and was renamed Paul by God, began to persecute the church ruthlessly.

> Now Saul was consenting to his death. At that time a *great persecution arose against the church* which was at Jerusalem; and they were all *scattered* throughout the regions of Judea and Samaria, except the apostles. As for Saul, he *made havoc of the church*, entering every house, and dragging off men and women, committing them to *prison*. Therefore those who were scattered *went everywhere preaching the word*.[386]

Years later, after Saul's (Paul's) conversion, he spoke clearly about this transition from physical Israel to the Christian church, which was composed of Gentile and Jewish believers:

> Then Paul and Barnabas grew bold and said, "It was necessary that the *word of God* should be *spoken to you first*; but since you reject it, and judge yourselves unworthy of everlasting life, *behold,*

---

[383] Matthew 21:43 (emphasis added; see also 23:37, 38)
[384] Romans 2:28 (emphasis added)
[385] Galatians 3:29 (emphasis added; see also Romans 9:6–8; Galatians 3:7–9; 4:7, 21–31; 6:16)
[386] Acts 8:1–4 (emphasis added)

we turn to the Gentiles. For so the Lord has commanded us: 'I have set you as a light to the Gentiles, that you should be for salvation to the ends of the earth.'"[387]

Therefore, the seventieth week, the last seven years of probation for the nation of Israel, came to an end in AD 34 at the stoning of Steven, and the gospel was preached to the Gentiles through the church.

"But in the middle of the week He shall bring an end to sacrifice and offering." The middle of seven years would be three-and-a-half years. Since the decree to rebuild Jerusalem was issued in the fall of 457 BC, as we have seen, 483 years would bring us to the fall of AD 27.

Therefore, from the fall of AD 27, going forward three-and-a-half years would reach the spring of AD 31. Jesus was crucified on Passover, the fourteenth day of the first month of the Jewish ceremonial year,[388] which is in the spring. Passover is close to the time the world celebrates Easter today. That year, Passover fell on Friday,[389] so the Passover lamb was to be slain that day.[390] We know Jesus was crucified on Friday[391] and died at the time of the slaying of the Passover lamb, which was at 3:00 p.m.[392]

When Jesus died, the earthly sanctuary services were fulfilled. That to which the sacrifices and offerings had been pointing forward had now taken place. Even though the sanctuary services still contain many lessons about the plan of salvation, the observance of the ceremonies and sacrifices is no longer needed because the true Lamb of God has been slain![393]

---

[387] Acts 13:46, 47 emphasis added)
[388] See 1 Corinthians 5:7
[389] See John 19:31
[390] See Mark 15:42
[391] See Luke 23:50–56
[392] See Matthew 27:46–50—the ninth hour of Jewish time is 3:00 p.m. our time, which was when the Passover lamb was to be slain; see also Leviticus 23:5
[393] See 1 Corinthians 5:7

Therefore, Jesus brought "an end to sacrifice and offering." This was signified at His death when the veil in the temple was torn from top to bottom. That veil could not possibly be torn accidently or by any human hands. The cloth was as thick as a man's hand is wide. It was torn by an angel to signify the fulfillment of the sacrificial ceremonies. They no longer needed to be carried out because the true Lamb of God had been slain. "And Jesus cried out with a loud voice, and *breathed His last*. Then the *veil of the temple* was *torn in two* from top to bottom."[394]

The Jews still conducted the sacrificial services until the sanctuary was destroyed in AD 70 by the Romans. However, they had lost their spiritual importance to Christian believers. In fact, to continue offering sacrifices would have been a denial of their faith in Jesus.

Thus, the Bible predicted the exact year, month, day, and hour of Christ's death, and it took place exactly as prophesied. No other prophecy gives such amazing details, yet Christ's death was the most important event to ever take place on earth and merits such detail.

The completed chart of the seventy-week prophecy of Daniel 9 is as follows:

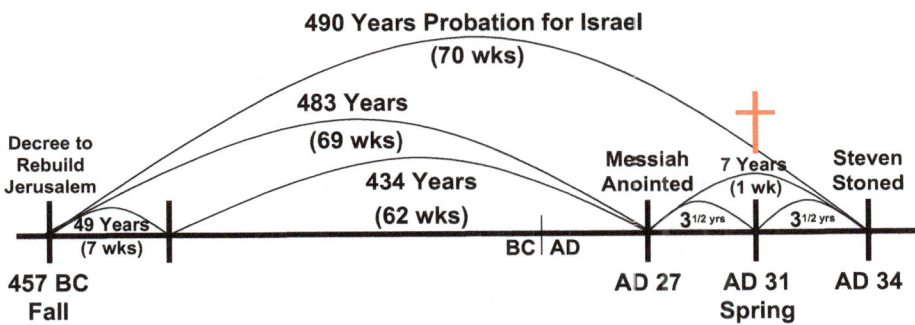

The essence of Christianity is the cross of Christ—not something you wear around your neck, but something you wear in your heart! The key to the Christian life is to surrender your will to Jesus, just as He surrendered His will to His Father and made the final decision to go to the cross. "Father, if it is Your will, take this cup away from Me; nevertheless *not My will, but Yours, be done*."[395]

---

[394] Mark 15:37 (emphasis added)
[395] Luke 22:42 (emphasis added)

When the Bible says one thing but we are used to doing another, we need to say, as Jesus did, "Not my will, but yours, be done." The apostle Paul learned this lesson and shared his experience: *"I have been crucified with Christ*; it is *no longer I who live*, but *Christ lives in me*; and the life which I now live in the flesh *I live by faith in the Son of God*, who *loved me* and *gave Himself for me."*[396]

This is the spiritual experience that will enable us to stand through the days ahead. This is what we need to pass the judgment and be ready when Jesus comes!

The last part of Gabriel's explanation was about the destruction of the Roman power, which was to be responsible for destroying the city of Jerusalem in AD 70. "And on the wing of abominations shall be *one who makes desolate*, Even until the consummation, which is determined, *Is poured out on the desolate."*[397]

The marginal reading translates the last part of this verse "Is poured out on the desolator." It only makes sense that the "one who makes desolate" is the "desolator." It was Rome that destroyed Jerusalem and made it desolate. Therefore, this prophecy says Rome (the desolator) will be destroyed in the end.

This was also pointed out in Daniel 2 when the stone, representing the kingdom of heaven, struck the metal man on his feet and toes of iron and clay and crushed it in pieces. You will recall the iron represented Rome. Subsequently, Gabriel is again reminding us of the end of the story, so to speak. Satan and his forces will not win in this cosmic battle between him and God. Jesus gained the victory on the cross. Praise the Lord!

The next questions to address are, How does this seventy-week prophecy answer the question left unanswered at the end of Daniel 8? How does this prophecy connect with the 2,300-year prediction, when judgment was to begin in the heavenly sanctuary?

The simple answer is that the 490 years (70 weeks) is the first part of the 2,300 years. In other words, the 2,300 years and 490 years began at the same time, in the fall of 457 BC, when the decree to rebuild Jerusalem was issued by Artaxerxes. How do we know this? There are at least two reasons:

---

[396] Galatians 2:20 (emphasis added)
[397] Daniel 9:27 (emphasis added)

1. The only visions in the book of Daniel with which the angel Gabriel was involved were the visions of chapters 8 and 9, and the only part of the vision of chapter 8 Gabriel did not explain was the part about the 2,300 years. When he returned after Daniel's prayer in chapter 9, he said he had come to give him understanding of the vision he had partially explained before. Now he had come to explain the remaining part.

   While I was speaking in prayer, the man *Gabriel*, whom I had seen *in the vision at the beginning*, being caused to fly swiftly, reached me about the time of the evening offering. And he informed me, and talked with me, and said, "O Daniel, *I have now come forth to give you skill to understand*. At the beginning of your supplications the command went out, and I have come to tell you, for you are greatly beloved; therefore consider the matter, and *understand the vision*."[398]

2. The phrase "Seventy weeks are determined for your people and for your holy city" can also be translated "Seventy weeks are cut off for your people and for your holy city." The Hebrew word is חתך (*khaw-thak'*), which properly means to "cut off" and figuratively means to "decree" or "determine."[399] In order for the 490 years to be "cut off," they would have to be cut off from a longer time prophecy, and the only one in this vision is the 2,300 years. Therefore, the 70 weeks (490 years) are "cut off" from the 2,300 years. The equation would look like this:

   2,300 years
   − 490 years
   1,810 years

   Therefore, there would be 1,810 years remaining after the 490 years came to an end in AD 34, when probation for the Jewish nation ended and the gospel went to the Gentiles.

   AD 34
   + 1,810 years
   AD 1844

---

[398] Daniel 9:21–23 (emphasis added)
[399] See Strong's Greek and Hebrew Dictionary

The time chart for the 2,300 years would look like the following:

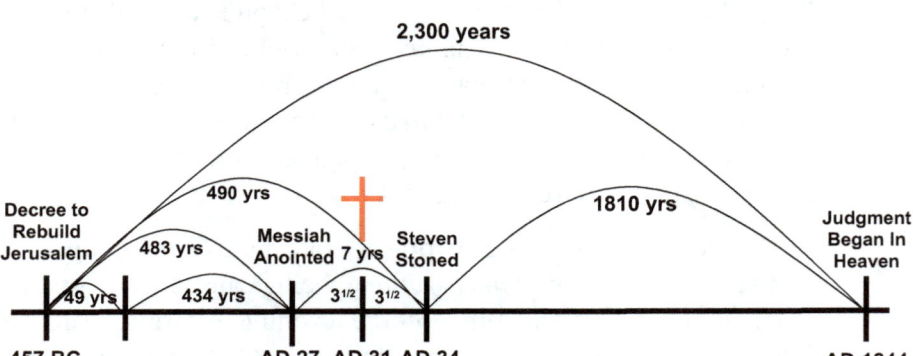

Therefore, we are not only living in the time of the toenails of Daniel 2 and the time of the little horn of Daniel 7, but we are also living in the time of the judgment, when Satan's power will be broken and the people of God will receive the kingdom of heaven. We are living at the very close of this earth's history. Jesus is coming soon!

> But the *court* shall be *seated*, And they shall take away his dominion, To consume and destroy it forever. Then the *kingdom and dominion*, And the greatness of the kingdoms under the whole heaven, Shall be *given to the people, the saints of the Most High*. His kingdom is an *everlasting kingdom*, And *all dominions shall serve and obey Him*.[400]

What a wonderful day that will be when the judgment is completed and Jesus comes to take us to be with Him forever! That is Christ's promise to you!

> *Let not* your heart be *troubled*; you believe in God, believe also in Me. In My Father's house are many mansions; if it were not so, I would have told you. *I go to prepare a place for you*. And if I go and prepare a place for you, *I will come again and receive you to Myself; that where I am, there you may be also*.[401]

---

[400] Daniel 7:26, 27 (emphasis added)
[401] John 14:1–3 (emphasis added)

The apostle Paul calls this the blessed hope of the Christian. "Looking for the *blessed hope* and *glorious appearing* of our *great God* and *Savior Jesus Christ*."[402]

Stay tuned, for this blessed hope is the topic of the next chapter.

---

[402] Titus 2:13 (emphasis added)

Chapter 8

The Blessed Hope

The book of Revelation is commonly known as the Apocalypse, which means "disclosure, appearing, coming." This is because it is a disclosure of Jesus and His work for us in preparation for His second coming. Because of some of the very graphic symbolic representations used, many people are afraid to read or study Revelation; they would rather ignore this book.

The reality is that Revelation is all about Jesus. In fact, the very first verse declares it is a "Revelation of Jesus Christ."[403] This revelation involves events in the past as well as prophecies of the future that show how Jesus is working for our salvation. The whole purpose of Revelation is to help us be ready for Christ's second coming. In fact, in the last chapter, Jesus makes this point three times:

"Behold, *I am coming quickly*! *Blessed is he who keeps the words of the prophecy of this book.*"[404]

"Surely *I am coming quickly*."[405]

"And behold, *I am coming quickly*, and *My reward is with Me*, to give to every one according to his work."[406]

Jesus said He will give out His rewards when He comes—not at death! We will study this later, but I want you to notice what happens just before He comes to give out His rewards, which were determined in the judgment. The previous verse is the pronouncement Jesus gives at the conclusion of the investigative judgment. There will only

---

[403] Revelation 1:1
[404] Revelation 22:7 (emphasis added)
[405] Revelation 22:20 (emphasis added)
[406] Revelation 22:12 (emphasis added)

be two groups of people on earth when He comes. "He who is *unjust*, let him be *unjust still*; he who is *filthy*, let him be *filthy still*; he who is *righteous*, let him be *righteous still*; he who is *holy*, let him be *holy still*."[407]

This pronouncement was given to the apostle John, the author of Revelation, over nineteen centuries ago. You might wonder how quickly is "quickly." Even though God revealed the exact time of Christ's death on Calvary, Jesus made it clear that His Father has not revealed the time of His second coming,[408] and I believe He has done this for our benefit. Believing He is coming soon is an encouragement for us to develop and maintain a close, personal, love-faith relationship with Him. The apostle Paul called the glorious second coming of Jesus the "blessed hope!"[409] For the believer in Jesus, it truly is a blessed hope.

Just a few days before Christ was crucified, He was sitting on the Mount of Olives with four of His disciples, and they asked about His return. "What will be the sign of Your coming, and the end of the age?"[410]

In answer, Jesus outlined more than twenty signs of His return. We will look at only a few of them, but in doing so, our conviction will grow that His coming truly is soon. "And you will hear of *wars* and *rumors of wars*. See that you are not troubled; for all these things must come to pass, but the end is not yet. For *nation* will rise *against nation*, and *kingdom against kingdom*."[411]

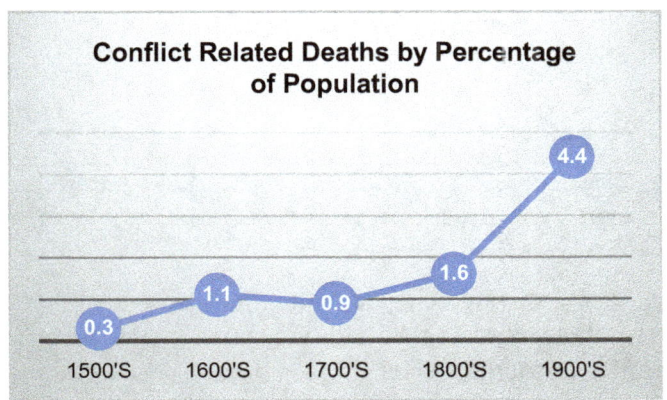

---

[407] Revelation 22:11 (emphasis added)
[408] See Matthew 24:36
[409] Titus 2:13 (emphasis added)
[410] Matthew 24:3
[411] Matthew 24:6, 7 (emphasis added)

There have been many wars throughout the history of this world. However, conflict-related deaths by percentage of population have been on a sharp rise. There never was a world war until the 1900s. World War I was declared to be the war that was to end all wars. Yet, since World War II, our world has seen at least seventeen major conflicts. And not only do we have continuing wars today, but many nations are talking about or planning and preparing for war. Threats of war are reported frequently in the news.

Jesus goes on to tell us more signs that will take place before He returns: "And there will be *famines*, *pestilences*, and *earthquakes* in various places."[412]

Despite global efforts, some 21,000 people die every day from hunger or malnutrition.[413] That means 7.6 million die per year of starvation. "Pestilence" is another word for pandemic diseases. Even as I write this book, the world is in the grip of the COVID-19 pandemic. By all projections, it will be with us for years to come, adding to the risk of famine. Time will tell, but it has changed life across the globe and united the world against a common threat. That global unity against a common enemy is also the fulfillment of prophecy. We will see this more fully when we study Revelation 13.

Jesus also talked about earthquakes as a sign of His soon return. The following chart of the US Geological Survey of Notable Earthquakes shows the dramatic increase of earthquakes in the last 200 years.

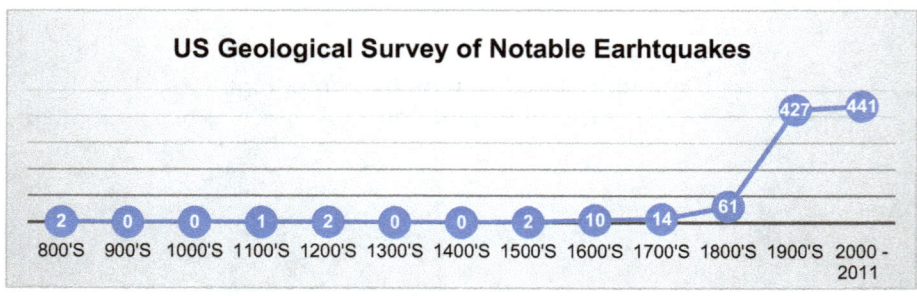

Nevertheless, Jesus made it clear that "all these are the *beginning of sorrows*."[414] In other words, there will be a smaller time of trouble before the great time of trouble, which is just before Jesus comes.[415] Talking about these times of trouble, Jesus said, "Then they will deliver you up to

---

[412] Matthew 24:7 (emphasis added)
[413] "World Hunger Day 2019," Voice of America, https://editorials.voa.gov/a/world-hunger-day-2019/4935420.html (accessed February 9, 2021)
[414] Matthew 24:8 (emphasis added)
[415] See Daniel 12:1

tribulation and kill you, and *you will be hated by all nations for My name's sake*. And then many will be offended, will betray one another, and will *hate one another*."[416]

If we get our self-worth from those around us, we have no solid anchor. The only way to handle such rejection, hatred, and persecution is by developing a strong relationship with Jesus. We must get our self-worth from knowing God's acceptance and the assurance of His love. Our self-worth should not be based on what others think of us, what we look like, how much money we have, or how popular we are, but on what God thinks of us. When we accept Christ as our personal Savior, He covers us with His perfect righteousness. Therefore, when God looks at us, He sees Jesus! Your value to God is beyond estimate, "for you were bought at a price,"[417] and that price was Jesus. He wants you to be with Him for eternity!

> *If we get our self-worth from those around us, we have no solid anchor. The only way to handle such rejection, hatred, and persecution is by developing a strong relationship with Jesus.*

Jesus continued to describe events that are important for us to know in order to be prepared for His second coming. "Then *many false prophets* will rise up and *deceive many*."[418] He did not say all "prophets" at the end of time would be false, just many of them. The Bible tells us how we can know if a prophet is true or false. The biblical tests of a prophet are as follows:

1. "To the *law* and to the *testimony*! If they do not speak *according to this word*, it is because there is *no light in them*."[419]

    The first five books of the Bible were written by Moses and called the "books of the law." The writings of the prophets were called the "testimony." Therefore, "To the law and to the testimony" is a reference to the entire Bible. Light is a symbol of truth, so a prophet's words must be tested by the Bible.

---

[416] Matthew 24:9, 10 (emphasis added)
[417] 1 Corinthians 6:20
[418] Matthew 24:11 (emphasis added)
[419] Isaiah 8:20 (emphasis added)

2. "If there arises among you a *prophet* or a *dreamer of dreams*, and he gives you a *sign or a wonder*, and the sign or the wonder *comes to pass*, of which he spoke to you, saying, '*Let us go after other gods*'—which you have not known—'and let us serve them,' *you shall not listen to the words of that prophet* or that dreamer of dreams, for the LORD your God is testing you to know whether you love the LORD your God with all your heart and with all your soul. You shall walk after the LORD your God and fear Him, and keep His commandments and obey His voice; you shall serve Him and hold fast to Him."[420]

   In other words, miracles (signs and wonders) are not necessarily an indication that a person's messages are from God. Satan and his evil angels can work miracles as well. Miracles only show that a supernatural power is at work. The only way to determine if it is from God or Satan is to test it by the Bible. God will not contradict His Word!

3. "When a *prophet* speaks in the name of the LORD, if the thing *does not happen or come to pass*, that is the thing which *the LORD has not spoken*; the prophet has spoken it presumptuously; you shall not be afraid of him."[421]

   A true prophet's predictions will always come to pass, unless they are based on a condition that does not come to pass (e.g., repentance).

4. "*Beware of false prophets*, who come to you in *sheep's clothing*, but inwardly they are ravenous wolves. *You will know them by their fruits.*"[422]

   Not only do their words need to match the Bible, but their lives and the results of their work must match as well. A true prophet will be a genuine, humble follower of Jesus, living a holy life and having an influence for righteousness.

5. "Beloved, *do not believe every spirit*, but *test the spirits*, whether they are of God; because *many false prophets* have gone out into the world. By this you know the Spirit of God: Every spirit that *confesses that Jesus Christ has come in the flesh is of God*, and every

---

[420] Deuteronomy 13:1–4 (emphasis added).
[421] Deuteronomy 18:22 (emphasis added; see also Jeremiah 28:9).
[422] Matthew 7:15, 16 (emphasis added).

spirit that does not confess that Jesus Christ has come in the flesh is not of God."[423]

It is important to test everyone who teaches the Bible, including me and what I am teaching in this book. When the apostle Paul and his ministry associate, Silas, went to Berea to preach about Jesus, the Bereans were commended because "they received the word with all readiness, and *searched the Scriptures daily* to find out *whether these things were so.*"[424]

Jesus made it clear there would be many false prophets in the end of time, but He did not say that all end-time prophets would be false. We must test everything according to the law and testimony. Jesus continued talking about the time just before He returns. "And because *lawlessness will abound*, the *love of many will grow cold*. But he who endures to the end shall be saved."[425]

In 2018, in the United States alone, there were 1,210,000 violent crimes reported; and who knows how many were not reported. Mass shootings are becoming increasingly common. Violence and evil were the reasons God destroyed the world (all but eight people)[426] with a flood in the days of Noah.[427] Jesus said just before He returns, the world would be just like it was in the days of Noah.[428]

The people at the time of the flood were oblivious to the destruction that was coming their way, even though Noah had been prophesying about it for 120 years. They closed their minds to the word of God through Noah. Instead, they carried on as if life would continue the way it was without interruption. "They ate, they drank, they married wives, they were given in marriage, *until the day that Noah entered the ark*, and the *flood came* and *destroyed them all.*"[429]

Jesus wants us to learn the lessons of history so we do not repeat their mistakes. He goes on to say the condition of the world will be as it was in the days of Lot. Lot was a believer in God, but he settled in the very wicked city of Sodom, which was known for its prevalent homosexual lifestyle, and this was one of the reasons God destroyed that city by fire.[430]

---

[423] 1 John 4:1–3 (emphasis added)
[424] Acts 17:11 (emphasis added)
[425] Matthew 24:12, 13 (emphasis added)
[426] See Genesis 6:5, 11–13
[427] See 2 Peter 2:5
[428] See Matthew 24:37
[429] Luke 17:27 (emphasis added)
[430] See Genesis 19:1–26; Romans 1:26, 27

God loves all sinners, no matter the sin, and desires that we all repent so we will not be destroyed like the people of Sodom were.[431]

> *Likewise as it was* also in the *days of Lot*: They ate, they drank, they bought, they sold, they planted, they built; but on the day that Lot went out of *Sodom it rained fire and brimstone from heaven* and destroyed them all. *Even so will it be in the day when the Son of Man is revealed.*[432]

Christ's second coming will take most people by surprise—not because they have not been warned, but because they ignored the warnings, signs, and messages. This was the point He was emphasizing when He said, "But know this, that if the master of the house had known what hour the *thief* would come, *he would have watched* and not allowed his house to be broken into. Therefore *you also be ready*, for the Son of Man is coming *at an hour you do not expect.*"[433]

Jesus was almost redundant with His insistence that we "watch" for His coming so it will not take us by surprise. He knows how easy it is to become absorbed with the things of daily life and neglect preparation for His coming. Therefore, He repeatedly said, *"Watch therefore, for you do not know* what hour your *Lord is coming.... Therefore you also be ready*, for the *Son of Man is coming* at an hour you *do not expect."*[434]

The idea of Jesus coming as a thief in the night does not indicate He will come in a secret manner. Instead, He warns us to prepare so it will not take us by surprise. The apostle Paul makes it clear:

> For you yourselves know perfectly that the *day of the Lord so comes as a thief in the night*. For when they say, "Peace and safety!" then *sudden destruction* comes upon them, as labor pains upon a pregnant woman. And they shall not escape. But *you*, brethren, *are not in darkness*, so that this Day should overtake you *as a thief*. You are all sons of light and sons of the day. We are not of the night nor of darkness. Therefore *let us not sleep*, as others do, but *let us watch* and be sober.[435]

---

[431] See 2 Peter 3:9
[432] Luke 17:28–30 (emphasis added)
[433] Matthew 24:43, 44 (emphasis added)
[434] Matthew 24:42, 44 (emphasis added)
[435] 1 Thessalonians 5:2–6 (emphasis added)

There will be only two groups of people alive when Jesus comes. One group will be looking for His coming, studying the truths of the Bible, and prepared. For these people, His coming will not be as a thief. It will not be a surprise to them. However, there will be many who are in the dark, so to speak, regarding the truths of the Bible and asleep spiritually. For these people, Christ's coming will be a surprise, like an unexpected thief.

The term "thief in the night," in reference to Christ's coming, is not referring to the manner of His coming. He is not coming secretly to snatch His people to heaven. The apostle Peter makes that clear:

> But the *day of the Lord* will come as a *thief in the night*, in which the *heavens will pass away* with a *great noise*, and the *elements will melt with fervent heat*; both the earth and the works that are in it will be burned up. Therefore, since all these things will be dissolved, what manner of persons ought you to be *in holy conduct and godliness, looking for and hastening the coming of the day of God*, because of which the heavens will be dissolved, being on fire, and the elements will melt with fervent heat?[436]

Coming as a "thief in the night" is certainly not secretive, according to the Bible. In fact, when Jesus comes, everybody will see Him, hear Him, and know Him. Notice what the angels tell Jesus' disciples on the day He ascended to heaven: "This *same Jesus*, who was taken up from you into heaven, will *so come in like manner as you saw Him go into heaven*."[437]

They saw Him ascend into heaven surrounded by a cloud of angels, and we will see Him descend from heaven surrounded by a cloud of angels.

> Then the sign of the Son of Man will appear in heaven, and then all the tribes of the earth will mourn, and they will *see* the *Son of Man coming on the clouds of heaven* with *power* and *great glory*.[438]

> Behold, *He is coming with clouds*, and *every eye will see Him*, even they who pierced Him. And all the tribes of the earth will mourn because of Him.[439]

> For as the *lightning* comes *from the east and flashes to the west*, so *also* will the *coming of the Son of Man be*.[440]

---

[436] 2 Peter 3:10–12 (emphasis added)
[437] Acts 1:11 (emphasis added)
[438] Matthew 24:30 (emphasis added)
[439] Revelation 1:7 (emphasis added)
[440] Mathew 24:27 (emphasis added)

Even with your eyes closed, you can see a flash of lightning. Everyone will see Him come. For those who are ready, it will be the most exciting day of their lives. However, for those who are not ready, they will be terror stricken.

> And the *kings* of the earth, the *great* men, the *rich* men, the *commanders*, the *mighty* men, every *slave* and every *free* man, *hid themselves* in the caves and in the rocks of the mountains, and said to the mountains and rocks, "Fall on us and *hide us from the face of Him who sits on the throne and from the wrath of the Lamb*! For the great day of His wrath has come, and *who is able to stand*?"[441]

Notice it is not just the believers who will see Him coming. Even though the lost will want to hide from Jesus, the Lamb of God, they will not be able to do so. The searching question is asked: "Who is able to stand?" Revelation gives us the answer, and we will study that in the next couple chapters.

As we have seen, Jesus is not only coming personally and visibly for everyone on earth, but His coming will be the loudest day ever witnessed! The apostle Paul describes it this way:

> For the *Lord Himself will descend* from heaven with a *shout*, with *the voice of an archangel*, and with the *trumpet of God*. And the *dead in Christ will rise first*. Then we who are *alive and remain* shall be *caught up together* with them in the clouds *to meet the Lord in the air*. And thus we shall always be with the Lord.[442]

When Jesus comes, He will shout, the archangel and trumpet will sound, and those who have died "in Christ" will be resurrected to immortal, eternal life, to be with Jesus forever—never to die, never to suffer, never to have pain or sorrow again![443] What a wonderful day that will be for those who are ready! Then the living saved and the resurrected saved will be taken up from this earth together to meet Jesus in the clouds.

There are a couple things to notice in this verse: First, as we saw earlier, Jesus gives the reward of eternal life when the trumpet sounds and He descends in the cloud of angels—not at death. Paul makes this perfectly clear. You will notice he calls death a "sleep." We will study more about that later.

---

[441] Revelation 6:15–17 (emphasis added)
[442] 1 Thessalonians 4:16, 17 (emphasis added)
[443] See Revelation 21:3–5

Behold, I tell you a mystery: We shall not all *sleep*, but we shall all be *changed*—in a moment, in the twinkling of an eye, *at the last trumpet*. For the *trumpet will sound*, and the *dead will be raised incorruptible*, and *we shall be changed*. For this *corruptible* must put on *incorruption*, and this *mortal* must put on *immortality*. So *when* this corruptible has put on incorruption, and this mortal has put on immortality, *then* shall be brought to pass the saying that is written: *"Death is swallowed up in victory. O Death, where is your sting? O Hades, where is your victory?"*[444]

Second, Jesus will not touch this earth when He returns. He will be in the clouds, and the redeemed will be transported up into the clouds to meet Him there. In fact, Jesus warned us about being deceived upon this point. If a dazzlingly glorious being appears in different places on the planet, speaking the same beautiful words Jesus spoke when He was here 2,000 years ago, you can know it is a deception of Satan because Jesus said, "Therefore if they say to you, 'Look, He is in the desert!' do not go out; or 'Look, He is in the inner rooms!' do not believe it."[445]

Evil people and Satan himself will pretend to be Jesus, but they will not be able to replicate the manner of His coming. Let us review what happens when Jesus comes:

1. Every eye will see Him
2. Righteous dead raised
3. Righteous living changed
4. Immortality bestowed
5. Wicked living destroyed
6. Righteous taken up into the cloud
7. Righteous go to heaven with Jesus

Just as the majority of people were deceived and unprepared for Christ's first coming, so the majority are being deceived regarding His second coming. The *Left Behind* movies and books have become popular in recent years among Christians, but most people fail to read the subtitle, which says, "A *NOVEL* OF THE EARTH'S LAST DAYS."[446]

The theory that is promoted in this material is commonly called the "secret rapture" or simply "rapture." There are various versions of the theory, and none of them agree. However, there are some common elements at which we

---

[444] 1 Corinthians 15:51–55 (emphasis added)
[445] Matthew 24:26
[446] Tim LaHaye and Jerry B. Jenkins, Left Behind (Carol Stream, IL: Tyndale House Publishers, 1995), front cover (emphasis added)

will look. If you remember, we dealt with this briefly in chapter 4. This theory was developed by Francisco Ribera, a Jesuit priest in the 1500s.

The commonly held elements of the theory state Jesus will come secretly to snatch away Christians from the earth and take them to heaven; then there will be seven years of great tribulation before Jesus returns to set up His kingdom on the earth. During the seven years of tribulation, the antichrist will appear, all the Jews will be converted, and those who were not ready for the rapture will have time to get ready for His final coming. The problem with this theory is it does not fit what the Bible teaches. The theory is based on four points:

1. Seven years of tribulation: It is very true that this planet will be plunged into a time of great tribulation just before Jesus returns.

   > At that time Michael shall stand up, the great prince who stands watch over the sons of your people; and there shall be a *time of trouble*, *Such as never was* since there was a nation, even to that time. And at that time your people shall be delivered, everyone who is found written in the book.[447]

   The time of trouble is described more fully in Revelation 16, which outlines the seven last plagues to come in one day (year).[448] However, nowhere in the Bible do we have a seven-year period of tribulation described. The teachers of the rapture theory get the seven years from Daniel 9. They cut off the final 7 years from the 490 years and apply them to the antichrist at the end of time.

   However, as we studied in our previous chapter, the prophecy pinpoints the death of Christ exactly in the middle of the last 7 years of the 490-year prophecy. Therefore, they take the prophecy that belongs to Christ and apply it to antichrist, as seen below:

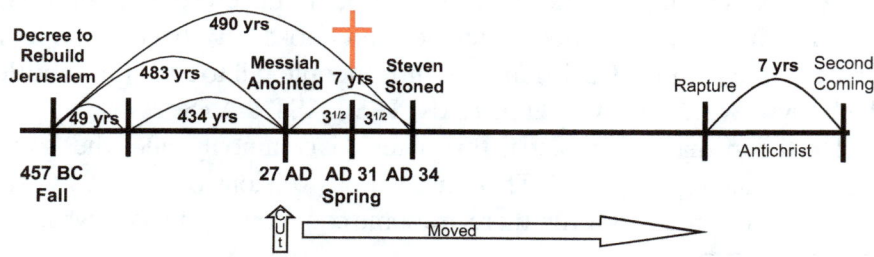

The Rapture theory cuts the last 7 years off the 490 years, which pinpoints the Cross of Christ, and moves them 2,000 years to the end of time, applying them to the Antichrist.

---

[447] Daniel 12:1 (emphasis added)
[448] See Revelation 18:8

The greatest danger about this theory, beyond the fact it is not biblical, is it offers a fraudulent second chance for salvation. According to the theory, if you miss out on the rapture, you have seven years to change your mind and get ready for Christ's coming. The Bible says that today is the day of salvation.[449] We cannot safely put off our spiritual preparation. Jesus said His coming would be like the flood in Noah's day and the destruction of Sodom in Lot's day. There was no second chance then, and there will be no second chance when Jesus comes again. Before He comes, the results of the investigative judgment will have already been announced. There will be no changing sides at that time. "He who is unjust, let him be *unjust still*; he who is filthy, let him be *filthy still*; he who is righteous, let him be *righteous still*; he who is holy, let him be *holy still*."[450]

2. The rapture theory teaches that antichrist does not appear until after the Christians are raptured to heaven at the beginning of the seven years of tribulation. This ignores what Daniel 7 and 8 teach regarding the papacy as antichrist.[451] In fact, according to this theory, the papacy is not antichrist, never has been, and never will be. That sets him up to be the world leader at the end of time. We will see this more clearly as we continue to study.

3. The rapture theory teaches that the second coming of Jesus is divided into two parts, but that is never even insinuated in the Bible. There is only one second coming! Let us look again at Paul's description of that great event. Remember Paul calls death a "sleep." "For if we believe that Jesus died and rose again, even so God will bring with Him those who sleep in Jesus."[452]

The question is, From where is God bringing His resurrected believers, and to where is He taking them? The rapture theory says He is bringing them with Him from heaven to earth when He comes in glory, but is that what the text says? The text compares Christ's death and resurrection to what happens to those who die in Him; and we know Jesus went from earth to heaven at His resurrection, not from heaven to earth. We will see this more clearly

---

[449] See Hebrews 3:15
[450] Revelation 22:11 (emphasis added)
[451] Review chapters 3–6 of this book
[452] 1 Thessalonians 4:14

in chapter 13. Besides, the next three verses make it perfectly clear from where the redeemed are taken and to where they are taken.

> For this we say to you by the word of the Lord, that *we who are alive and remain* until the coming of the Lord will by no means precede those who are *asleep*. For the Lord Himself will descend from *heaven* with a shout, with the voice of an archangel, and with the trumpet of God. And the dead in Christ will rise first. Then we who are alive and remain shall be *caught up together* with them *in the clouds to meet the Lord in the air*. And thus we shall always be with the Lord.[453]

Thus, at Jesus' glorious appearing, the redeemed are taken from this world up to meet Him in the air. And He tells us where He will take us at that time: heaven.[454]

> ***The greatest danger about this theory, beyond the fact it is not biblical, is it offers a fraudulent second chance for salvation. According to the theory, if you miss out on the rapture, you have seven years to change your mind and get ready for Christ's coming. The Bible says that today is the day of salvation.[448] We cannot safely put off our spiritual preparation.***

4. The rapture theory is also based on the teaching that all Israel will be saved and the prophecies of Revelation from chapter 6 onward apply only to the Jews. This idea effectively destroys any significance of the mark of the beast, the image of the beast, spiritual Babylon, and the message Jesus sends to the world to "Come out of her my people."[455] This is a very clever scheme Satan uses to cause people to disregard the message of love Jesus wants the entire world to hear—every race and nationality, not just Jews.[456] We will study this more later.

---

[453] 1 Thessalonians 4:15–17 (emphasis added)
[454] See John 14:1–3
[455] Revelation 18:4
[456] See Revelation 14:6–12

Paul does state, "all Israel will be saved."[457] However, we must remember the context in which this was written. In the same book, Paul clarifies this by saying, "For they are *not all Israel* who are *of Israel.*"[458] According to the Bible, true believers in Jesus are what compose true "Israel," no matter what their nationality might be. Paul uses the illustration of grafting a branch onto a tree. We who are not of Jewish descent are grafted into true Israel.[459] Let's review a couple New Testament passages that clarify the issue of true Israel:

> For *he is not a Jew who is one outwardly*, nor is circumcision that which is outward in the *flesh*; but *he is a Jew who is one inwardly*; and circumcision is that of the *heart*, in the Spirit, not in the letter; whose praise is not from men but from God.[460]
>
> For *you are all sons of God through faith in Christ Jesus*. For as many of you as were baptized into Christ have put on Christ. *There is neither Jew nor Greek*, there is neither slave nor free, there is neither male nor female; for you are all one in Christ Jesus. And *if you are Christ's, then you are Abraham's seed*, and *heirs according to the promise.*[461]

All the promises given to Abraham belong to those who accept Jesus as their personal savior. They are the true "heirs"—true Israel. The "all Israel" who will be saved are those who are genuine believers in Jesus. Not one of them will be lost! This is especially important when we study Revelation. The entire book is addressed to everyone worldwide. It describes the identifying characteristics of God's last-day people: "And the dragon was enraged with the woman, and he went to make war with the rest of her offspring, who *keep the commandments of God* and *have the testimony of Jesus Christ.*"[462]

God does not save people because of their nationality. Salvation is by grace through faith alone, without regard to race or nationality. Therefore, the rapture theory does not stand the test of Scripture.

The glorious appearing of Jesus in the clouds of heaven is the blessed hope of the true believer in Jesus. Paul encourages us to be "looking for

---

[457] Romans 11:26
[458] Romans 9:6 (emphasis added)
[459] See Romans 11:17–23
[460] Romans 2:28, 29 (emphasis added)
[461] Galatians 3:26–29 (emphasis added)
[462] Revelation 12:17 (emphasis added)

the *blessed hope* and *glorious appearing* of our *great God and Savior Jesus Christ.*"[463] The second coming of Jesus is truly a blessed hope!

Some people wonder about a certain expression Jesus used: "One will be *taken* and the other *left.*"

> For as in the days before the *flood*, they were eating and drinking, marrying and giving in marriage, until the day that Noah entered the ark, and *did not know* until the *flood came* and *took them all away*, so also will the *coming of the Son of Man* be. Then two men will be in the field: one will be *taken* and the other *left*. Two women will be grinding at the mill: one will be *taken* and the other *left*.[464]

In the days of Noah, the flood waters destroyed the wicked and "took them all away"; so it will be when Jesus comes. The lost will be destroyed by the brightness of His coming.[465] The saved will go to heaven with Jesus.[466] The point Jesus was trying to make is there will only be two groups of people on earth when He comes: those who have rejected His love and those who have accepted His gift of grace.

We own today but not tomorrow. "Behold, *now* is the accepted time; behold, *now* is the *day of salvation.*"[467] Jesus wants you to be with Him throughout eternity. That is why He is coming back. He cannot wait to take you home with Him!

> *Let not your heart be troubled*; you believe in God, believe also in Me. In My Father's house are many mansions; if it were not so, I would have told you. *I go to prepare a place for you.* And if I go and prepare a place for you, *I will come again* and *receive you to Myself; that where I am, there you may be also.*[468]

Jesus is coming again soon! Is there anything that would keep you from being ready for the coming of Christ? In the next chapter, we will discover "who is able to stand"—who will be ready when Jesus returns—so keep reading.

---

[463] Titus 2:13 (emphasis added)
[464] Matthew 24:38–41 (emphasis added)
[465] See 2 Thessalonians 2:8
[466] See John 14:1–3
[467] 2 Corinthians 6:2 (emphasis added)
[468] John 14:1–3 (emphasis added)

Chapter 9

Who Is Able to Stand?

Jesus is coming again, not to live on earth as He did 2,000 years ago, but in a cloud of angels to take to heaven those who are ready to meet Him. That will be the most spectacular day this world has ever witnessed! He is coming with unspeakable glory and brilliance. Those who are spiritually prepared for Him will rejoice and declare, "Behold, this is our God; *We have waited for Him*, and He will save us. This is the LORD; We have waited for Him; *We will be glad and rejoice in His salvation.*"[469]

They will stand praising God for deliverance, their hearts filled with abundant joy and overwhelming love. It will be the greatest day of their lives! Those who are ready will be caught up into that cloud of angels, along with the resurrected saved from all ages in the past, to meet the Lord in the air and be transported to heaven, where Jesus lives. He promised, "I will come again and receive you to Myself; that where I am, there you may be also."[470]

However, for those who are not spiritually prepared, it will be the most terrifying day of their lives. They will attempt to run and hide.

> The *kings* of the earth, the *great* men, the *rich* men, the *commanders*, the *mighty* men, every *slave* and every *free* man, *hid themselves* in the caves and in the rocks of the mountains, and said to the mountains and rocks, "*Fall on us and hide us* from the *face of Him who sits on the throne* and from the wrath of the Lamb! For the great day of His wrath has come, and *who is able to stand?*"[471]

God's wrath is different from human wrath; the hearts of those who are unprepared spiritually when Jesus comes will be filled with terror, but not because God is angry with them. When their eyes behold Christ in His glory and they perceive His love, purity, and holiness, the guilt of their stubborn rebellion and unconfessed and unforsaken sins will grip their hearts with fear. They will want to do the same as Adam and Eve did after they sinned: run and hide.[472] They will flee like cockroaches when the light is turned on.

---

[469] Isaiah 25:9 (emphasis added)
[470] John 14:3
[471] Revelation 6:15–17 (emphasis added)
[472] See Genesis 3:7, 8

The answer to the question "Who is able to stand?" is found in the next several verses of Revelation. I don't know about you, but I want to be among those who are "able to stand." We will see those who are able to stand are those who receive the "seal of the living God."

> After these things I saw *four angels* standing at the *four corners of the earth*, holding the *four winds* of the earth, that the wind should not blow on the earth, on the sea, or on any tree. Then I saw another angel ascending from the east, having the *seal of the living God*. And he cried with a loud voice to the four angels to whom it was granted to harm the earth and the sea, saying, *"Do not harm the earth, the sea, or the trees till we have sealed the servants of our God on their foreheads."*[473]

Obviously, this sealing is a worldwide event that involves all four directions of the compass. It is not limited to one nationality or people group. The messages of Revelation are for "every nation, tribe, tongue, and people"![474]

This is a highly symbolic vision that God gave to the apostle John, but the symbols are easily understood if we let the Bible interpret itself. In the Bible, winds are symbolic of war, strife, human passions, and disasters of various kinds.[475] Earth, sea, and trees are symbolic of nature, nations, and people.[476]

Therefore, these four angels are commissioned to hold in check Satan's power to destroy and cause havoc, chaos, war, violence, and bloodshed until God's seal is placed upon the foreheads of His people. When God's people are sealed, the four angels will begin to loosen their grip on the winds of strife, and this planet will begin to experience unusual times—times of stress and unprecedented crises. Are we there yet? Everyone recognizes we are living in extraordinary times. Could we be approaching that time of trouble of which Daniel spoke? "And there shall be a time of trouble, such as never was since there was a nation, even to that time."[477]

The time of trouble will be held back until God's people are sealed on their foreheads. This seal is what enables us to stand when the winds blow. God does not want anyone to be lost, so He commissions His angels

---

[473] Revelation 7:1–3 (emphasis added)
[474] Revelation 14:6 (see also 5:9; 10:11; 13:7, 8, 16)
[475] See Isaiah 49:36; 51:1; Daniel 7:2
[476] See Revelation 12:16; 17:15; Daniel 4:20–22; 7:2–8; Isaiah 17:12, 13; Psalm 1:1–6
[477] Daniel 12:1

to keep holding back the winds of strife until everyone has had a chance to know Him and choose to receive His seal of eternal life.

The prophet Ezekiel also gave a description of the sealing of God's people, but with different terminology:

> And He called to the man clothed with linen, who had the *writer's inkhorn* at his side; and the LORD said to him, "Go through the midst of the city, through the midst of Jerusalem, and *put a mark on the foreheads* of the men who *sigh and cry* over all the abominations that are done within it."[478]

God's seal—His mark—is placed on the foreheads of those who have come to recognize the sinfulness of sin. They are repulsed by any form of it. They have fully given themselves over to Jesus and His righteousness. They love the sinner but have learned to hate the sin. They have seen what it cost God to provide our redemption from sin and want to be fully free from it.

The apostle John heard the number of those who were sealed: "And I heard the number of those who were sealed. *One hundred and forty-four thousand* of all the tribes of the children of Israel were sealed:"[479]

We will come back to the symbolic number 144,000, but for now, notice the seal of God is placed on the forehead. The part of the brain behind the forehead is called the frontal lobe. That is where spiritual and moral decisions are made. It is significant that the only other place where the 144,000 is specifically mentioned in Revelation is in chapter 14. Notice in this passage what is placed on their foreheads: "Then I looked, and behold, a *Lamb* standing on Mount Zion, and with Him *one hundred and forty-four thousand*, having *His Father's name written* on their *foreheads*."[480]

Jesus, the Lamb of God, is pictured standing on the heavenly Mount Zion, where the New Jerusalem is located.[481] With Him are the redeemed from this earth, called the 144,000.[482] However, notice what is found on their foreheads: the name of God the Father!

When God places His name or seal on someone, it indicates the person is His forever—his or her destiny is fixed for eternity.[483] When you sign your name to a document, that means the document belongs to

---

[478] Ezekiel 9:3, 4 (emphasis added)
[479] Revelation 7:4 (emphasis added)
[480] Revelation 14:1 (emphasis added)
[481] See Hebrews 12:22
[482] See Revelation 14:2–5
[483] See Revelation 22:4

you; you take ownership of it. Similarly, when God puts His name on you, He is declaring to the universe that you are His child. His truth has settled into your heart and mind, and you are spiritually prepared to stand when Jesus returns.

There are several aspects to this seal that are inseparably connected. In a nutshell, the seal of the Living God is summarized by Paul's declaration that "Christ in you" is "the hope of glory."[484] When Jesus is living out His life in you by faith, you are ready to stand in the day of trial.

Names carry connotations of character. For example, the names "Jezebel" and "Hitler" convey evil characters. However, the name "Jesus" conveys a righteous character. Therefore, when God writes His name on your forehead, He is not only declaring you belong to Him, but He is giving you His spotless character. He is giving you His mind—His way of thinking, acting, and speaking. The Bible calls this "sanctification," the process of forming the character of Jesus in you. I want to be like Jesus, don't you?

The apostle Paul declared, "For this is the will of God, *your sanctification*."[485] God wants all of us to have pure, righteous, and holy characters, but we cannot sanctify ourselves. The prophet Jeremiah reminded us of this impossibility: "Can the Ethiopian change his skin or the leopard its spots? Then *may you also do good who are accustomed to do evil?*"[486]

The apostle Paul also said, "Because the carnal mind is *enmity against God*; for it is *not subject to the law of God, nor indeed can be*. So then, those who are in the flesh cannot please God."[487] Our only hope of sanctification is through faith in Jesus!

When the apostle Paul was recounting to King Agrippa His conversion, he revealed the mission on which Jesus had sent him: "To open their eyes, in order to turn them from darkness to light, and from the power of Satan to God, that they may receive forgiveness of sins and an inheritance among those who are *sanctified by faith in Me*."[488] Sanctification is by faith just as much as justification is. Sanctification is the work of the Holy Spirit in our hearts. When we surrender to Him full control of our thoughts, feelings, and actions, we are sealed for redemption.

---

[484] Colossians 1:27
[485] 1 Thessalonians 4:3 (emphasis added)
[486] Jeremiah 13:23 (emphasis added)
[487] Romans 8:7, 8 (emphasis added)
[488] Acts 26:18 (emphasis added)

In Him you also trusted, after you heard the word of truth, the gospel of your salvation; in whom also, *having believed, you were sealed with the Holy Spirit of promise*, who is the *guarantee of our inheritance* until the redemption of the purchased possession, to the praise of His glory.[489]

The Holy Spirit is our sanctifier. This is what gives us hope. We can come to God just as we are, but He does not leave us trapped in sin. By keeping our minds focused on the beauty of His character, we are transformed into His likeness![490] And more than that, He gives us a sign by which we can know He is the One who sanctifies us: "Moreover I also gave them *My Sabbaths*, to be *a sign between them and Me*, that they might *know that I am the LORD who sanctifies them*."[491]

The Sabbath is God's sign between Himself and us, openly declaring He is the One who transforms us into the likeness of Christ's character as we cling to Him by faith. Clearly, the Sabbath is designed to lead us into the spiritual experience of being sanctified by faith in Jesus. We are not sanctified by our own human effort. Our works have no sanctifying power. Our only hope of true sanctification is through the power of the Holy Spirit. We can rest in Him! "There remains therefore a *rest* for the *people of God*. For he who has entered *His rest* has himself also *ceased from his works* as God did from His."[492]

In Hebrews 4:9, the word "rest" in the Greek language, in which the New Testament was written, is σαββατισμός (*sabbatismos*), which means a "Sabbath rest" or "Sabbath keeping." This differs from the other occurrences of "rest" in Hebrews 4 (κατάπαυσις, *katapausis*).The Sabbath was designed by God to be a taste of heaven on earth—one day a week to focus our minds on eternal realities instead of the temporal things of this world.

After creating our world in six literal days, Jesus our Creator[493] rested from His work, and He invites us to enter His rest. Jesus set aside His work so He could spend undivided time with Adam and Eve. After spending six days creating all things in the physical world, He gave it all to Adam and Eve as a gift. However, He did not stop there. He spent the seventh day giving Himself, a gift in time.

---

[489] Ephesians 1:13, 14 (emphasis added; see also 4:40; 2 Corinthians 1:22)
[490] See 2 Corinthians 3:18
[491] Ezekiel 20:12 (emphasis added)
[492] Hebrews 4:9, 10 (emphasis added)
[493] See John 1:1–3; Colossians 1:16, 17; Hebrews 1:1, 2

> Thus the heavens and the earth, and all the host of them, were finished. And on the *seventh day* God ended His work which He had done, and He *rested on the seventh day* from all His work which He had done. Then God *blessed the seventh day* and *sanctified it*, because in it He rested from all His work which God had created and made.[494]

God "rested" on the seventh-day Sabbath, "blessed" it, and "sanctified it." He made it His holy or sanctified day. The word "rested" in the Old Testament is the Hebrew word תבש (*shâbath*), "which means desist from exertion, cease, celebrate, keep Sabbath, rest."[495] Jesus rested (kept the Sabbath) on the seventh day after He had finished creating our planet, just as He rested in the tomb on the seventh-day Sabbath after completing our redemption. He invites us to enter His rest—to put our full trust and confidence in Him and His Word. The Sabbath rest is not just physical but also spiritual.

The Sabbath is a weekly reminder that our only hope of salvation is in Jesus. We must learn to rest in His grace and not rely upon our best efforts, which are as worthless as filthy rags. Another word for this type of rest is "faith." The Jews of old failed to enter God's rest because of unbelief.

> Therefore, since a promise remains of *entering His rest*, let us fear lest any of you seem to have come short of it. For indeed the *gospel was preached* to us as well as to them; but the word which they heard did not profit them, *not being mixed with faith* in those who heard it. *For we who have believed do enter that rest*.[496]

Just as God offered His gospel rest to the Jews of old, so He still offers it to us. Please notice the rest that Jesus offers is not an excuse for disobedience. Instead, it offers the only power for obedience to all of God's commandments of love.

"There *remains* therefore a *rest for the people of God*. For he who has *entered His rest* has himself also *ceased from his works* as God did from His. Let us therefore be *diligent* to *enter that rest*, lest anyone fall according to the same *example of disobedience*."[497] If we never rested or slept, we would

---
[494] Genesis 2:1–3 (emphasis added)
[495] See Strong's Greek and Hebrew Dictionary
[496] Hebrews 4:1–3 (emphasis added)
[497] Hebrews 4:9–11 (emphasis added)

soon be unable to work; so it is spiritually. Our resting (faith) in God's grace enables and strengthens us to be obedient to Him (sanctification).

> *The Sabbath is a weekly reminder that our only hope of salvation is in Jesus. We must learn to rest in His grace and not rely upon our best efforts, which are as worthless as filthy rags.*

Now, let us return to that intriguing number, 144,000. This has been the subject of much discussion. It is not the purpose of this chapter to answer all the questions. Some wonder if there will be only 144,000 people saved at the end of time. If that were the case, they would give up in discouragement, thinking there was no hope for them. Others think the 144,000 are a special group among the saved when Jesus comes. Some think the 144,000 are only Jews because it says, "And I heard the number of those who were sealed. One hundred and forty-four thousand *of all the tribes of the children of Israel* were sealed:"[498]

It is evident the 144,000 is a symbolic number depicting the redeemed who are alive when Jesus comes. John was shown in vision that there were 12,000 from each of the twelve tribes of Israel who were sealed (12 × 12,000 = 144,000). It is interesting that the list of the twelve tribes in Revelation 7 is different from the original list in Genesis 49. The tribe of Dan is listed in Genesis, but not in Revelation. Instead of Dan, John lists Manasseh, one of the sons of Joseph.

Jacob said the following about Dan: "Dan shall be a *serpent* by the way, A *viper* by the path, that bites the horse's heels So that its rider shall fall backward."[499] A serpent is what Satan used to deceive Eve. In the same way, Dan was under the control of Satan's power.

In the New Testament, we find a similar scenario. Jesus chose twelve disciples, but one (Judas) became His betrayer and was replaced by Matthias.[500] Therefore, those who composed the twelve disciples after Matthias took Judas' place were the true believers in Jesus. The same is true for the twelve tribes of Israel. True Israel consists of those who have put their faith fully in God and not in themselves. We studied this more fully in chapter 7, but just to jog your memory, let us review a couple texts:

---

[498] Revelation 7:4 (emphasis added)
[499] Genesis 49:17 (emphasis added)
[500] See Acts 1:15–26

> For he is *not a Jew* who is one *outwardly*, nor is circumcision that which is *outward* in the flesh; but *he is a Jew who is one inwardly*; and circumcision is that of the *heart*, in the Spirit, not in the letter; whose praise is not from men but from God.[501]
>
> And *if you are Christ's*, then you are *Abraham's seed*, and *heirs according to the promise*.[502]

The true Israel of God are those who "are Christ's"—those who belong to Jesus. This was true in Old Testament as well as New Testament times. The true Israel of God consist of believers in Jesus from "every nation, tribe, tongue, and people."[503] When we go beyond what the Bible teaches, we get into trouble.

After describing 12,000 from each tribe, John described a great multitude of people, which no one can number, who will be saved when Jesus comes:

> After these things I looked, and behold, a *great multitude which no one could number*, of *all nations, tribes, peoples, and tongues*, standing before the throne and before the Lamb, *clothed with white robes*, with palm branches in their hands, and crying out with a loud voice, saying, "Salvation belongs to our God who sits on the throne, and to the Lamb!"[504]

Then the explanation was given regarding those clothed with white robes from every nation on earth:

> These are the ones who *come out of the great tribulation*, and *washed their robes and made them white in the blood of the Lamb*. Therefore they are before the throne of God, and serve Him day and night in His temple. And He who sits on the throne will dwell among them. They shall *neither hunger anymore nor thirst anymore*; the *sun shall not strike them, nor any heat*; for the Lamb who is in the midst of the throne will shepherd them and lead them to living fountains of waters. *And God will wipe away every tear from their eyes*.[505]

---

[501] Romans 2:28, 29 (emphasis added)
[502] Galatians 3:29 (emphasis added)
[503] Revelation 14:6
[504] Revelation 7:9, 10 (emphasis added)
[505] Revelation 7:14–17 (emphasis added)

This passage makes it clear that the great multitude and the 144,000 have exactly the same experiences and characteristics. Notice the following two comparisons:

1. They both go through a great time of trouble. The 144,000 live at the time when the four winds of strife are let loose on the earth. The great multitude "come out of great tribulation." And the promise that they will not hunger and thirst anymore and the sun or heat will not strike them could mean they will go through the seven last plagues, which end just as Christ comes.[506] Those plagues include the sun scorching people.
2. The 144,000 are sealed with the seal of the Living God, which means they are sanctified. By faith in Jesus, they have gained the victory over every besetting sin. Those of the great multitude are also sanctified—they have "washed their robes and made them white in the blood of the Lamb." Robes, in the Bible, are a symbol of our actions and character.[507] In other words, the great multitude has gained victory over sin. They are also sealed with the seal of the Living God.

Therefore, the number "144,000" is a symbolic number representing God's redeemed from around the world when Jesus comes. Their faith will have been strengthened and purified in the fires of affliction. I don't know about you, but I want to be part of them! God wants everyone who is alive when Jesus comes to be part of that group. However, we know the majority will not choose to be sanctified (purified of sin).

It is significant to note *how* God sanctifies something or someone. When Moses was herding sheep in the wilderness, He saw a bush that was on fire but not burning up. As he drew close to examine it, God spoke to him out of the burning bush and said, "Do not draw near this place. Take your sandals off your feet, for *the place where you stand is holy ground.*"[508]

The ground was holy because God was there. His presence made it holy. When God is present, sin, sorrow, suffering, evil, and death must flee! During creation week, when Jesus sanctified the seventh day (made it holy), He did so by putting His presence in it. On the seventh day, God gives us the gift of Himself in time!

---

[506] See Revelation 16:1–21
[507] See Revelation 19:7, 8
[508] Exodus 3:5 (emphasis added)

God's purpose for the seventh-day Sabbath is our sanctification—to help us fall in love with Him more and more each week as we spend twenty-four hours with Him in a special way that is not possible on any other day of the week. On this day like no other, He brings His sanctifying power into our lives. He "blessed" the seventh day—something He did not do for any other day. When we learn to keep the Sabbath as He designed it to be kept, it becomes a powerful tool in His hands for our redemption. It is the day packed with His blessings.

> If you turn away your foot from the *Sabbath*, From doing your pleasure on *My holy day*, And call the *Sabbath* a *delight*, The *holy day of the LORD honorable*, And shall *honor Him*, not doing your own ways, Nor finding your own pleasure, Nor speaking your own words, *Then you shall delight yourself in the LORD*; And I will cause you to ride on the high hills of the earth, And feed you with the heritage of Jacob your father. The mouth of the LORD has spoken.[509]

The Sabbath is our "date-day" with God. As we honor Him by honoring His holy day, we will fall in love with Him over and over and find our highest delight in Him!

Now can you see why Satan is angry with the Sabbath? Can you see why he would want to inspire antichrist to attempt to change the Sabbath, God's holy day, to Sunday, which is a common workday devoid of God's rest, blessing, and sanctification? He has effectively replaced God's presence in time with a manmade institution. He has put humanity where only God belongs.

There is far more to the Sabbath than just a day. It is God's sign or seal. In the Bible, the words "sign" and "seal" are interchangeable. An example of this is when the apostle Paul argued that Abraham was declared righteous by faith before he was circumcised. His circumcision was the sign or seal of that righteousness, which he had already received by faith. "And he received the *sign* of circumcision, a *seal* of the *righteousness of the faith* which he had while still uncircumcised, that he might be the father of all those who believe, though they are uncircumcised, that righteousness might be imputed to them also,"[510]

Abraham was declared righteous by faith, not by works (circumcision). Likewise, the Sabbath is God's sign or seal of sanctification. We are not sanctified by works or mere Saturday "keeping," but true Sabbath

---

[509] Isaiah 58:13, 14 (emphasis added)
[510] Romans 4:11 (emphasis added)

keeping is the sign or seal that God is our sanctifier—not ourselves. We are sanctified by faith, not by works.

Sanctification is the process of overcoming sin and developing the character of Jesus. The biblical definition of sin is "the transgression of the law" of God.[511] Therefore, the seal of God is the process of sealing His law in our hearts. "Bind up the testimony, *seal the law* among my disciples."[512] When we look at the Ten Commandments, we find God's seal is in the Sabbath commandment.

Kings, presidents, and prime ministers around the world have seals that indicate their scope of authority. Most of these include their name, title, and the territory over which they govern. For example:

- Name = Joe Biden (currently)
- Title = President
- Territory = United States of America

The Sabbath commandment is the only commandment that contains these three items:

- Name = "Lord your God"
- Title = Creator ("the Lord made…")
- Territory = "the heavens and the earth, the sea, and all that is in them"

When God gave the Ten Commandments from Mount Sinai, He included the Sabbath in His principles of righteousness. Those commandments are the foundation of His government—the rule of His kingdom. The basis for the Sabbath commandment is what Jesus did during creation week. It is interesting that the one commandment God said to remember is the one most largely forgotten.

> *Remember the Sabbath day*, to keep it *holy*. Six days you shall labor and do all your work, but the *seventh day is the Sabbath of the LORD your God*. In it you shall do no work: you, nor your son, nor your daughter, nor your male servant, nor your female servant, nor your cattle, nor your stranger who is within your gates. For *in six days the LORD made* the heavens and the earth, the sea, and all

---

[511] 1 John 3:4, KJV
[512] Isaiah 8:16 (emphasis added)

that is in them, and *rested the seventh day*. Therefore the LORD *blessed the Sabbath day* and *hallowed it*.[513]

The Ten Commandments are summarized by love, the Sabbath included.[514] However, God knew "love" needed to be defined. He did not dare leave it up to us to guess. In trying to understand the law, a lawyer asked Jesus, "Which is the great[est] commandment?"

> Jesus said to him, "'You shall *love the LORD your God* with all your heart, with all your soul, and with all your mind.' This is the first and great commandment. And the *second* is like it: 'You shall *love your neighbor as yourself.*' On these two commandments hang all the Law and the Prophets."[515]

Christ quoted directly from the book of the law in the Old Testament.[516] This is the same place where the Ten Commandments are found, so it is obvious love does not replace the Ten Commandment, but helps us understand their intent. The first four commandments address our love-relationship with God. If we love God with all our heart, soul, and strength, we will want to keep the four commandments that deal with our relationship with Him:

1. He will be supreme in our lives.[517]
2. We will not pray to or worship any idols or statues.[518]
3. Our language will be pure—not using God's name in vain.[519] And we will not be a false follower of Jesus.[520]
4. We will remember to keep the Sabbath day holy. Our date day with God will be a high priority in our lives.[521] We will not let anything encroach on it or interfere with it. It will be our greatest delight to spend that weekly, twenty-hour time with our Creator and Redeemer.

The last six commandments address our love-relationships with our fellow mankind. If we love our neighbors as ourselves, we will want to

---

[513] Exodus 20:8–11 (emphasis added)
[514] See Romans 13:10
[515] Matthew 22:37–40 (emphasis added)
[516] See Deuteronomy 6:5; 10:12; 30:6; Leviticus 19:18
[517] See Exodus 20:3
[518] See Exodus 20:4–6
[519] See Exodus 20:7
[520] See Matthew 15:8, 9
[521] See Exodus 20:8–11

keep these six commandments as well. However, we need to understand the spiritual implications of these commandments, not just the letter of the law. The spiritual implications have an infinite depth of meaning. They define love.

5. We will love and respect our parents as well as all others in authority.[522]
6. Not only will we not murder, but we will not be angry or carry a grudge.[523]
7. We will be emotionally and physically involved in sexual intimacy with only our marriage partner, husband or wife. God created Adam and Eve, not Adam and Steve.[524]
8. We will not take anything that does not belong to us. We will respect the property of others.[525]
9. Our speech will always be characterized by truth and love.[526]
10. We will be content with the position and possessions God has given us and not have corrupt motives.[527]

"God is love,"[528] and love is what the Ten Commandments are all about, including the Sabbath commandment. We need to understand this more fully. True Sabbath keeping is the *antidote* for legalism!

---

[522] See Exodus 20:12 and Romans 13:1
[523] See Exodus 20:13; Matthew 5:21, 22
[524] See Exodus 20:14; Romans 1:26, 27
[525] See Exodus 20:15
[526] See Exodus 20:16
[527] See Exodus 20:17
[528] 1 John 4:8

Chapter 10

God's Mark

The Sabbath is far more than just a day—infinitely more! Therefore, let us dig into it further. First of all, the Sabbath is the sign that distinguishes God's people from the world—the seal that we are worshipping the true Creator. "I am the LORD your God: Walk in My statutes, keep My judgments, and do them; *hallow My Sabbaths*, and they will be a *sign* between Me and you, *that you may know that I am the LORD your God.*"[529]

The Sabbath is God's mark of authority, and by keeping it holy, we recognize His authority and lovingly submit ourselves to it. It is the sign that He is our God. We belong to Him twice-over: He created us and redeemed us! We do not belong to ourselves.[530] We acknowledge His authority by keeping the Sabbath as God's holy day for public, corporate worship.[531]

There are two biblical reasons for worshipping God: One is that Jesus died for our salvation. John recorded all of heaven worshipping Him as the Lamb of God who died for our sins, saying, "Worthy is the Lamb who was slain to receive power and riches and wisdom, and strength and honor and glory and blessing!"[532]

The second reason for worshipping God is that He is our Creator. He made everything that exists. Therefore, the heavenly beings fall down before Him and worship Him, saying, "You are worthy, O Lord, to receive glory and honor and power; for *You created all things*, And by Your will they exist and were created."[533]

The fact that Jesus is our Creator draws our minds back to creation week when He set aside the seventh day as His holy day for worship. This is so important that He sends out a message to the entire world at the end of time, calling us again to worship Him as Creator.

> Then I saw another angel flying in the midst of heaven, having the *everlasting gospel* to *preach* to those who dwell on the earth to *every nation, tribe, tongue, and people*—saying with a loud voice, "Fear God and give glory to Him, for the hour of His judgment has

---

[529] Ezekiel 20:19, 20 (emphasis added)
[530] See 1 Corinthians 6:19, 20
[531] See Leviticus 23:3
[532] Revelation 5:12
[533] Revelation 4:11 (emphasis added)

come; and *worship Him who made heaven and earth, the sea and springs of water.*"[534]

God is the One who wants us to worship Him as Creator, and the only way to truly do that is to worship Him on the day He created for worship. Otherwise, we are placing a human institution in the place of God's. This is exactly what antichrist has done. Here is what they claim regarding the creation of this world:

> In 1950, Pope Pius XII proclaimed there was no opposition between evolution and Catholic doctrine. In 1996, St. John Paul II endorsed Pius' statement.[535]
>
> Pope Francis has waded into the controversial debate over the origins of human life, saying the big bang theory did not contradict the role of a divine creator, but even required it.... "When we read about Creation in Genesis, we run the risk of imagining God was a magician, with a magic wand able to do everything. But that is not so," Francis said.[536]

God has called us back to the Sabbath at the end of time because it is His memorial of creation. And the fact that He created this world in six days and rested on the seventh is the distinguishing mark that He is the true God. "For thus says *the LORD, Who created* the *heavens*, Who is God, Who *formed* the *earth* and *made it*, Who has *established it*, Who did not create it in vain, Who formed it to be inhabited: *'I am the LORD, and there is no other.*'"[537] If you take the word of mankind as truth, God's power is limited, but if you take His Word as truth, His power is unlimited.

Just as God forbade Adam and Eve from eating of a particular tree in the Garden of Eden as a sign of their loyalty to Him, so He has asked us to set aside a particular day as a sign of our loyalty to Him. The forbidden fruit was not poisonous, or else they would have died then and there. There was nothing wrong with the fruit of that particular tree, except God chose it as a test of their loyalty. Likewise, the Sabbath is no different than any other day of the week, except He has chosen that day to rest, bless, and sanctify. It is a test of our loyalty to God.

The reality is we need to worship God every day of the week. However, the Sabbath is His special day chosen for corporate worship. It is a specific

---
[534] Revelation 14:6, 7 (emphasis added)
[535] Josephine McKenna, "Pope says evolution, Big Bang are real," USA Today, October 28, 2014
[536] Ibid.
[537] Isaiah 45:18 (emphasis added)

twenty-four-hour period each week set aside to develop our relationship with Him. "Six days shall work be done, but *the seventh day is a Sabbath* of solemn rest, a *holy convocation*. You shall do no work on it; it is the Sabbath of the LORD in all your dwellings."[538]

Some people wonder if we can know which day is the Sabbath day, the memorial of creation. All reputable Bible scholars and commentaries will agree it is Saturday, but let us see some of the evidence for ourselves.

First, the seven-day weekly cycle came directly from creation week. Other than this weekly cycle, the way we tell the passing of time is by the rotation of the earth along its own axis, the moon around the earth, and the earth around the sun. There is no celestial mechanism that calibrates a seven-day cycle. Creation week included the seventh-day Sabbath, not just the six days of creating physical aspects of our world.

However, some people wonder if somehow, society lost track of time over the thousands of years of this earth's history. The cross of Christ helps us understand which day of the week is the Sabbath. After Jesus breathed His last, Joseph of Arimathea obtained permission from Pilate to take His body down from the cross.

> *The forbidden fruit was not poisonous, or else they would have died then and there. There was nothing wrong with the fruit of that particular tree, except God chose it as a test of their loyalty. Likewise, the Sabbath is no different than any other day of the week, except He has chosen that day to rest, bless, and sanctify. It is a test of our loyalty to God.*

> Then he took it down, wrapped it in linen, and laid it in a tomb that was hewn out of the rock, where no one had ever lain before. *That day was the Preparation*, and the *Sabbath drew near*. And the women who had come with Him from Galilee followed after, and they observed the tomb and how His body was laid. Then they returned and prepared spices and fragrant oils. And *they rested on the Sabbath according to the commandment*.[539]

---

[538] Leviticus 23:3 (emphasis added)
[539] Luke 23:53–56 (emphasis added)

The day following the Sabbath, Jesus came victoriously out of the tomb, triumphing over death.

> Now on the *first day of the week*, very early in the morning, they, and certain other women with them, came to the tomb bringing the spices which they had prepared. But they found the stone rolled away from the tomb. Then they went in and did not find the body of the Lord Jesus. And it happened, as they were greatly perplexed about this, that behold, two men stood by them in shining garments. Then, as they were afraid and bowed their faces to the earth, they said to them, "Why do you seek the living among the dead? *He is not here, but is risen!*"[540]

The days of the week at the time of the crucifixion of Christ are clear evidence of which day the Sabbath is:

1. **Friday** was called the "Preparation" day because that was the day the Bible instructs us to prepare for the Sabbath, our date-day with God. The day on which Jesus was crucified is still called "Good Friday." The day after Preparation Day was Sabbath.
2. **Sabbath** followed Friday. His followers "rested on the Sabbath according to the commandment." The Sabbath commandment had obviously not been changed before Christ's death, and we know the day following Friday is Saturday.
3. **Sunday** was the day Jesus came forth from the tomb. Today, it is commonly known as Easter Sunday. The translators of the Bible rendered it "the first day of the week." However, the original Greek text says, "the first day after the Sabbath." The entire week rotated around the Sabbath. The only days with names were the Preparation day and the Sabbath day. The other days were numbered with reference to the Sabbath, as well as creation (i.e., first day, second day, etc.). Clearly, the biblical Sabbath is the seventh day of the week—Saturday.

Some people suggest the day of worship was changed to Sunday to honor the resurrection of Christ. It is wonderful to celebrate His resurrection, but Sunday worship is not the way the Bible instructs us to do it. The biblical way to celebrate the resurrection is baptism—joining Jesus in His

---

[540] Luke 24:1–6 (emphasis added)

death, burial, and resurrection by watery immersion.[541] This is symbolic of being resurrected to a new life in Christ.

Other people wonder if the calendar has been changed, and the answer is, Yes it has. In October of 1582, ten days were dropped from the calendar in order to align it with the seasons. Up until then, they had not added an extra day to February every four years. Therefore, Thursday, October 4, 1582 was followed by Friday, October 15, 1582. You will notice that even though ten days were dropped out, the weekly cycle was not interrupted; Thursday was followed by Friday.

It is interesting that in over 140 languages, the word for the seventh day of the week is "Sabbath." It would be one thing if it was in just one or two languages, but to find it in over 140 languages clearly indicates a common origin—Creation. Here are several examples:

Language	Word for 7th Day	Meaning
Greek	*Sabbaton*	Sabbath
Spanish	*Sabado*	Sabbath
Portuguese	*Sabado*	Sabbath
Italian	*Sabato*	Sabbath
French	*Samedi*	Sabbath
German	*Samstag*	Sabbath
Russian	*Subbota*	Sabbath
Polish	*Sobota*	Sabbath
Persian	*Shambin*	Sabbath
Hindi	*Szombat*	Sabbath
Arabic	*As Sabit*	Sabbath

What about the example and teaching of Jesus, the apostles, and the early church? Did they change the day of worship from Sabbath to Sunday? Let us begin with looking at Christ's example: "So He came to Nazareth, where He had been brought up. And *as His custom was*, He went into the synagogue on the *Sabbath day*, and stood up to read."[542]

Jesus was faithful in keeping the Sabbath holy. However, He was reprimanded by the religious leaders for healing on the Sabbath. He stripped the Sabbath of human traditions and restrictions and showed that the Sabbath was not a do-nothing day but a day to worship and bless others.[543]

---
[541] See Romans 6:3–8
[542] Luke 4:16 (emphasis added)
[543] See Matthew 12:12

He clearly demonstrated the Sabbath was to be a blessing for the human race, not a burden. It was designed by God to meet our specific needs. "And He said to them, 'The *Sabbath was made for man*, and *not man for the Sabbath*. Therefore the *Son of Man* is also *Lord of the Sabbath*.'"[544]

When Jesus was prophesying about the destruction of Jerusalem, which was fulfilled in AD 70, He encouraged His followers to pray they would be able to keep the Sabbath amid that crisis. That prophecy was fulfilled thirty-nine years after the cross. If He was going to change the Sabbath to Sunday, He would not have said, "And let him who is in the field not go back to get his clothes. But woe to those who are pregnant and to those who are nursing babies in those days! And *pray that your flight may not be in winter or on the Sabbath*."[545] It is clear Jesus expected His faithful followers to still keep that weekly date with Him thirty-nine years after the cross.

The apostles also were faithful in keeping the Sabbath holy. Notice Paul followed the example of Jesus. On one of his missionary journeys, he stopped at Thessalonica for a few weeks, and the following is recorded of his stay there: "Then Paul, as his custom was, went in to them, and for three Sabbaths reasoned with them from the Scriptures."[546] Paul's custom was the same as was Jesus' custom. He was a true follower of Christ's example.

On another of his missionary journeys, Paul came to Antioch, and again, as his custom was, he "went into the synagogue on the Sabbath day and sat down."[547] The synagogue would be compared to our present-day church. After worshipping for a while, Paul was invited to speak. He took the opportunity to teach that Jesus was the promised Messiah. After the service was over, the record states, "So when the Jews went out of the synagogue, the *Gentiles* begged that these words might be preached to them the *next Sabbath*."[548]

If the Sabbath was just for the Jews and Sunday for the Gentiles, they would not have begged Paul to preach to them the next Sabbath. Notice what took place on the next Sabbath: "On the *next Sabbath* almost the *whole city* came together to *hear the word of God*."[549]

---

[544] Mark 2:27, 28 (emphasis added)
[545] Matthew 24:18–20 (emphasis added)
[546] Acts 17:2
[547] Acts 13:14
[548] Acts 13:42 (emphasis added)
[549] Acts 13:44 (emphasis added)

These were not isolated events. This was Paul's "custom." When he came to the town of Philippi in Macedonia, they stayed there for several days. Evidently there was no synagogue there, but that did not keep Paul from seeking a place to worship with others on the Sabbath. "And on the Sabbath day we went out of the city to the riverside, where prayer was customarily made; and we sat down and spoke to the women who met there."[550]

When Paul came to Corinth, he stayed there a year and six months teaching the Word of God.[551] And during that entire time, he kept the Sabbath. "And he reasoned in the synagogue every Sabbath, and persuaded both Jews and Greeks."[552]

Paul held eighty-four meetings on Sabbaths, according to the book of Acts. Nowhere in the New Testament does it say the church kept Sunday as the holy day of worship. There are eight texts in the New Testament that mention the first day of the week, and not one of them tells us to worship on Sunday in honor of the resurrection of Jesus.

Sunday is commonly called the "Lord's Day," but there is no place in the Bible where that is found. The only place in the Bible where the term "Lord's Day" is found does not tell us the day to which it referred. "I was *in the Spirit* on the *Lord's Day*, and I heard behind me a loud voice, as of a trumpet, saying, 'I am the *Alpha and the Omega*, the *First and the Last*.'"[553]

John was taken into vision on the "Lord's Day," and Jesus spoke directly to Him. It does not say whether the Lord's Day was Sunday or Sabbath. Jesus is the Lord of everything, but it is significant to note that the only day He specifically claimed to be Lord of is the Sabbath day. "And He said to them, 'The Son of Man is also Lord of the Sabbath.'"[554]

That is in harmony with all the prophets. Notice what one wrote centuries before:

> If you turn away your foot from the *Sabbath*, From doing your pleasure on *My holy day*, And call the *Sabbath* a delight, The *holy day of the LORD honorable*, And shall honor Him, not doing your own ways, Nor finding your own pleasure, Nor speaking your own words, Then you shall *delight yourself in the LORD*.[555]

---

[550] Acts 16:13
[551] See Acts 18:11
[552] Acts 18:4 (emphasis added)
[553] Revelation 1:10, 11 (emphasis added)
[554] Luke 6:5
[555] Isaiah 58:13, 14 (emphasis added)

It was not until AD 325, in the Council of Laodicea, that Sylvester, Bishop of Rome, officially declared Sunday the Lord's Day. However, if God's law was to be changed, it would have had to been done before Jesus died on Calvary. Paul made this clear: "For where there is a *testament*, there must also of necessity be the *death of the testator*. For a *testament is in force after men are dead*, since it has no power at all while the testator lives."[556]

The illustration used here is very interesting. My wife and I have a document that is called "Our Last Will and Testament." As long as we are alive, we can change it, but once we are dead, it cannot be altered in the slightest. The new covenant was ratified by Christ's death without changing the law; therefore, the law could not be changed after His death.

Instead, the law is to be written on our hearts. "For this is the *covenant* that I will make with the house of Israel after those days, says the Lord: I will put *My laws* in their *mind* and *write* them on their *hearts*; and *I will be their God*, and *they shall be My people*."[557]

However, some people still honestly wonder if the law of God and specifically the Sabbath was done away with when Jesus died. If that was the case, His followers would not have kept the Sabbath according to the Ten Commandments immediately after His death.[558] Nevertheless, there is a passage that is quoted to promote the idea that the law was nailed to the cross. Let us look at that passage closely:

> Having *wiped out* the *handwriting of requirements* that was *against us*, which was contrary to us. And He has taken it out of the way, having *nailed it to the cross*. Having disarmed principalities and powers, He made a public spectacle of them, triumphing over them in it. So *let no one judge you* in *food* or in *drink*, or regarding a *festival* or a *new moon* or *sabbaths*, which are a *shadow of things to come*, but the *substance is of Christ*.[559]

Remember, we must let the Bible be its own interpreter, so let us evaluate each aspect of this passage:

"Having wiped out the handwriting of requirements that was against us": Two sets of laws were given to Israel at Mount Sinai. The Ten Commandments were written by the finger of God on tables of stone. The

---

[556] Hebrews 9:16, 17 (emphasis added)
[557] Hebrews 8:10 (emphasis added)
[558] See Luke 23:56
[559] Colossians 2:14–17 (emphasis added)

ordinances were written by Moses on parchment scrolls. The two sets of laws were stored in two different places in order to show their distinction. The Ten Commandments were kept inside the ark of the covenant.[560] The book of law that Moses wrote was kept on the outside of the ark. With that said, which set of laws was "against us"? Here is the answer:

> So it was, when *Moses* had completed *writing the words of this law in a book*, when they were finished, that Moses commanded the Levites, who bore the ark of the covenant of the LORD, saying: "*Take this Book of the Law*, and put it *beside the ark of the covenant* of the LORD your God, that it may be there as a witness *against you*."[561]

The "handwriting of requirements" that was wiped out and nailed to the cross was the book of the law that Moses wrote. It contained the ceremonial laws of sacrifices and services of the sanctuary. All those sacrifices and services were symbolic of Jesus' death on Calvary and His ministry for us in the heavenly sanctuary.

Therefore, when Jesus, the true Lamb of God, died, there no longer was a need for the ceremonial laws to be observed. If you remember, the angel Gabriel prophesied this when he said, "But in the middle of the week He shall *bring an end to sacrifice and offering*."[562] To continue offering sacrifices after Christ's death would indicate a denial of our faith in Him as our Redeemer.

It was the ceremonial law, written by Moses under inspiration of the Holy Spirit, that was nailed to the cross. This ceremonial law was a prophecy of the gospel of God's grace through Jesus Christ. And when Jesus was nailed to the cross, the prophecy was fulfilled. The ceremonial laws pointing forward to Christ's death were symbolically nailed to the cross with Him.

Now, let us look at a very easily misunderstood scripture: "So *let no one judge you* in *food* or in *drink*, or regarding a *festival* or a *new moon* or *sabbaths*, which are a *shadow of things to come*, but the *substance is of Christ*." The ceremonial law contained ordinances regarding food and drink offerings,[563] which, again, were fulfilled in Christ.

---

[560] See Hebrews 9:4; Exodus 25:16; 32:15, 16
[561] Deuteronomy 31:24–26 (emphasis added)
[562] Daniel 9:27
[563] See Numbers 28, 29

It was *symbolic* for the present time in which both *gifts* and *sacrifices* are offered which cannot make him who performed the service perfect in regard to the conscience—concerned only with *foods* and *drinks*, various washings, and fleshly ordinances imposed *until the time of reformation*.[564]

The sanctuary services included six feasts and one fast. The feasts were Passover, Unleavened Bread, First Fruits, Pentecost, Trumpets, and Tabernacles. The fast was the Day of Atonement. Along with the new moons, these were all part of the ceremonial law fulfilled by Jesus and done away with at the cross.

What about the "sabbaths"? Were they done away with at the cross as well? Many people get confused by this because they do not realize there were three types of sabbaths. There was the seventh-day, weekly Sabbath (singular); there was a land sabbath every seven years, when no crops were to be planted and the land was to be given a rest for a year; and there were the yearly, ceremonial, festival sabbaths (small "s" and plural). The Lord made this very clear. He first refers to the weekly Sabbath: "*Six days shall work be done*, but the *seventh day is a Sabbath* of solemn rest, a holy convocation. You shall do no work on it; it is *the Sabbath of the LORD* in all your dwellings."[565]

Then the lord continues and describes all the yearly, ceremonial days, which were also called "sabbaths." However, these were separate from the weekly, seventh-day Sabbath. In the same chapter, the Lord calls the Day of Atonement "a sabbath": "It shall be to you a sabbath of solemn rest, and you shall afflict your souls; on the ninth day of the month at evening, from evening to evening, you shall celebrate your sabbath."[566] Therefore, the yearly sabbaths (festivals) were fulfilled by Jesus and done away with at the cross.

There is one last piece of evidence that helps to clarify this issue. Going back to Paul's easily misunderstood passage in Colossians 2, we find all these food and drink offerings, festivals, new moons, and sabbaths were " a shadow of things to come, but the substance is of Christ."[567]

Paul told us what this "shadow" is. Remember, the earthly sanctuary was patterned after the heavenly sanctuary in order to teach us what Jesus is doing for us there. "For if He [Jesus] were on earth, He would not be a

---

[564] Hebrews 9:9, 10 (emphasis added)
[565] Leviticus 23:3 (emphasis added)
[566] Leviticus 23:32 (emphasis added)
[567] Colossians 2:17

priest, since there are priests who offer the gifts according to the law; who serve the *copy* and *shadow* of the *heavenly things*, as Moses was divinely instructed when he was about to make the tabernacle."[568]

Therefore, the law that was nailed to the cross was not the Ten Commandments, but the ceremonial law of the sanctuary services. We see harmony throughout the Bible on this topic.

One more thought regarding the Sabbath is that it is God's "holy day," not a "holiday." There is a big difference! A heart that is touched by God's grace will love Him and long to keep His Commandments; they will be a delight, not a burden. "For this is the *love of God*, that we *keep His commandments*. And His commandments *are not burdensome*."[569]

In Jesus' day, the Jews, especially the religious leaders, made the mistake of trusting in their goodness (their good works) to somehow gain favor with God. In order to make sure they kept the Sabbath perfectly, they loaded it down with hundreds of manmade rules and regulations until it had become a heavy burden. It was these rules that Jesus violated. Notwithstanding, for Jesus, the Sabbath was a delight, not a burden. He demonstrated the proper attitude toward keeping the Sabbath holy. And as we keep it God's way, we will find it a wonderful blessing made for our eternal good! "Therefore the Lord blessed the Sabbath day and hallowed it."[570]

God blessed the seventh day, but what are the blessings packed into the Sabbath? I'd like to look at three: rest, relationships, and worship.

Adam and Eve were created on the sixth day. God could have stopped his creation with six days, but he created a special day at the end of the week and established it as a day set apart from all the other days—sanctified and holy. It is a day when we are to cease our regular labor to sustain life and devote the day to physical, mental, social, and spiritual restoration by building our relationships with God and each other. It is a day for holy worship.

There are two special gifts God gave to us during creation week: the Sabbath and marriage. He designed both sacred institutions to be sources of tremendous blessing, but they are under extreme attack by Satan today. Why? Because he hates happy relationships and wants our worship. You know relationships are made of time—no time, no relationship. If we want

---

[568] Hebrews 8:4, 5 (emphasis added; see also 10:1–4)
[569] 1 John 5:3 (emphasis added)
[570] Exodus 20:11

a close family, we must spend time together. In the same way, if we want a close relationship with God, we must spend regular time with Him.

The Sabbath is God's authorized break time—twenty-four hours when it is okay to say "No" to the chores; "No" to work and the world's demands upon our time and attention. It is a day to say "Yes" to time with God, family, and others.

> *There are two special gifts God gave to us during creation week: the Sabbath and marriage. He designed both sacred institutions to be sources of tremendous blessing, but they are under extreme attack by Satan today. Why? Because he hates happy relationships and wants our worship.*

Let us look at how the Bible tells us to say "No" to the world's encroachment upon God's Sabbath and "Yes" to His blessing. We want to throw the doors of our lives wide open so we can get all the life-giving blessings God wants us to have.

There are two ways to make sure you get the blessings God put into the Sabbath: "Remember the Sabbath day, to keep it holy."[571] "Remember" means we anticipate the joy of the Sabbath. We look forward to it with delight and keep it in mind all through the week. In fact, the whole week rotates around the Sabbath. Remembering also means being ready for the Sabbath when it begins. It is a date-day with God.

When does the Sabbath day begin? According to the Bible, days begin and end at sunset, and the Sabbath is no different. The Sabbath begins at sunset on Friday and ends at sunset on Saturday. "From evening to evening, you shall celebrate your sabbath."[572]

How else do we get ready for the Sabbath?

> *Six days you shall labor* and do all your work, *but the seventh day is the Sabbath of the LORD your God. In it you shall do no work*: you, nor your son, nor your daughter, nor your male servant, nor your female servant, nor your cattle, nor your stranger who is within your gates.[573]

---

[571] Exodus 20:8
[572] Leviticus 23:32 (see also Mark 1:32; Genesis 1:23, 31)
[573] Exodus 20:9, 10 (emphasis added)

We should treat the Sabbath as it really is: a weekly appointment with the most important, powerful, and loving Being in the universe! And if we treat it this way, we will want to complete our work in six days and not waste it with secular affairs. Ezekiel referred to the "six working days": "Thus says the Lord GOD, 'The gateway of the inner court that faces toward the east shall be shut the six working days; but on the Sabbath it shall be opened.'"[574]

The Bible calls Friday the "Preparation Day," the day on which we should make sure things are prepared for the Sabbath.[575] With that said, for what are we preparing? We are preparing to draw closer and closer to Jesus. Therefore, we want to remove as many of the distractions of everyday life as possible.

What are some biblical ways we can prepare for the Sabbath day? There is an interesting story in Nehemiah. Israel had again fallen into apostasy, and Nehemiah was trying to bring them back to loyalty to God, so he rebuked the religious leaders of Jerusalem.

> Men of Tyre dwelt there also, who brought in fish and all kinds of goods, and *sold them on the Sabbath* to the children of Judah, and in Jerusalem. Then I contended with the nobles of Judah, and said to them, *"What evil thing is this that you do, by which you profane the Sabbath day?* Did not your fathers do thus, and did not our God bring all this disaster on us and on this city? Yet you bring added wrath on Israel *by profaning the Sabbath."* So it was, at the gates of Jerusalem, as it began to be dark before the Sabbath, that I commanded the gates to be shut, and charged that *they must not be opened till after the Sabbath*. Then I posted some of my servants at the gates, so that no burdens would be brought in on the Sabbath day.[576]

Buying and selling is to be done outside of Sabbath hours. It is not a day for trips to Walmart or the hardware store. Is that because these things are not good things? No, that is not the reason. God has declared the Sabbath to be holy and used for holy purposes. If I am spending my time at Walmart or the hardware store, I am not dedicating that time to the Lord, serving the Lord, or worshiping the Lord. Plus, I am putting myself in an atmosphere that is anything but holy.

---

[574] Ezekiel 46:10 (emphasis added)
[575] See Luke 23:54–56
[576] Nehemiah 13:16–19 (emphasis added)

All business matters should be put aside and left for another day. The Sabbath is not the day to watch your stock portfolio, discuss business deals, or call clients or employees. God wants us to use this time differently than we would any other day of the week. The Sabbath is holy time, and we want to respect it. It is God's property—His holy day.

Another story of preparation comes from when God protected and cared for Israel in the wilderness for forty years. He rained manna down for them every day except Sabbath.

> Then the LORD said to Moses, "Behold, *I will rain bread from heaven* for you. And the people shall go out and gather a certain quota *every day*, that I may test them, whether they will walk in My law or not. And it shall be on the *sixth day* that they shall prepare what they bring in, and it shall be *twice as much as they gather daily*."[577]

No manna fell on the Sabbath. Instead, the Israelites were to prepare twice as much on Friday so they would have food to eat on Sabbath without having to prepare it. Therefore, as far as is possible and practical, food preparation is best done before the Sabbath arrives. You want to spend as little time in the kitchen as possible on your date-day with God. This way, the Sabbath becomes a very special day as free as possible from the cares of this world. It becomes a foretaste of heaven!

The second way to ensure the blessings of the Sabbath is to "keep it holy." We need to remember that it is a holy day, not a holiday.

> If you turn away your foot from the Sabbath, *from doing your pleasure* on My holy day, and *call the Sabbath a delight*, the *holy day of the LORD honorable*, and shall honor Him, *not doing your own ways, nor finding your own pleasure, nor speaking your own words*, then *you shall delight yourself in the LORD*; and I will cause you to ride on the high hills of the earth, and feed you with the heritage of Jacob your father. The mouth of the LORD has spoken.[578]

In the Bible, the foot was a sign of ownership. God says, "You do not own it, so take your foot off it. Do not trample on it. Recognize the Sabbath is the Lord's Day." Therefore, it is to be a day kept *wholly* for Him in a delightful manner. Doing this will place you on spiritually high places. The Sabbath was given to us to bring us into and keep us in a saving relationship with God—a growing faith relationship.

---

[577] Exodus 16:4, 5 (emphasis added)
[578] Isaiah 58:13, 14 (emphasis added)

You see, in life, there is the temporal; and then there is the eternal. Most of our time is spent in the pursuit of the temporal—money, houses, promotions, cars, etc. While these are necessary things, we need to recognize the danger of allowing them to swallow up the things of God—the things that really matter for eternity.

People can get so bogged down in pursuing the necessary that they lose sight of what is really important. This is why God wants us to take the twenty-four hours of the seventh day and spend it wholly with Him. This puts a limit on the influence of the temporal in our lives, stopping the pursuit thereof from taking over. It is a practical way to put our trust in Him to provide for our needs.

The Sabbath is a weekly reminder that we are saved by grace through faith, not by our own human effort. It is a lesson in trusting in Jesus. Put God first and see how He blesses your life.

> Therefore *do not worry*, saying, "What shall we eat?" or "What shall we drink?" or "What shall we wear?" For *after all these things the Gentiles seek*. For your heavenly Father knows that you need all these things. But *seek first the kingdom of God* and *His righteousness*, and *all these things shall be added to you*.[579]

What are some practical ways to keep the Sabbath holy? Let me just share some ideas that my family does. We begin the Sabbath hours with a time of worship and prayer as the sun sets on Friday evening. The whole day is different. The secular TV programs are off on the Sabbath (of course, a Christian TV channel like *Hope Channel* or *3ABN* would be different). The music we play is of a sacred nature. News reports are off, and secular things are put aside—out of sight.

It can be a time for reading and studying the Bible or other spiritual books, or for memorizing Scripture. It is also a wonderful time to spend out in nature with family and friends, enjoying the beautiful things God has created.

On Sabbath morning, we do as Jesus did. It was His custom to be in church on the Sabbath, and we want to do the same.[580] The Sabbath is the day of sacred worship. When we gather on Sabbath, it is for more than study; it is for worshipping our great and loving God!

Church attendance and Christian fellowship are vital parts of enjoying the Sabbath. The Sabbath is the day that God invites us to come together

---

[579] Matthew 6:31–33 (emphasis added)
[580] See Luke 4:16

in fellowship as believers. This is especially important as we near the end of time. "And let us consider one another in order to stir up love and good works, *not forsaking the assembling of ourselves together*, as is the manner of some, but exhorting one another, and *so much the more as you see the Day approaching*."[581]

As we near the day of Christ's return, we will need the fellowship of Christian friends even more. And besides that, we will be keeping the Sabbath in heaven, so why not start now? Talking about the new heaven and the new earth, the prophet said, "'And it shall come to pass that from one New Moon to another, and from *one Sabbath to another*, all flesh shall come to *worship before Me*,' says the LORD."[582]

The Sabbath is also a time to encourage others. Jesus healed many people on the Sabbath. It is a good time to get involved with visiting lonely people, ministering to prisoners, helping the homeless, and relieving sickness and suffering. Jesus said, "It is lawful to do good on the Sabbath."[583]

Now, if someone asked me to help him paint his fence on the Sabbath, although that might be a service to him, I would probably tell him I could do that another day. However, if someone was sick and needed food or medical attention, I would do everything I could to help. Or, if someone was stuck along the side of the road with a flat tire, I would stop to help.

On the one hand, you can be so rigid that the Sabbath becomes a burden, and that is not what God wants. On the other hand, you can be so lax that the Sabbath becomes no different from the other days of the week, and God is not calling us to that either. If you seek the Lord, He will lead you to make the Sabbath all He intends it to be.

The Sabbath will be what you make it. Approach it with joy, and it will become the best day of your week. Remember what God says about His people in the last days: they "keep the commandments of God and the faith of Jesus."[584]

The Sabbath is a gift given directly by God. I invite you to enjoy it. It is a foretaste of heaven! I invite you to "Remember the Sabbath day to keep it holy." It is designed to help you fall in love with Jesus more and more every week. Therefore, Satan hates it, and in the next chapter, we will see his final attack against it.

---

[581] Hebrews 10:24, 25 (emphasis added)
[582] Isaiah 66:23 (emphasis added)
[583] Matthew 12:12
[584] Revelation 14:12

Chapter 11

A Counterfeit Mark

We have studied about the mark (seal) that God wants to put on our foreheads, but Revelation describes another mark—a counterfeit mark—that Satan and his forces want us to receive instead. God's seal is characterized by love; Satan's mark is characterized by force. God will only accept service motivated by love, but Satan uses a variety of motives, including rewards, flattery, peer pressure, fear, and force to induce us to follow him.

In Revelation 13, we find two fierce beasts collaborating with Satan to force the world to receive the counterfeit mark on their foreheads or right hands. This is his final battle against God and His people. That warfare is introduced in chapter 12 yet described in detail in chapters 13–19. Let us look at the introduction to that war: "And the *dragon* was wroth with the *woman*, and *went to make war* with the remnant of her seed, which *keep the commandments of God*, and have the *testimony of Jesus Christ*."[585]

It is important to identify the opposing forces in this conflict: the dragon against the woman. The symbols of the "dragon" and the "woman" are easily understood by letting the Bible interpret itself. Revelation tells us who the dragon represents:

> *God's seal is characterized by love; Satan's mark is characterized by force. God will only accept service motivated by love, but Satan uses a variety of motives, including rewards, flattery, peer pressure, fear, and force to induce us to follow him.*

> And there was war in heaven: Michael and his angels fought against the *dragon*; and the *dragon* fought and his angels, And prevailed not; neither was their place found any more in heaven. And the *great dragon* was cast out, that *old serpent*, called the *Devil*, and

---

[585] Revelation 12:17, KJV (emphasis added; the KJV is the best translation of this verse)

Satan, which deceiveth the whole world: he was cast out into the earth, and his angels were cast out with him.[586]

The human instrumentality Satan uses to do his work is also described as a dragon. For example, when Jesus was born in Bethlehem, Satan did all in his power to kill Him as an infant. He inspired Herod, the Roman king of the Judean area, to kill all the children two years old and under in Bethlehem and its surrounding territories.

However, God sent an angel to warn Joseph and Mary to escape from Bethlehem and go to Egypt before the massacre took place. The prophecy in Revelation 12 describes Satan's attempt to kill baby Jesus this way: "And the dragon stood before the woman which was ready to be delivered, for *to devour her child as soon as it was born*."[587]

Therefore, it is ultimately Satan who is at war with Jesus and the remnant of the woman's offspring, even though he uses Rome as his human instrumentality to conduct his warfare. Throughout the Bible, God's people are represented by a woman—His church. Let us look at a couple examples:

Let us be glad and rejoice, and give honour to him: for the marriage of the Lamb is come, and his *wife* hath made *herself* ready. And to *her* was granted that she should be arrayed in fine linen, clean and white: for the fine linen is the righteousness of *saints*.[588]

For I am jealous over you with godly jealousy: for I have espoused you to one husband, that I may present you as a *chaste virgin* to Christ.[589]

---

[586] Revelation 12:7–9, KJV (emphasis added)
[587] Revelation 12:4 (emphasis added)
[588] Revelation 19:7, 8, KJV (emphasis added)
[589] 2 Corinthians 11:2 (emphasis added)

Therefore, the final battle at the end of time is between Satan and his forces on one side and God and His people who "keep the commandments of God and have the testimony of Jesus Christ" on the other.

Some people like to read the last chapter of a book first to find out who wins before they wade through the rest of the book. As such, here is a peek at the outcome of this war: "These shall make *war* with the *Lamb*, and *the Lamb shall overcome them*: for he is Lord of lords, and King of kings: and *they that are with him are called, and chosen, and faithful*."[590]

Jesus is the Lamb of God who takes away our sins. The Lamb will be victorious, and those who have chosen Him as their Savior will be victorious with Him! Nevertheless, how could a Lamb win in a battle against a ferocious beast? It is because self-sacrificing love is stronger than force. Truth triumphs over falsehood.

Now that we have identified the two sides in the battle (Satan vs. God), we are ready to launch into Revelation 13, where we find Satan's forces and battle plans defined. This gives God's people an incredible advantage. By knowing the enemy's plans, God has blessed us with the ability to avoid his traps and defeat his purposes. This is the value of studying prophecy.

In Revelation 13, we find Satan will use two powers at the end of time that will work together to annihilate God's people. These powers are represented as beasts. The first beast is described in verses 1–10, and the second beast is described in verses 11–18. By letting the Bible be its own interpreter, we will be able to identify what these beasts represent. The first one has the famous number 666, and the second one makes an image to it and enforces its mark of authority. Let us start with the first beast:

> And I stood upon the sand of the sea, and saw a *beast* rise up out of the *sea*, having *seven heads* and *ten horns*, and upon his horns *ten crowns*, and upon his heads the *name of blasphemy*. And the beast

---
[590] Revelation 17:14 (emphasis added)

which I saw was like unto a *leopard*, and his *feet* were as the feet of a *bear*, and his mouth as the mouth of a *lion*: and the *dragon* gave him his *power*, and his *seat*, and *great authority*.[591]

Notice from where this beast comes. It arose out of the "sea." Revelation tells us what bodies of water like seas represent. "The *waters* which you saw, where the harlot sits, are *peoples, multitudes, nations*, and *tongues*."[592]

Just as the four beasts of Daniel 7 came up out of the sea,[593] so does this beast. This is the first clue that this beast is related to the beasts of Daniel 7. They all arise in an area of the world that is heavily populated, with a wide variety of nations speaking different languages.

The reason we began our study of prophecy with the book of Daniel is because it lays the foundation for understanding the prophetic symbols of Revelation. If you will recall our study of Daniel 7 (chapters 3 and 4 of this book), we saw a lion, bear, leopard, and dragon. These four beasts represented four kingdoms:[594]

- Lion = Babylon (605–539 BC)
- Bear = Media-Persia (539–331 BC)
- Leopard = Greece (331–168 BC)
- Dragon = Rome (168 BC–AD 476)

The first beast of Revelation 13 is a conglomeration of all the characteristics of those nations. Papal Rome did not destroy the pagan religions of the kingdoms. Instead, they incorporated parts of their pagan beliefs and practices into their church life.

We also saw the fourth beast of Daniel 7 (empirical Rome) divided into the ten nations of Europe, but then a religious-political power arose (papal Rome) and was instrumental in destroying three of those European nations. Therefore, only seven survived.

Revelation describes this power with seven heads and ten horns. The ten horns have crowns on them, indicating they are monarchies—ruled by kings and queens. They are not democracies ruled by officials elected by the people. This is an important distinction, as we will see shortly.

Another clue is this first beast of Revelation 13 has *"on his heads a* blasphemous *name."* Blasphemy is a prominent characteristic of the beast. The

---

[591] Revelation 13:1, 2 (emphasis added)
[592] Revelation 17:15 (emphasis added)
[593] See Daniel 7:3
[594] See Daniel 7:23

apostle John described this characteristic: "And he was given a mouth speaking *great things* and *blasphemies*, and he was given authority to *continue for forty-two months*. Then he opened his mouth in *blasphemy against God*, to blaspheme His *name*, His *tabernacle*, and *those who dwell in heaven*."[595]

This is a direct parallel to the little-horn antichrist power of Daniel 7, which had "a mouth speaking pompous words"[596] and spoke "words against the Most High."[597] When sinful humans take upon themselves the name "Holy Father," they are blaspheming the name of God. When they claim to have the power to forgive sins, they are blaspheming God's tabernacle, where Jesus is our only Mediator and Intercessor. He is the only one who can forgive our sins. When mere humans claim to change God's holy law of Ten Commandments, which the angels in heaven delight to obey,[598] they blaspheme those who dwell in heaven.

Notice this beast "was given authority to continue for forty-two months." In the biblical reckoning of time, each month had thirty days. Therefore, 42 x 30 = 1,260 days. In Bible prophecy, a day is symbolic of a literal year. Seven times between the books of Daniel and Revelation, the papacy is described as having persecuting power for 1,260 years.[599]

The papacy solidified its persecuting power in AD 538, when the Roman Emperor Justinian gave the pope his throne and political power over western Europe. However, that persecuting power is described as coming to a temporary end with a deadly wound at the conclusion of those 1,260 years: "And I saw one of his heads as if it had been mortally wounded, and his deadly wound was healed. And all the world marveled and followed the beast."[600]

It was in 1798 (exactly 1,260 years after 538) that Napoleon sent his armed forces, under the leadership of General Berthier, into Rome and took the pope off his throne, removing his political powers; the pope died in exile shortly after. The Church of Rome could no longer dominate the nations of Europe as they had done for the previous 1,260 years.

The world rejoiced, thinking the papal power was dead and would never rise to power again. They were tired of being controlled, manipulated, and forced to carry out the wishes and enforce the doctrines and decrees of the Church of Rome.

---

[595] Revelation 13:5–6 (emphasis added)
[596] Daniel 7:8
[597] Daniel 7:25
[598] See Psalm 103:20
[599] See Daniel 7:25; 12:7; Revelation 11:2; 11:3; 12:6; 12:14; 13:5
[600] Revelation 13:3

However, God knew better. He knew the deadly wound would eventually be healed and the world would again follow the pope's lead, as we see happening today. The world is basically falling at the feet of the pope, recognizing him as the spiritual and moral leader of the planet. By recognizing the pope's authority to change God's law, they are, in effect, bowing to Satan and joining his rebellion against it. "*So they worshiped the dragon who gave authority to the beast; and they worshiped the beast*, saying, 'Who is like the beast? Who is able to make war with him?'"[601]

Nobody can worship the beast and have one's name recorded in the Lamb's book of life at the same time; the two are exclusive. Therefore, it is important to understand this prophecy and to heed the warnings. Clearly, this is a salvation issue! "*All who dwell on the earth will worship him*, whose names have *not* been written in the *Book of Life of the Lamb slain from the foundation of the world.*"[602]

The deadly wound took away the pope's political/persecuting power. Therefore, the healing of the deadly wound will involve the restoring of his political/persecuting power. In plain words, contrary to popular opinion, the papacy will become a persecuting power again. "It was granted to him to make war with the saints and to overcome them. And authority was given him over every tribe, tongue, and nation."[603]

Let me remind you that the prophecies are not speaking of the Catholic people. There are many true Christians in the Catholic Church who are serving God to the best of their ability with the knowledge they have. What the prophecies are pointing out is the religious-political papal system centered in the Vatican in Rome. God is not pointing this out to condemn anyone but to save all who will come unto Him for truth, forgiveness from sin, and His power for victory over all weaknesses. He will accept anyone, no matter who they are or what their pasts have been!

Another characteristic of the sea beast is the well-known number 666. It is "the number of his name. Here is wisdom. Let him who has understanding *calculate* the *number of the beast*, for it is the *number of a man*: His number is *666.*"[604] One of the official titles (names) of the pope (a man) is "*Vicarius Filli Dei*," which means "Vicar of the Son of God."[605]

---

[601] Revelation 13:4 (emphasis added)
[602] Revelation 13:8 (emphasis added)
[603] Revelation 13:7 (emphasis added)
[604] Revelation 13:17, 18 (emphasis added)
[605] For more information about this, see Edwin de Kock's book, *The Truth About 666 and the Story of the Great Apostasy*

When one calculates the Roman numeric value of this name, it looks like the following:

```
V =   5        F =   0        D = 500
I =   1        I =   1        E =   0
C = 100        L =  50        I =   1
A =   0        I =   1            501
R =   0        I =   1
I =   1           53
U =   5
S =   0
    112
```

When you add these numbers together (112 + 53 + 501), they equal 666. This would be a very weak argument if it stood alone, but combined with all the other points of evidence, we can see it fits perfectly.

Revelation 13 concludes its initial description of the first beast by drawing our attention back to the deadly wound that was inflicted on the Papacy in 1798: "If anyone has an ear, let him hear. He who *leads into captivity* shall *go into captivity*; he who *kills with the sword* must be *killed with the sword*. Here is the patience and the faith of the saints."[606]

The papacy was responsible for killing at least 50 million Christians during the 1,260 years of their supremacy. The pope used the sword of the state; and it was the sword of the state[607] that removed him and took his power away in 1798. The first beast, the sea beast of Revelation 13, clearly represents the papal power of the Vatican in Rome.

This sets the stage for the introduction of the second beast of Revelation 13. The second beast is seen coming up out of the earth at the very time the first beast, the sea beast, receives his deadly wound: in 1798.

The question is, What world-dominating nation was arising at the time the deadly wound was inflicted on the papacy? We will look at ten identifying characteristics that will help us identify who this beast rising from the earth represents. There is only one power that lines up with all ten characteristics.

The earth beast is introduced this way: "Then I saw *another beast* coming up out of the *earth*, and he had *two horns like a lamb* and *spoke like a dragon*."[608]

---

[606] Revelation 13:9, 10 (emphasis added)
[607] See Romans 13:4
[608] Revelation 13:11 (emphasis added)

1. This beast represents a nation: In Bible prophecy, a beast represents a nation, kingdom, or political power. Remember, Daniel lays the foundation for understanding Revelation. Notice how Daniel identifies what a beast represents: "Thus he said: 'The fourth *beast* shall be A fourth *kingdom* on earth.'"[609]

2. It represents a nation at the end of time: The mark of the beast is an end-time event, and it is this beast that forces it upon the world.

   > He *causes all*, both small and great, rich and poor, free and slave, to receive a *mark on their right hand or on their foreheads*, and that no one may buy or sell except one who has the *mark or the name of the beast*, or the number of his name.[610]

3. It is the world's most powerful end-time nation: This is evident from the fact that it *"causes all,"* or forces all to receive the mark of the sea beast – the mark of Papal authority. Yes, you have guessed it already. This earth beast represents The United States of America. But let us see how the rest of the identifying characteristics fit.

4. It comes "up out of the earth":[611] The papal power arose out of the "sea"—a very populated part of the earth with many nations and different languages[612]—Europe. The "earth," in contrast, would indicate a very unpopulated part of the world, like North

---

[609] Daniel 7:23 (emphasis added)
[610] Revelation 13:16, 17 (emphasis added)
[611] Revelation 13:11
[612] See Revelation 17:15

America was when the pilgrims landed here. They left Europe to seek freedom of religion and escape persecution. They were seeking a church without a pope and a state without a king. They wanted freedom to worship God according to the dictates of their consciences.

> And when God's hand seemed pointing them across the sea, to a land where they might found for themselves a state, and leave to their children the precious heritage of religious liberty, they went forward, without shrinking, in the path of providence.[613]

The Declaration of Independence states, "We hold these truths to be self-evident, that all men are created equal, that they are endowed by their Creator with certain inalienable rights, that among these are Life, Liberty, and Pursuit of Happiness."

Our founding fathers specifically worded the Constitution to guarantee freedom of religion. "Congress shall make no law respecting the establishment of religion, or prohibiting the free exercise thereof."

The principle of religious liberty is what has made this nation the greatest on earth! The United States arose to a nation at the very time the deadly wound was inflicted on the papacy. Notice the sequence of dates:

1776—Declaration of Independence
1789—Constitution ratified
1791—Bill of Rights adopted
1798—Deadly wound inflicted on the papacy

There is no other world-dominating nation that arose at the end of the 1700s other than the United States of America, the greatest nation on earth today. I am proud to be an American, even though I know what our nation will do in the near future. Thankfully, some Americans (myself included) will refuse to take part in certain activities of the lamb-like beast.

---

[613] Ellen G. White, The Great Controversy (Mountain View, CA: Pacific Press Publishing Association, 1911), p. 291.

5. Lamb-like: "He had two horns like a lamb."[614] Being compared to a lamb gives us several clues:

    - A lamb is a young animal, indicating this would be a new nation
    - A nation characterized by freedom, innocence, gentleness, and energy
    - A Christian nation as it began

6. A democracy or republic: This is indicated by the fact that the horns on this beast did not have crowns, in contrast to the horns on the first beast that had crowns. The papacy arose amid European nations ruled by kings and queens. They were monarchies, as prophetically indicated by crowns on the horns. However, the horns on the earth beast did not have crowns, which would indicate a different form of government—a government that was to be for the people and by the people.

    > *I am proud to be an American, even though I know what our nation will do in the near future.*

7. Eventually leads (controls) the world: The United States has dominated the world politically and economically for many years, but soon we will also dominate the world in regard to religious worship, forcing everyone to fall in step with the pope's agenda. "And he exercises all the authority of the first beast in his presence, and causes the earth and those who dwell in it to worship the first beast, whose deadly wound was healed."[615]

8. Speaks as a dragon: "He had two horns like a lamb and spoke like a dragon."[616] We have already identified the dragon as Satan, the devil. Even though the United States began with Christlike characteristics, it is predicted to change and take on Satan's characteristics. For a long time, it was difficult to imagine this taking place in our great nation, but we see it happening today before our very eyes. There is no way a nation speaks more clearly than by the laws it passes. Our constitutional rights are being increasingly eroded, and the masses are seemingly willing to submit to greater control.

---

[614] Revelation 13:11
[615] Revelation 13:12
[616] Revelation 13:11

This nation will soon pass laws restricting religious freedoms and enforcing papal-endorsed religious observances.

> He performs great signs, so that he even makes fire come down from heaven on the earth in the sight of men. And he *deceives* those who dwell on the earth—by those signs which he was granted to do in the sight of the beast, *telling those who dwell on the earth to make an image to the beast who was wounded by the sword and lived*. He was granted power to give breath to the image of the beast, that the image of the beast should both *speak* and *cause* as many as would *not worship* the image of the beast to be *killed*. He *causes* all, both small and great, rich and poor, free and slave, to *receive a mark on their right hand or on their foreheads*, and that *no one may buy or sell* except one who has the *mark* or the name of the *beast*, or the number of his name.[617]

9. Makes an image to the sea beast: An image is a likeness of something. Here, we see predicted that the United States will be instrumental in creating a likeness to the religious-political, dominating power the papacy demonstrated during the 1,260 years of their control. It is hard to comprehend the United States doing such a thing, but the prophecy has so far been fulfilled in every detail. This assures us the future details will be fulfilled exactly as predicted as well.

    The golden image King Nebuchadnezzar set up on the Plain of Dura, to which he forced all to bow and worship or be thrown into the fiery furnace, is a precursor to this end-time image. If you remember, three Hebrew captives (Shadrach, Meshach, and Abed-Nego) were among those who were ordered to fall down and worship the image, but they refused to do so. Therefore, they were thrown into the furnace, but Jesus came to them and saved them from the flames.[618]

    The reason Shadrach, Meshach, and Abed-Nego refused to bow to the golden image was because they loved God with all their heart, soul, and strength. Therefore, they refused to break His Ten Commandments. They would rather die than be disloyal to their Creator and Redeemer. This incident in Daniel helps us

---

[617] Revelation 13:13–17 (emphasis added)
[618] See Daniel 3

understand the image to the beast in Revelation also has to do with loving God and being loyal to Him by keeping His Ten Commandments, even if it means not being able to buy or sell or facing a death decree.

The image to the beast will be formed when church and state unite to enforce religious practices. The prophecy makes it clear what religious practices will be enforced, but before we get to that subject, let us look at this church-state union more carefully.

This unity of church and state is brought out more clearly in Revelation 17, which describes a woman riding a beast:

> So he carried me away in the Spirit into the wilderness. And I saw a *woman* sitting on a *scarlet beast* which was full of names of *blasphemy*, having *seven heads* and *ten horns*. The *woman* was arrayed in purple and scarlet, and adorned with gold and precious stones and pearls, having in her hand *a golden cup* full of *abominations* and the *filthiness of her fornication*.[619]

We have seen before that a woman is symbolic of the church. In Revelation, there are two very different women depicted. We already discovered a pure woman described in chapter 12. This woman (true church) is persecuted and has to go into hiding for 1,260 years, and the "remnant" of this church at the end of time "keep the commandments of God, and have the testimony of Jesus Christ."[620]

The other woman is the corrupt woman who we read about in Revelation 17. This woman is full of abominations and fornication. She represents a corrupt, false church. It is significant that she is represented as a fornicator (harlot) because a harlot is one who is involved in an illegitimate, unlawful, unholy relationship.

---

[619] Revelation 17:3, 4 (emphasis added)
[620] Revelation 12:17

The marriage vow between a man and a woman is symbolic of the covenant relationship God wants with His people. When we allow anything or anyone to come between us and our faith relationship with God, we are committing spiritual fornication.

In the Old Testament, the nation of Israel is repeatedly depicted as a harlot because they repeatedly forsook the covenant relationship they had made with God.

> Do not rejoice, O *Israel*, with joy like other peoples, For you have *played the harlot against your God*. You have made love for hire on every threshing floor.[621]
>
> You also *played the harlot with the Assyrians*, because you were insatiable; indeed you *played the harlot with them* and still were not satisfied.[622]

Israel played the harlot with the pagan gods of the nations around them. They also played the harlot by seeking protection from their enemies, turning to the Assyrians and Egyptians instead of seeking the God of heaven.

This is exactly how the corrupt church of Revelation 17 plays the harlot. She turns to the state for support instead of turning to God Almighty.

> Then one of the seven angels who had the seven bowls came and talked with me, saying to me, "Come, I will show you the judgment of the *great harlot* who sits on many waters, *with whom the kings of the earth committed fornication*, and the inhabitants of the earth were made drunk with the wine of her fornication."[623]

The prophecy clearly reveals that this corrupt church turns to the power of the state to do its bidding. The woman represents the church, and the beast represents the power of the state. This puts the church in an unlawful, inappropriate relationship with the state because, instead of turning to the state for help, she should turn only to God "in truth."[624]

---

[621] Hosea 9:1 (emphasis added)
[622] Ezekiel 16:28 (emphasis added)
[623] Revelation 17:1, 2 (emphasis added)
[624] Psalm 145:18

This is where Satan's deceptions will be so close to the truth it will be very difficult to discern between the two. In turning to the state for help, the religious leaders will call for prayer, fasting, and serious repentance. Many politically accepted sins will be denounced as the cause of the troubles coming upon our nation and the world at large. However, this will be a counterfeit revival just before the true outpouring of the Holy Spirit takes place. Even though it will have the appearance of a holy and righteous revival, those who take part in it will embrace two deadly errors. First, they will reject the seventh-day, Saturday Sabbath of the fourth commandment. Second, they will solicit the power of the state to force compliance to God's commandments as changed by human agents. God never uses force! Eventually, those who adhere to the Bible Sabbath will be denounced as dangerous troublemakers because they refuse to comply with the popular revival, and the religious leaders will solicit the power of the state to force them to comply.

The prophecy depicts this corrupt woman as riding the beast. This is symbolic of an apostate church controlling and using the state for her purposes, and this is exactly what the Church of Rome did during the 1,260 years of papal supremacy. This was the power that was removed from her when she received the deadly wound in 1798, and this is the power that will soon be restored to her as the deadly wound is healed. All the people of the world will follow her lead, except the remnant people of God, those who "keep the commandments of God, and have the testimony of Jesus Christ."[625]

This corrupt woman has a very descriptive name written on her forehead: "And on her forehead a name was written: MYSTERY, BABYLON THE GREAT, THE MOTHER OF HARLOTS AND OF THE ABOMINATIONS OF THE EARTH."[626]

Please remember she is called "Babylon the Great" because we will come back to that in the next chapter. For now, notice she is "the Mother of Harlots." The Church of Rome considers herself the "Mother Church" and calls the Protestant churches her wayward daughters. Therefore, this woman called "Babylon the Great" is comprised not only of the Church of Rome, but also

---

[625] Revelation 12:17
[626] Revelation 17:5

of the Protestant churches who join with Rome to control and use the power of the state for their purposes.

The Protestant churches and the Church of Rome have been moving closer together for many years. The name "Protestant" was given to those who held to the Bible alone for their faith and practice, protesting the evils of the Vatican. However, today, the Protestant churches are no longer protesting. Instead, they are uniting with the Catholic Church. Notice a summary statement regarding this phenomenon. Much more has taken place regarding the ecumenical movement since this was written, but the following statement demonstrates that this prophecy in Revelation is being fulfilled before our eyes:

> The most significant event in nearly 500 years of church history was revealed as a fiat accompli on March 29, 1994. On that day leading American evangelicals and Catholics signed a joint declaration titled "Evangelicals and Catholics Together: The Christian Mission in the 3rd Millennium." *The document, in effect, overturned the Reformation* and will unquestionably have far-reaching repercussions throughout the Christian world for years to come.[627]

More recently, on January 5, 2021, the Vatican issued a statement regarding unity with Lutheranism.[628] This statement looks good on the surface, but when one understands the Catholic doctrine of justification, it becomes clear the Lutherans have compromised biblical truth to obtain unity with Rome.

The combined force of churches will again become a persecuting power against those who refuse to go along with their agenda. It will be done in such a way as to make it appear that those who refuse to cooperate with their plans are enemies of the state. This is exactly what happened to Jesus. "And one of them, Caiaphas, being high priest that year, said to them, 'You know nothing at all, nor do you consider that *it is expedient for us that one man should die for the people, and not that the whole nation should perish.*'"[629]

---

[627] David Hunt, A Woman Rides the Beast (Eugene, OR: Harvest House Publishers, 1994), p. 5 (emphasis added)

[628] See "Catholics and Lutherans reaffirm commitment to communion," Vatican News, https://1ref.us/1op (accessed February 7, 2021).

[629] John 11:49, 50 (emphasis added)

Likely, the same argument will be used by Babylon the Great against the remnant who "keep the commandments of God, and have the testimony of Jesus Christ." "I saw the *woman*, drunk with the *blood of the saints* and with the *blood of the martyrs of Jesus*. And when I saw her, I marveled with great amazement."[630]

10. <u>Forces the world to receive the mark of the beast</u>: As there are two women depicted in Revelation, representing two churches, so there are two marks described in Revelation as well. We have already studied God's mark (seal). We will see His mark contrasts with the mark of the beast.

> He *causes* all, both small and great, rich and poor, free and slave, *to receive a mark* on their *right hand* or on their *foreheads*, and that no one may buy or sell except one who has the mark or the name of the beast, or the number of his name.[631]

Let us notice one similarity and several differences between God's mark and the papal mark. The similarity is they both can be placed on the forehead. However, that is as far as the similarities go. You will notice the papal mark is also placed on the right hand, whereas God's mark is not.

First, I want to clarify that this is not a tattoo, computer chip, or biometric identification system injected into a person's body. The forehead is where the frontal lobe of the brain resides—where we make spiritual and moral decisions. Having these marks placed on the forehead indicates a particular spiritual and moral decision has permanently been made.

It is interesting that God's mark is only placed on the forehead, not on the right hand. However, the papal mark is placed on the right hand *or* the forehead. The United States combined with the papal power will "cause all… to receive a mark." The word "cause" indicates using pressure or force. This is something God does not do, but it is a tactic the papacy has used since its beginning. Receiving the mark of the beast on the right hand would indicate a person does not really believe the papal way to be the right way, but in order to be able to buy and sell so they can feed their families and save their lives, they will go along with it. It will

---

[630] Revelation 17:6 (emphasis added)
[631] Revelation 13:16, 17 (emphasis added)

constitute performing a religious act from pressure or force and not by faith. When the mark is on the forehead, the person is convinced it is right and buys into papal authority, but when it is on the right hand, the person is coerced to go along with it.

The central issue regarding the mark of the beast is worship. That was the issue with Nebuchadnezzar's golden image, as well as when Daniel was thrown into the lion's den. Both events were prophetic of the issue that will promulgate at the end of time, which Revelation clearly identifies as worship. Notice how the issue of worship is repeatedly mentioned regarding the beast, with its image and mark, on one side and the Creator God on the other:

> So they *worshiped* the dragon who gave authority to the beast; and they *worshiped* the beast, saying, "Who is like the beast? Who is able to make war with him?"[632]
>
> All who dwell on the earth will *worship* him, whose names have not been written in the Book of Life of the Lamb slain from the foundation of the world.[633]
>
> And he exercises all the authority of the first beast in his presence, and causes the earth and those who dwell in it to *worship* the first beast, whose deadly wound was healed.[634]
>
> He was granted power to give breath to the image of the beast, that the image of the beast should both speak and cause as many as would not *worship* the image of the beast to be killed.[635]
>
> Then a third angel followed them, saying with a loud voice, "If anyone *worships* the beast and his image, and receives his mark on his forehead or on his hand, he himself shall also drink of the wine of the wrath of God."[636]
>
> Then the beast was captured, and with him the false prophet who worked signs in his presence, by which he deceived those who received the mark of the beast and those who *worshiped* his image. These two were cast alive into the lake of fire burning with brimstone.[637]

---

[632] Revelation 13:4 (emphasis added)
[633] Revelation 13:8 (emphasis added)
[634] Revelation 13:12 (emphasis added)
[635] Revelation 13:15 (emphasis added)
[636] Revelation 14:9, 10 (emphasis added)
[637] Revelation 19:20 (emphasis added)

A Counterfeit Mark

Nowhere is there a stronger warning in the Bible. And in contrast to worshipping the beast and his image, we have the appeal of God to worship Him as our Creator:

> Then I saw another angel flying in the midst of heaven, having the everlasting gospel to preach to those who dwell on the earth to every nation, tribe, tongue, and people—saying with a loud voice, "Fear God and give glory to Him, for the hour of His judgment has come; and *worship* Him who made heaven and earth, the sea and springs of water."[638]

> And I saw thrones, and they sat on them, and judgment was committed to them. Then I saw the souls of those who had been beheaded for their witness to Jesus and for the word of God, *who had not worshiped the beast or his image*, and had not received his mark on their foreheads or on their hands. And they lived and reigned with Christ for a thousand years.[639]

Now we come to the crucial question: What is the mark of the beast? What is the mark of papal authority? It has to do with worship. We have seen God's mark or sign of authority is Sabbath worship, and you have already, undoubtedly guessed the mark of papal authority is Sunday worship.

What does the Roman Catholic Church claim as the sign of its authority? Notice these statements from their official documents:

> [Q] How *prove* you that the church hath power to command feasts and holy days?
>
> [A] By the very act of *changing the Sabbath into Sunday*, which Protestants allow of: and therefore fondly contradict themselves by keeping Sunday strictly and breaking most other feasts commanded by the same church.[640]

> [Q] Have you any other way of *proving* that the church has power to institute festivals of precept?
>
> *[A] HAD she not had such power* she could not have substituted the observance of *Sunday*, the first day of the week, for

---

[638] Revelation 14:6, 7 (emphasis added)
[639] Revelation 20:4 (emphasis added)
[640] Henry Tuberville, An Abridgment of the Christian Doctrine, (New York: John Doyle, 1833), p. 58 (emphasis added)

the observance of *Saturday*, the seventh day, *a change for which there is no scriptural authority*.[641]

> Protestants reject Divine Tradition, the Unwritten Word, which Catholics accept as of equal authority with the Written Word, the Bible.... The Bible still teaches that the Sabbath or Saturday should be kept holy. There is no authority in the New Testament for the substitution of Sunday for Saturday. Surely it is an important matter. It stands there in the Bible as one of the Ten Commandments of God. There is no authority in the Bible for abrogating this Commandment, or for transferring its observance to another day of the week.
>
> For Catholics it is not the slightest difficulty.... The Church is above the Bible; and this transference of Sabbath observance from Saturday to Sunday is proof positive of that fact. Deny the authority of the Church and you have no adequate or reasonable explanation or justification for the substitution of Sunday for Saturday in the Third—Protestant Fourth—Commandment of God.[642]
>
> Perhaps the boldest thing, the most revolutionary change the Church ever did happened in the first century. The *holy day, the Sabbath*, was *changed* from *Saturday* to *Sunday*... not from any direction noted in the Scriptures, but from the *Church's sense of its own power*... People who think that the Scriptures should be the sole authority, should logically become Seventh-day Adventists and keep Saturday holy.[643]

The second beast of Revelation 13, representing the United States, will "cause" (force) the world to accept and receive the mark of papal authority—Sunday sacredness. "He causes all, both small and great, rich and poor, free and slave, to receive a mark on their right hand or on their

---

[641] Stephen Keenan, A Doctrinal Catechism, 3rd ed., (New York: T. W. Strong [late Edward Duningan & Bro.], 1876), p. 174 (emphasis added). The Catholic Record has been approved and recommended by Archbishops Falconio and Sbaretti, late Apostolic Delegates to Canada, the Archbishops of Toronto, Kingston, Ottawa, and St. Boniface, the Bishops of London, Hamilton, Peterborough and Odgensburg, N. Y., and the clergy throughout the Dominion (https://1ref.us/1oq, accessed February 4, 2021)

[642] *Catholic Record*, Vol. 45, Number 2342, London, Ontario, September 1, 1923 (emphasis added; these may be old documents, but the Church of Rome still stand behind them)

[643] *Saint Catherine Catholic Church Sentinel*, Vol. 50, Number 22, Algonac, MI, May 21, 1995 (emphasis added)

foreheads, and that no one may buy or sell except one who has the mark or the name of the beast, or the number of his name."[644]

At that time, the choice will be clear: either accept the sign of papal authority and be able to feed your family or accept the sign of God's authority and be persecuted and maybe even put to death. "He was granted *power* to give breath to the image of the beast, that the image of the beast should both speak and cause as many as would not worship the image of the beast to be killed."[645]

It has been difficult to imagine The United States using economic and life-threatening laws to force people to accept the sign of papal authority. However, the way our nation is headed today, it is becoming clear this prophecy could be fulfilled sooner rather than later. It doesn't take much imagination to see how it will happen. As society continues to unravel and fall into chaos and violence, nations continue to escalate the threats of war, and nature continues to become more destructive and deadly, the cry will go out from our religious leaders that these are God's judgments upon our land, and they will appeal to the people as well as to our legislators to turn form sin and return to worshiping and serving God.

Then, as this world continues to implode upon itself, our religious leaders will persuade our national leaders to institute laws requiring us to stop working on Sunday and go to church instead. The argument will be that we have to get back to God or we will only experience more severe judgments. They will naturally choose Sunday as the national day of worship because it is the day on which most Christians worship already. Even though their intent will be to bring us back to God, knowingly or unknowingly, they will be enforcing the papal sign of authority.

There is much more that could be said about the beast and its image and mark, but the purpose of this book is not to condemn and belittle, but to reflect God's heart of love for erring human beings (myself included). God is sending one, last, final message of appeal to the world. His heart of love yearns for everyone to respond positively to His invitation. Will you? We will look at His invitation more fully in the next chapter, but here is a peek at it:

> After these things I saw another angel coming down from heaven, having great authority, and the earth was illuminated with his glory. And he cried mightily with a loud voice, saying, *"Babylon the great*

---
[644] Revelation 13:16, 17
[645] Revelation 13:15 (emphasis added)

is fallen, is fallen, and has become a *dwelling place of demons*, a prison for every foul spirit, and a cage for every unclean and hated bird! For all the *nations* have drunk of the wine of the wrath of *her fornication*, the *kings of the earth have committed fornication with her*, and the merchants of the earth have become rich through the abundance of her luxury." And I heard another voice from heaven saying, "*Come out of her, my people*, lest you share in her sins, and lest you receive of her plagues."[646]

> **There is much more that could be said about the beast and its image and mark, but the purpose of this book is not to condemn and belittle, but to reflect God's heart of love for erring human beings (myself included).**

Do you hear the pathos in the voice from heaven inviting you to come out of Babylon—the mother and her daughters? It is a salvation issue, and God wants you in heaven with Him! Jesus does not want anyone to be lost! "Therefore *He is also able to save to the uttermost* those who *come to God through Him*, since He always lives to make intercession for them."[647]

In calling us out of Babylon, God is also inviting us into a personal and collective experiential relationship with Him. He describes those who respond to His invitation this way: "Here is the patience of the saints; here are those who keep the commandments of God and the faith of Jesus."[648]

The word "saints" in the Bible means "true and genuine believers in Jesus." That is what you can be through God's power in your life. Will you invite Jesus into your heart? Do you choose to receive His mark—His seal? Will you take a stand for Him? He gave all for you!

We have nothing to fear for the future as long as we keep our eyes on Jesus! His promise to us during this time of trouble is our bread and water will be sure[649] and He will be our shelter and defense.[650] At that time, our only hope will be to put our trust and dependence fully upon God and God alone. You can be assured He will not let you down. He gave all for

---

[646] Revelation 18:1–4 (emphasis added)
[647] Hebrews 7:25 (emphasis added)
[648] Revelation 14:12
[649] See Isaiah 33:16
[650] See Psalm 91:1–16

you! This is why it is so important that we learn to put our full faith in Him today.

> Today, the issue of loyalty centers in worship.
> In the days of Noah, God invited His people to take a stand.
> In the days of Lot, God invited His people to take a stand.
> In the days of Daniel, God invited His people to take a stand.
> In the days of Jesus, God invited His people to take a stand.
> In the days of the early Christian Church, God invited His people to take a stand.
> In the Dark Ages, God invited His people to take a stand.
> In these last days, God invites His people to take a stand.
> What about you? Which mark will you receive? Keep reading. The best is yet to come!

Chapter 12

Three, No, Four Angels Shout!

God always sends messages to prepare His people for major events that will affect their eternal destiny. The Scriptures assure us of this.

> Surely the Lord GOD does nothing, Unless He reveals His secret to His servants the prophets."[651]
>
> Declaring the end from the beginning, And from ancient times things that are not yet done, Saying, "My counsel shall stand, And I will do all My pleasure."[652]

When the world had become so wicked that it was necessary for God to destroy it with a flood, He sent Noah to build an ark and preach repentance and righteousness (for 120 years) in order to prepare the people of his day to be ready.[653] God hoped their hearts would be so touched and humbled by Noah's warnings that they would choose to enter the ark and be saved from the flood. Unfortunately, when the invitation was given, only Noah and his wife, their three sons, and their wives were willing to enter the ark and be saved.

Likewise, before the city of Jerusalem and its magnificent temple were destroyed by Nebuchadnezzar's army, God sent messages and warnings through several different prophets over a period of many years, pleading with His people to forsake the pagan gods of the nations around them and return to Him, their only hope of salvation; but they stubbornly refused.

> And the *LORD God of their fathers sent warnings* to them by His messengers, rising up early and sending them, because *He had compassion on His people* and on His dwelling place. *But they mocked the messengers of God, despised His words, and scoffed at His prophets*, until the wrath of the LORD arose against His people, *till there was no remedy*.[654]

Again, God sent John the Baptist to prepare the people of his day, through repentance and righteousness, to receive Jesus the Messiah when

---

[651] Amos 3:7
[652] Isaiah 46:10
[653] See Genesis 6:11–22; Luke 17:26, 27; Hebrews 11:7; 1 Peter 3:20; 2 Peter 2:5
[654] 2 Chronicles 36:15, 16 (emphasis added)

He came to this earth the first time.[655] Again, God hoped their hearts would be touched by John's warnings and invitations, but "He came to His own, and His own did not receive Him."[656]

Likewise, in harmony with His caring heart, God has sent messages to us at the end of time in order to prepare us for the global crisis ahead and Christ's second coming. The first three of these messages are found in Revelation 14, and they are commonly called the "three angels' messages." In Revelation 18, we find another angel's message, an amplification of the second angel's message. Notwithstanding, let us begin by reading the three angels' messages:

> Then I saw *another angel* flying in the midst of heaven, having the *everlasting gospel* to preach to those who dwell on the earth to *every nation, tribe, tongue, and people*—saying with a loud voice, "*Fear God* and *give glory to Him*, for *the hour of His judgment has come*; and *worship Him who made* heaven and earth, the sea and springs of water."[657]
>
> And *another angel followed*, saying, "*Babylon is fallen, is fallen*, that great city, because she has *made all nations* drink of the wine of the wrath of *her fornication*."[658]
>
> Then *a third angel followed them*, saying with a loud voice, "If anyone *worships the beast and his image*, and *receives his mark on his forehead or on his hand*, he himself shall *also drink of the wine of the wrath of God*, which is poured out full strength into the cup of His indignation. He shall be tormented with fire and brimstone in the presence of the holy angels and in the presence of the Lamb. And the smoke

---

[655] See Matthew 3:1–3; Mark 1:1–4; Luke 3:1–6; John 1:6–8
[656] John 1:11
[657] Revelation 14:6, 7 (emphasis added)
[658] Revelation 14:8 (emphasis added)

of their torment ascends forever and ever; and they have no rest day or night, who worship the beast and his image, and whoever receives the mark of his name." Here is the *patience of the saints*; here are those *who keep the commandments of God* and *the faith of Jesus*.[659]

The next several verses describe the event for which these messages are to prepare us—the most climactic event ever to happen on earth. The symbolism of harvesting grain is used to describe the second coming of Jesus in the clouds to take the redeemed to heaven:

> Then I looked, and behold, a white cloud, and on the cloud sat One like the *Son of Man*, having on His head a golden crown, and in His hand a *sharp sickle*. And another angel came out of the temple, crying with a loud voice to Him who sat on the cloud, "Thrust in Your sickle and *reap*, for the time has come for You to reap, for *the harvest of the earth is ripe*." So He who sat on the cloud thrust in His sickle on the earth, *and the earth was reaped*.[660]

The final verses in Revelation 14, which reflect the harvest of grapes, describe what will happen to the lost when Jesus comes:

> And another angel came out from the altar, who had power over *fire*, and he cried with a loud cry to him who had the *sharp sickle*, saying, "Thrust in your sharp sickle and *gather the clusters of the vine of the earth*, for her *grapes are fully ripe*." So the angel thrust his sickle into the earth and gathered the vine of the earth, and *threw it into the great winepress of the wrath of God*.[661]

In Matthew 13, Jesus tells the parable of a farmer (representing God) who sowed good seed (truth) in his field (the human population), but his enemy (Satan) sowed weeds. This helps us understand the meaning of Revelation's symbol of the harvest.

> The enemy who sowed them is the devil, *the harvest is the end of the age*, and the *reapers are the angels*. Therefore as the *tares are gathered and burned in the fire*, so it will be at *the end of this age*. The *Son of Man* will send out His angels, and they will gather out of His kingdom *all things that offend*, and *those who practice lawlessness*, and will cast them into the furnace of fire.[662]

---

[659] Revelation 14:9–12 (emphasis added)
[660] Revelation 14:14–16 (emphasis added)
[661] Revelation 14:18, 19 (emphasis added)
[662] Matthew 13:39–42 (emphasis added)

The harvest will take place when the characters of both the sinful and righteous have become fully ripe, never to be changed. Unfortunately, the harvest of the righteous will be very small in comparison with the harvest of the sinful.[663] At the end of time, society will be in such moral decline that it will be as if we are in a freefall. And it is during this final freefall of the world that Satan will make his last desperate attempt to take total control of this planet.

Therefore, God gave the three angels' messages to prepare us to be part of the harvest of the righteous, rather than that of the wicked, when Jesus returns. Let us look at each of these messages carefully, beginning with the first one:

> Then I saw another angel flying in the midst of heaven, having the everlasting gospel to preach to those who dwell on the earth to every nation, tribe, tongue, and people—saying with a loud voice, "Fear God and give glory to Him, for the hour of His judgment has come; and worship Him who made heaven and earth, the sea and springs of water."[664]

This message is so important that it is described as being delivered by a flying angel in the midst of heaven. We should pay careful attention to it. Let us look at the following six points of the message, each of which is significant for us who are living in the end time:

1. Everlasting gospel: The gospel is the good news about salvation from sin through Jesus. This is the truth that Satan hates and has tried to corrupt through the beast power. It is the "everlasting" gospel because God's plan of salvation was not an emergency measure conceived as an afterthought when Adam and Eve sinned. The gospel is the natural response of His character of self-sacrificing love. It was a plan that was made in eternity past and will remain throughout eternity future.

   The gospel of Jesus Christ has always been the only way to salvation, in Old Testament and New Testament times.[665] The apostle Peter boldly declared, "Nor is there salvation in any other, for there is *no other name under heaven given among men by which we must be saved.*"[666]

---

[663] See Matthew 7:13, 14
[664] Revelation 14:6, 7
[665] See Galatians 1:8, 9; Romans 4; Hebrews 11
[666] Acts 4:12 (emphasis added)

The good news is that God is love, and everything that comes from Him is filled with love. This is why the apostle Paul was so completely sold out to the gospel!

> So, *as much as is in me*, I am ready to *preach the gospel* to you who are in Rome also. For I am not ashamed of the *gospel of Christ*, for *it is the power of God to salvation for everyone who believes*, for the Jew first and also for the Greek. For *in it the righteousness of God is revealed* from faith to faith; as it is written, "*The just shall live by faith.*"[667]

> *It is the "everlasting" gospel because God's plan of salvation was not an emergency measure conceived as an afterthought when Adam and Eve sinned. The gospel is the natural response of His character of self-sacrificing love.*

The gospel of Jesus offers us the righteousness of God by faith alone—not by faith *plus* works. It is by a faith *that* works.[668] Faith in Jesus brings us the power of God for victory over every temptation and sin. It transforms the character of the believer into the self-sacrificing, loving attributes of Jesus because He is living out His life within us by faith.[669]

2. Every nation, tribe, tongue, and people: God is passionate that every human being be saved. He insists that this good news (gospel) must go to everyone. Satan has perverted the gospel and deceived the whole world.[670] Therefore, the truth of the everlasting gospel must go to every ethnic group (nation), tribal group, language group, and people group. Jesus emphasized this by saying, "And this *gospel of the kingdom* will be preached in *all the world* as a witness to *all the nations*, and *then* the *end will come.*"[671] The everlasting gospel that is to go to "all the world" at the end of time includes the final four points of the first angel's message:

3. Fear God: It is clear God does not want us to be afraid of Him, so what does it mean to "fear God"? When God thundered the Ten Commandments from Mount Sinai with lightning flashes and

---

[667] Romans 1:15–17 (emphasis added)
[668] See Ephesians 2:4–10
[669] See Galatians 2:20
[670] See Revelation 12:9
[671] Matthew 24:14 (emphasis added)

trumpet blasts, the people were terrified and drew back in panic and fear. "And Moses said to the people, '*Do not fear*; for God has come to test you, and *that His fear may be before you*, so *that you may not sin.*'"[672]

Therefore, we are not to be afraid of God, but we are to fear Him. The kind of fear that is appropriate supplies the power to overcome every temptation in Satan's tool bag. The admonition to fear God is found throughout the Bible, from Genesis to Revelation. It contains two interconnected fundamental concepts:

First, it is an encouragement to get to know God in such a profound, experiential way that you are awestruck by His greatness, unlimited power, infinite wisdom, and endless knowledge, as well as His immeasurable love, boundless compassion, and constant longsuffering.

I like to compare this awe of God with the experience of standing on the rim of the Grand Canyon for the first time. Even though I was standing behind a guard rail and thus perfectly safe, the vast expanse of space that lay before me made me take a step back from the edge. I was awestruck by the wonder of what I was beholding. When we get to know God as He really is, we will be profoundly awestruck.

Another illustration is a small child who has come to love and trust his big, muscular father. The two are walking hand in hand amid a crowded shopping mall. The father is so strong that in an instant, he could crush out the life of his child; yet because he loves his son, he uses his strength to protect him instead. The son knows of his dad's loving care and super strength, so he has nothing of which to be afraid as long as he holds onto his father's hand. Solomon expressed that very thought toward God: "In the *fear of the LORD* there is *strong confidence*, And *His children* will have a *place of refuge*. The *fear of the LORD* is a *fountain of life*, To *turn one away* from the *snares of death*."[673]

True fear of God as holy means that you recognize Him as the ultimate power in the universe. Such fear overcomes any other fear. If He is for you, nobody else can touch you without

---

[672] Exodus 20:20 (emphasis added)
[673] Proverbs 14:26, 27 (emphasis added)

His permission. If He is against you because you have rebelled against Him, you can run, but you cannot hide![674]

The second aspect of "fear God" is expressed by the prophet Isaiah: "*Hear* the *word* of the LORD, You who *tremble at His word*:"[675] To "Hear the word of the Lord" conveys the idea of not only listening to it, but obeying it as well. To fear God involves taking Him seriously because He means every word He says!

This is extremely important today. The knowledge of and respect for the Word of God is at a dangerously low level in America. According to the Barna Research in Faith and Christianity, only 48% of Americans use the Bible even three to four times a year, and only 14% of all adults use the Bible daily.[676] According to a 2017 Gallup Research Report, only 24% of Americans believe the Bible is the literal Word of God, which is lower than the portion of those who consider the Bible to be nothing but a myth (26%).[677]

Jesus demonstrated a very different attitude toward the Scriptures. When confronted by Satan's temptations, He showed His thorough knowledge of and belief in the Bible by quoting from the Old Testament, saying, "It is written, 'Man shall not live by bread alone, but by every word that proceeds from the mouth of God.'"[678]

Christians are followers of Jesus Christ and profess to be like Him, but the trend in our society is far from the example He set for us. The aged apostle Paul commends the young Timothy for his example of knowing the Old Testament Scriptures:

> And that *from childhood* you have *known the Holy Scriptures*, which are *able to make you wise for salvation* through *faith* which is in *Christ Jesus*. *All Scripture* is given by *inspiration of God*, and is profitable for *doctrine*, for *reproof*, for *correction*, for *instruction in righteousness*, that the man of God may be *complete*, thoroughly *equipped for every good work*.[679]

---

[674] Roy Gane, Isaiah (Nampa, ID: Pacific Press Publishing Association, 2021), p. 48
[675] Isaiah 66:5 (emphasis added)
[676] See "State of the Bible 2018: Seven Top Findings," Barna, https://1ref.us/1o8 (accessed February 8, 2021)
[677] See Lydia Saad, "Record Few Americans Believe Bible Is Literal Word of God," Gallup, https://1ref.us/1o9 (accessed February 8, 2021)
[678] Matthew 4:4
[679] 2 Timothy 3:15–17 (emphasis added)

Fearing God is to get to know Him and learn to love Him with all your heart, soul, and strength. It is learning to trust Him—having explicit confidence in His Word, no matter what. Fearing God is having complete faith in His gift of salvation and absolutely no confidence in one's own ability to deserve or earn Christ's gift of righteousness. The fear of the Lord involves following and obeying God's Word and Ten Commandments, as opposed to following and obeying mankind's commandments. Therefore, fearing God is an essential ingredient of the everlasting gospel.

4. Give glory to Him: When Jesus was born in Bethlehem, angels burst forth singing, "Glory to God in the highest, And on earth peace, goodwill toward men!"[680] They were overwhelmed with wonder and admiration that our Creator God would stoop to be born as a baby into this corrupt and sinful world. They could not hold back their thanksgiving and praise; and we will be unable to hold back our praise when we get to know God as He really is. When we compare ourselves with Him, we will realize He deserves all the glory and we deserve none.

The heavenly beings love to give glory to our Creator God, saying, "You are *worthy*, O Lord, to receive *glory* and *honor* and *power*; For *You created all things*, And *by Your will* they *exist* and were *created*."[681]

Just as we cannot create ourselves physically, so we cannot recreate ourselves into the likeness of Christ's righteousness. We are totally dependent upon God for everything. And when we recognize that fact, it frees us from the stress of trying to do it on our own. My favorite Christian author put it this way:

> What is justification by faith? It is the *work of God in laying the glory of man in the dust, and doing for man that which it is not in his power to do for himself*. When men see their own nothingness, they are prepared to be clothed with the righteousness of Christ.[682]

---

[680] Luke 2:14
[681] Revelation 4:11 (emphasis added)
[682] Ellen G. White, The Faith I Live By (Washington, DC: Review and Herald Publishing Association, 1958), p. 111 (emphasis added)

When we give glory to God, we place Him on the throne of our hearts, where He belongs, and remove all selfish pride and human authority from that position.

There is another way we can give glory to God besides verbal praise for His greatness. We can do so by the way we live our lives. The law of our physical being is the law of cause and effect. This is why the apostle Paul admonishes us:

> Therefore, whether you *eat* or *drink*, or *whatever you do*, do *all to the glory of God*.[683]
>
> For you were bought at a price; therefore *glorify God in your body and in your spirit*, which are God's.[684]

God made us physical, mental, spiritual, and social beings, and by developing habits that promote health in all areas of life, we bring glory to Him. It vindicates His principles of righteousness. The demonstration of God's principles in our lives is not for the world only, but also for the universe, so that "the *manifold wisdom of God* might be *made known* by the *church* to the principalities and powers in the *heavenly places*."[685] It is truly awesome to realize the way we live our lives has an impact upon the whole universe!

God does not want us to give glory to Him because His ego needs stroking. He wants us to give glory to Him because of what it does for us. Giving glory to God lifts our minds from the corruption, pain, sorrow, suffering, dysfunction, violence, anger, hatred, sin, and evil of this world to the love, joy, peace, and harmony of heaven. It redirects our attention from the low thoughts of this world and focuses our sights on Him. We need to keep "looking unto Jesus, the author and finisher of our faith, who for the joy that was set before Him endured the cross, despising the shame, and has sat down at the right hand of the throne of God."[686]

The law of the mind is by beholding we become changed. Therefore, giving glory to God keeps our minds focused on His character of love and principles of righteousness. As we continue to behold Him, we become like Him. Again, the apostle Paul wrote, "But we all, with unveiled face, beholding as in a mirror the

---

[683] 1 Corinthians 10:31 (emphasis added)
[684] 1 Corinthians 6:20 (emphasis added)
[685] Ephesians 3:10 (emphasis added)
[686] Hebrews 12:2

glory of the Lord, are being *transformed into the same image from glory to glory*, just as by the Spirit of the Lord."[687]

This transformation takes place as we open our hearts to Jesus and allow Him to have full control of our lives. Therefore, the law of the spiritual is the union of the human with the divine.[688] "Christ in you" is "the hope of glory."[689] When Jesus is living out His life in us, our lives will be a glory to God and prepare us to live with Him in the glories of heaven. Therefore, giving glory to God is part of the everlasting gospel, the good news to the world. It is part of God's plan to rescue us from society's freefall.

5. The hour of His judgment has come: We spent a whole chapter dealing with the judgment, which began in 1844 and takes place in the heavenly sanctuary, so we will not repeat that here. However, I do want to point out the first angel's message is given during the time when the judgment is in progress ("has come" is present tense). Therefore, the first angel's message is to go to the entire world from 1844 onward. In other words, this is God's message especially for us today.

   Notice it says, "the hour of *his* judgment has come." Ultimately, God is the one who is being judged, even though our lives are being evaluated in the judgment. If we genuinely have faith in Jesus, that faith will have a life-changing effect on our lives. Therefore, our lives will be evidence that His Word is true. We will be part of the vindication of God. Satan has accused Him before the universe that His laws restrict, oppress, and limit happiness. It is amazing that God puts Himself on trial through the lives of His followers. I don't know about you, but I want my life to demonstrate the effectiveness of God's grace.

6. Worship Him who made: We have already studied about worshipping God as our Creator and seen the only way to do so is to worship Him on the day He made holy and established for worship: the Sabbath.

   I want to draw your attention to two significant points. First is the similarity between this final command in the first angel's message and the reason God gives for keeping the Sabbath day

---

[687] 2 Corinthians 3:18 (emphasis added)
[688] See 2 Peter 1:4
[689] Colossians 1:27

holy in the fourth commandment: the fact that He is our Creator. Notice how the fourth commandment concludes: "For *in* six days the LORD made the heavens and the earth, the sea, and all that *is* in them, and rested the seventh day. Therefore the LORD blessed the Sabbath day and hallowed it."[690]

As we have seen, worship will be the decisive issue between the saved and the lost at the end of time. The saved will worship God as Creator and receive His seal of authority; the lost will worship the beast and his image and receive his mark of authority. Therefore, worshipping God as Creator is part of the everlasting gospel to be proclaimed to the world at the end of time.

I like to compare the first angel's message to a loving father instructing his small child that the backyard of their home, which is adequately fenced, is the safest place to play; the second angel's message is like the father telling the child to stay out of the front yard, which does not have a fence, because the street is full of traffic; and the third angel's message is like the father yelling as loudly as he can for the child to get out of the street because a truck is about to hit him. The father does not yell because he is angry; he yells because he loves his child so much. We will see how this comparison plays out as we look at the second and third angels' messages.

The second angel's message reads like this: "And *another angel* followed, saying, '*Babylon is fallen, is fallen,* that

> *I like to compare the first angel's message to a loving father instructing his small child that the backyard of their home, which is adequately fenced, is the safest place to play; the second angel's message is like the father telling the child to stay out of the front yard, which does not have a fence, because the street is full of traffic; and the third angel's message is like the father yelling as loudly as he can for the child to get out of the street because a truck is about to hit him. The father does not yell because he is angry; he yells because he loves his child so much.*

---

[690] Exodus 20:11

great city, because she has made *all nations* drink of the wine of the wrath of her *fornication.*"[691] We studied about the end-time Babylon in the previous chapter. To refresh your memory, Babylon is composed of a mother church and her daughter churches.

The daughter churches came out of the mother church but still hold to some of her teachings and practices. Here, the additional announcement is made that "Babylon is fallen, is fallen." The announcement of the fall of Babylon is repeated in order to give it emphasis.

The word "Babylon" definitively means "confusion." The churches composing spiritual Babylon have confused ideas of biblical truth. In order to attract pagans to Christianity in the early days of the Church of Rome, the church leaders compromised their beliefs with popular worldly beliefs and practices.

> The church took the pagan philosophy and made it the buckler of faith against the heathen. She took the pagan, Roman Pantheon, temple of all the gods, and made it sacred to all the martyrs; so it stands to this day. She took the pagan Sunday and made it the Christian Sunday. She took the pagan Easter and made it the feast we celebrate during this season.... Hence the church in these countries would seem to have said, "Keep that old, pagan name. It shall remain consecrated, sanctified." And thus the pagan Sunday, dedicated to Balder, became the Christian Sunday, sacred to Jesus.[692]

Therefore, confusion was brought into the church by combining pagan sun worship with Christianity. When Babylon's daughter churches came out of her, they unfortunately retained some of these pagan beliefs (i.e., confused ideas of salvation, Sunday worship, etc.). In the next two chapters, we will look at more of the confused ideas from paganism.

Babylon will have its final fall from the truth as it is in Jesus when the churches resort to employing the power of the state to enforce the observance of some of these pagan practices—when the image of the papacy is formed and his mark of authority (Sunday) is enforced. When this takes place, the third angel's message will have special significance. That message is the strongest warning found in all of Scripture!

> Then a *third angel* followed them, saying with a loud voice, "If *anyone worships the beast and his image,* and *receives his mark* on

---

[691] Revelation 14:8 (emphasis added)
[692] William L. Gildea, "Paschale Gaudium," The Catholic World, 53 (March 1894), 809

his forehead or on his hand, he himself *shall also drink of the wine of the wrath of God*, which is poured out *full strength* into the cup of His indignation."[693]

One might wonder why worshipping the beast and his image and receiving his mark would be so offensive to God that He would pour His wrath upon them. It is not because He is angry with them but because He knows what that type of worship will ultimately do to those He loves. He knows that we become like the object we worship. If everyone worships a power that is coercing, persecuting, and replacing God with sinful humans, society will become violent, hateful, and angry. This world will become unfit for habitation. Therefore, He sends His wrath, which will cause all of us to demonstrate the principles that govern our lives.

What is the wrath of God? "Then I saw another sign in heaven, great and marvelous: *seven angels* having *the seven last plagues*, for *in them the wrath of God is complete*."[694] In the first plague, terrible sores break out upon masses of people. The second plague causes the sea to become like blood and everything in it to die. The same thing happens to the rivers and springs in the third plague. In the fourth plague, the sun scorches the population with intense heat.

There will be seven plagues altogether, but it is enough to say they will cause everyone to openly demonstrate their characters. A sudden crisis does not develop character; it only reveals character. And this is what the seven last plagues will do to the entire human race. Up until then, God's judgments have been mixed with mercy, but the seven last plagues will be "full strength"—not mixed with mercy.

Now let us continue reading the third angel's message, for it reveals the fate of those who worship the beast and his image and receive his mark:

> He shall be *tormented with fire and brimstone* in the presence of the holy angels and in the presence of the Lamb. And the *smoke of their torment ascends forever and ever*; and they have *no rest day or night*, who worship the beast and his image, and whoever receives the mark of his name.[695]

---

[693] Revelation 14:9, 10 (emphasis added)
[694] Revelation 15:1 (emphasis added; you can read about the seven last plagues in Revelation 16)
[695] Revelation 14:10, 11 (emphasis added)

This is the most severe warning in all of Scripture, given out of God's heart of love. He does not want anyone to be lost but everyone to repent and be saved. We will see there is good news regarding hellfire and will explore that as we continue in the next couple chapters, but for now, let me draw your attention to the fact that the second and third angels' messages are given in symbolic language. We will explore what these symbols mean and what the entire Bible says about hellfire. When we put it all together like a jigsaw puzzle, it will form a beautiful picture of our loving God.

Let us move to the final verse of the third angel's message. This verse contains the major focus of the message: "Here is the *patience of the saints*; here are those who *keep the commandments of God* and the *faith of Jesus*."[696] These are the ones who are in contrast to those who worship the beast and receive his mark. They respond to God's messages of love and warning and give their hearts fully to Him. Patience is a virtue very much akin to faith and trust. Having faith in God to unravel difficult situations empowers a person to have patience under provocation.

It was Christ's faith in His heavenly Father that enabled Him to demonstrate patience during His mock trial and crucifixion. His demonstration of patience is a lesson we need to learn. "Now may the Lord direct your hearts into the *love of God* and into the *patience of Christ*."[697]

Patience is developed in us when we face challenging circumstances that test our faith. James, the brother of Jesus, indicated patience is one of the most important of the character traits for which God is looking in His people, especially at the end of time.

> My brethren, count it all joy when you *fall into various trials*, knowing that the *testing of your faith produces patience*. But let patience have its perfect work, that you may be perfect and *complete, lacking nothing*.[698]
>
> You also be *patient*. Establish your *hearts*, for the *coming of the Lord is at hand*. Do not *grumble against one another*, brethren, lest you be *condemned*. Behold, the Judge is standing at the door! My brethren, take the *prophets*, who spoke in the name of the Lord, as an *example of suffering and patience*.[699]

---

[696] Revelation 14:12 (emphasis added)
[697] 2 Thessalonians 3:5 (emphasis added)
[698] James 1:2–4 (emphasis added)
[699] James 5:8–10 (emphasis added)

Not only will the Sabbath be a test for God's people at the end of time, but we will also be severely tested by how we treat our persecutors.[700] Will we treat them with patience and love like Jesus treated those who nailed Him to the cross when He said, "Father, forgive them, for they do not know what they do"?[701] Though God's people will be unable to buy or sell and threatened with death, they will be patient. They will demonstrate the character of Jesus.

The final verse of the third angel's message states the Lord's people at the end will "keep the commandments of God."[702] It would be good for us to refresh our memories of the Ten Commandments, spoken by God from Mount Sinai and written on tables of stone by His own finger.[703] God intends to give us the new-covenant experience by writing His Ten Commandments on our hearts.[704]

1. You shall have *no other gods before Me*.
2. You shall *not make for yourself a carved image*—any likeness of anything that is in heaven above, or that is in the earth beneath, or that is in the water under the earth; *you shall not bow down to them nor serve them*. For I, the LORD your God, am a jealous God, visiting the iniquity of the fathers upon the children to the third and fourth generations of those who hate Me, but showing mercy to thousands, to those who love Me and keep My commandments.
3. You shall *not take the name of the LORD your God in vain*, for the LORD will not hold him guiltless who takes His name in vain.
4. *Remember the Sabbath day, to keep it holy*. Six days you shall labor and do all your work, but *the seventh day is the Sabbath of the*

---

[700] See Matthew 5:44
[701] Luke 23:34
[702] Revelation 14:12 (emphasis added)
[703] See Exodus 20:1–21; 31:18; Deuteronomy 9:10
[704] See Hebrews 8:10; 10:16

> *LORD your God*. In it you shall do no work: you, nor your son, nor your daughter, nor your male servant, nor your female servant, nor your cattle, nor your stranger who is within your gates. *For in six days the LORD made the heavens and the earth*, the sea, and all that is in them, and *rested the seventh day*. Therefore the LORD blessed the Sabbath day and hallowed it.
> 5. *Honor your father and your mother*, that your days may be long upon the land which the LORD your God is giving you.
> 6. You shall *not murder*.
> 7. You shall *not commit adultery*.
> 8. You shall *not steal*.
> 9. You shall *not bear false witness* against your neighbor.
> 10. You shall *not covet* your neighbor's *house*; you shall not covet your neighbor's *wife*, nor his male servant, nor his female servant, nor his ox, nor his donkey, *nor anything that is your neighbor's*.[705]

I like to ask people, "If there was one place on the earth where all people kept all the commandments all the time from their hearts, would you want to live there?" The answer is invariably, "YES! Why not?" It would be like heaven because that is what heaven is like! And that is what God's people will be like at the end of time.

Jesus did not come in order to change God's law but rather to save us from breaking God's law—to save us from sin. The basic, biblical definition of sin is disobeying God's moral law. "Whosoever committeth sin transgresseth also the law: for *sin is the transgression of the law*."[706]

We will not be considered part of "those who keep the commandments of God" if we keep only eight or nine out of ten. That would be like telling the police officer you stop at red traffic lights eight or nine times out of ten.

> For whoever shall *keep the whole law*, and yet *stumble in one point*, he is *guilty of all*. For He who said, "do not commit adultery," also said, "do not murder." Now if you do not commit adultery, but you do murder, you have become a *transgressor of the law*.[707]

Why would someone want to find an excuse to disobey even one of the commandments? They are for our own good. And if we love God with all

---
[705] Exodus 20:3–17 (emphasis and numbering added)
[706] 1 John 3:4, KJV (emphasis added)
[707] James 2:10, 11 (emphasis added)

our hearts, it will be our greatest delight to obey Him. "For this is the *love of God*, that we *keep His commandments*. And His commandments are *not burdensome*."[708]

My favorite book on the life of Jesus speaks powerfully to this point:

> In the work of redemption there is no compulsion. No external force is employed. Under the influence of the Spirit of God, man is left free to choose whom he will serve. In the change that takes place when the soul surrenders to Christ, there is the highest sense of freedom. The expulsion of sin is the act of the soul itself. True, we have no power to free ourselves from Satan's control; but when we desire to be set free from sin, and in our great need cry out for a power out of and above ourselves, the powers of the soul are imbued with the divine energy of the Holy Spirit, and they obey the dictates of the will in fulfilling the will of God.
>
> The *only condition* upon which the *freedom of man is possible* is that of becoming *one with Christ*. "The *truth* shall make you *free*;" and Christ is the truth. *Sin can triumph only by enfeebling the mind, and destroying the liberty of the soul.* Subjection to God is restoration to one's self, —to the true glory and *dignity of man*. The divine law, to which we are brought into subjection, is "the *law of liberty*."[709]

God's people, at the time of the beast and his image and mark, will keep the Ten Commandments, but the question is, How can they do this? We face a predicament in the light of what the apostle Paul said about our natural hearts: "Because the *carnal mind* is *enmity against God*; for it is *not subject to the law of God, nor indeed can be*."[710]

The answer to our predicament is found in the final phrase of the third angel's message. The people of God will possess "the faith of Jesus."[711] This phrase has been translated two different ways: "the faith *of* Jesus" and "faith *in* Jesus." They both are meaningful, appropriate, and inseparably connected.

The quality of faith Jesus wants us to have in Him is the same quality of faith He had in His heavenly Father while He lived on earth. It was this

---

[708] 1 John 5:3 (emphasis added)
[709] Ellen G. White, The Desire of Ages (Mountain View, CA: Pacific Press Publishing Association, 1898), p. 466 (emphasis added)
[710] Romans 8:7 (emphasis added)
[711] Revelation 14:12

faith in His Father that enabled Him to do the things He did and overcome every temptation and trial Satan hurled at Him. When we develop that type of faith, trust, and confidence in Jesus, we will experience the same victory over sin He did and the same power to do God's will.

Faith is like a muscle. The more you exercise it, the stronger it becomes. It takes constant exercise to develop the strength of faith Jesus demonstrated. We need to be continually growing in faith. In this way, we are like trees. A tree that stops growing starts dying. In talking about the power of God found in the gospel of Christ, the apostle Paul emphasized the growth of faith: "For in it the righteousness of God is revealed *from faith to faith*; as it is written, '*The just shall live by faith.*'"[712]

Paul revealed that faith grows by studying the Word of God. In his day, few could afford to buy a copy of the hand-copied sacred scrolls, so they learned the Word of God by going to the synagogue and hearing it read. "So then *faith* comes by *hearing*, and hearing by the *word of God*."[713]

The apostle Peter also spoke of the need of growing in Jesus. "Therefore, laying aside all malice, all deceit, hypocrisy, envy, and all evil speaking, as newborn babes, *desire the pure milk of the word*, that you may *grow thereby*, if indeed you have tasted that the Lord is gracious."[714]

The faith Jesus had in His heavenly Father molded every aspect of His life: thoughts, words, and actions. His faith was demonstrated through total surrender to His Father.

> *Faith is like a muscle. The more you exercise it, the stronger it becomes. It takes constant exercise to develop the strength of faith Jesus demonstrated. We need to be continually growing in faith. In this way, we are like trees. A tree that stops growing starts dying.*

> *I can of Myself do nothing.* As I hear, I judge; and My judgment is righteous, *because I do not seek My own will but the will of the Father who sent Me.*[715]

---

[712] Romans 1:17 (emphasis added)
[713] Romans 10:17 (emphasis added)
[714] 1 Peter 2:1–3 (emphasis added)
[715] John 5:30 (emphasis added)

> When you lift up the Son of Man, then you will know that I am He, and that *I do nothing of Myself; but as My Father taught Me, I speak these things.*[716]

The prophet Isaiah revealed how Jesus learned to speak only what the Father wanted Him to speak, and it is also how we can learn to speak only what God wants us to speak: through spending time with Him daily in Bible study and prayer. Notice what he prophesied about Jesus:

> The Lord GOD has given Me The *tongue of the learned*, that I should know *how to speak a word in season to him who is weary*. He *awakens Me morning by morning*, He *awakens My ear to hear* as the learned. The Lord GOD has opened My ear; *and I was not rebellious, nor did I turn away*. I gave My back to those who struck Me, and My cheeks to those who plucked out the beard; I did not hide My face from shame and spitting.[717]

God will not open our ears to hear Him speak unless we ask Him to do so. He does not force His way into our hearts and minds, but He comes in when we invite Him in and spend time with Him in His Word. This is why it is so important to pray before we read the Bible. Jesus' faith in the love of His Father is what led Him to surrender to His will, even to the point of going to the cross.

We see Jesus struggling with this decision in the Garden of Gethsemane as He fell on His face, praying with such agony that He sweat drops of blood.[718] "He went a little farther and fell on His face, and prayed, saying, 'O My Father, if it is possible, let this cup pass from Me; nevertheless, not as I will, but as You will.'"[719]

It was the quality of Jesus' faith in His Father that enabled Him to surrender His will and go to the cross without argument, complaint, or resentment. This is the type of faith that will enable us to keep all ten of God's commandments, even in the face of persecution and death.

The faith of Jesus in His Father not only gave Him victory over all sin but also empowered Him for ministry. He came on a mission with a message, using God's method and motive. Regarding God's method of ministry, the disciple states, "And Jesus went about all Galilee, *teaching* in their

---

[716] John 9:28 (emphasis added)
[717] Isaiah 50:4–6 (emphasis added)
[718] See Luke 22:44
[719] Matthew 26:39

synagogues, *preaching* the gospel of the kingdom, and *healing* all kinds of sickness and all kinds of disease among the people."[720]

Therefore, Christ's method of ministry was to mingle with the people, showing sympathy for their problems. By healing their sicknesses and diseases, He was able to win their confidence and invite them to follow Him.

He empowered His disciples to use this method of ministry when He sent them out on their first missionary journey. "And when He had called His twelve disciples to Him, He gave them *power over unclean spirits*, to cast them out, and to *heal* all kinds of *sickness* and all kinds of *disease*."[721]

After Jesus went back to heaven, the apostles continued His mission of mercy, spreading His message of salvation, using His method of healing and exhibiting His motive of love.[722] To Jesus, healing the body and healing the soul are connected. Healing physical ailments is an illustration of the gospel because the character of Jesus is more than not doing wrong; it is doing right for everyone! The faith of Jesus will produce this type of character in His followers.

Receiving these three angels' messages will prepare God's people for Christ's second coming. Yet there is another angel's message that accompanies these three: an appeal for action!

After these things I saw *another angel* coming down from heaven, having great authority, and the earth was illuminated with his glory. And he *cried mightily with a loud voice*, saying, "*Babylon the great is fallen, is fallen*, and has become a dwelling place of demons, a prison for every foul spirit, and a cage for every unclean and hated bird! For *all the nations have drunk of the wine of the wrath of her fornication*, the *kings of the earth have committed fornication with her*, and the merchants of

---

[720] Matthew 4:23 (emphasis added)
[721] Matthew 10:1 (emphasis added)
[722] See Acts 28:8, 9

the earth have become rich through the abundance of her luxury." And I heard another voice from heaven saying, *"Come out of her, my people*, lest you share in her sins, and lest you receive of her plagues."[723]

The fourth angel's message repeats and greatly emphasizes the second angel's message. This angel "cried mightily with a loud voice." God is urgent in His warning. He appeals to us to come out of Babylon.

Please notice to whom God is appealing: "my people." His people at the end of time are in the churches that comprise Babylon. He wants them to come out of these churches because they will be instrumental in forming the image of the beast and enforcing its mark. God wants His people to come out before it is too late and the seven last plagues are poured out.

In calling His people out of Babylon, God is also calling them *into* something. He is calling them to unite with those who proclaim the three angels' messages. "Here is the patience of the saints; here are those who keep the commandments of God and the faith of Jesus."[724]

These are the ones with whom Satan is angry, the ones against whom he makes war, because they are faithful to Jesus. They are the remnant of God's true people. "And the dragon was wroth with the woman, and went to make war with the remnant of her seed, which keep the commandments of God, and have the testimony of Jesus Christ."[725]

Therefore, I invite you to respond to God's invitation to come out of the churches comprising Babylon and unite with His commandment-keeping people who have the faith of Jesus. Learning the truth without acting upon it gives Satan the opportunity to snatch the truth away.[726]

The wine in the cup of Babylon the harlot is the doctrines and teachings of paganism that have been incorporated into these churches. We have already discovered a couple of these teachings. In the following chapters, we will discover more.

---

[723] Revelation 18:1–4 (emphasis added)
[724] Revelation 14:12
[725] Revelation 12:17, KJV
[726] See Matthew 13:19

Chapter 13

Satan's 1,000-Year Vacation

In previous chapters, we discovered that "the wages of sin is death, but the gift of God is eternal life in Christ Jesus our Lord."[727] The question is, How will the wages of sin be carried out? We have studied the good news of God's gift of eternal life in Jesus, but now let us study the good news about the wages of sin, which is death.

Revelation 20 describes Satan as chained and in a bottomless pit for 1,000 years—not exactly the type of vacation for which he was hoping. After the 1,000 years is ended, he and those who follow him will be thrown into the lake of fire, aka hell. The churches comprising Babylon have greatly misrepresented death and hell. In fact, their teachings on these two subjects are part of the intoxicating wine in Babylon's cup that she offers to the world.

By looking at the 1,000 years of Satan's unwelcome vacation, we will discover the truth about death and hell.

> Then I saw an angel coming down from heaven, having the key to the *bottomless pit* and a *great chain* in his hand. He laid hold of the *dragon, that serpent of old, who is the Devil and Satan*, and *bound him for a thousand years*; and he *cast him into the bottomless pit*, and shut him up, and set a seal on him, so that *he should deceive the nations no more till the thousand years were finished*. But *after these things* he must be *released for a little while*.[728]

There are several points to consider in these verses. First, Satan is bound for 1,000 years, during which he is not able to deceive the nations. After the 1,000 years are ended, he is "released for a little while" and again able to deceive the nations, but only for a short time.

We will come back to the "great chain" with which Satan is bound and the "bottomless pit" later, but first let us read what the redeemed will be doing during the 1,000 years. The apostle John was given a vision of the redeemed during the 1,000-year period:

---

[727] Romans 6:23
[728] Revelation 20:1–3 (emphasis added)

> And I saw *thrones*, and they *sat on them*, and *judgment was committed to them*. Then I saw the souls of those who had been beheaded for their witness to Jesus and for the word of God, *who had not worshiped the beast* or his *image*, and *had not received his mark* on their foreheads or on their hands. And *they lived and reigned with Christ for a thousand years*.[729]

What an amazing privilege it will be to sit on thrones as judges and rulers for 1,000 years! Guess to whom they will be sitting along side of—Jesus! "To *him who overcomes* I will grant to *sit with Me* on *My throne*, as *I also overcame* and *sat down with My Father* on *His throne*."[730] The Bible reveals where God's throne is: "The LORD has established His throne in heaven, and His kingdom rules over all."[731]

To reiterate, while Satan is bound for 1,000 years, the redeemed will be with Jesus in heaven. Therefore, they must go to heaven at the beginning of that time. If we know when the redeemed go to heaven, then we will know when the 1,000-year period begins. The Bible tells us the redeemed go to heaven with Jesus at His second coming. He assured us, "In *My Father's house* are many mansions; if it were not so, I would have told you. I go to *prepare a place for you*. And if I go and prepare a place for you, *I will come again* and *receive you to Myself*; that *where I am*, there *you may be also*."[732]

When Jesus left this earth after His resurrection, He ascended to heaven and sat down with His Father on His throne. "Now this is the main point of the things we are saying: We have such a High Priest, who is seated at the right hand of the throne of the Majesty in the heavens."[733]

When Jesus comes back the second time, He will not set up His throne on this earth; neither will the redeemed sit on thrones in an earthly kingdom. When Jesus returns, He will take the redeemed to heaven to sit on thrones and judge for 1,000 years. The apostle Paul described Christ's return this way:

> But I do not want you to be ignorant, brethren, concerning those who have *fallen asleep*, lest you sorrow as others who have no hope. For if we believe that *Jesus died and rose again*, even so God will bring with Him those who *sleep in Jesus*. For this we say to you by

---

[729] Revelation 20:4 (emphasis added)
[730] Revelation 3:21 (emphasis added)
[731] Psalm 103:19
[732] John 14:2, 3 (emphasis added)
[733] Hebrews 8:1 (see also 1:3, 13; 10:12; 12:2; Colossians 3:1; Revelation 3:21)

the word of the Lord, that *we who are alive* and remain until the coming of the Lord will by *no means precede* those who are *asleep*. For the *Lord Himself* will *descend from heaven* with a shout, with the voice of an archangel, and with the trumpet of God. And the *dead in Christ will rise first*. Then we who are *alive and remain* shall be *caught up together with them in the clouds* to *meet the Lord in the air*. And thus we shall *always be with the Lord*.[734]

Repeatedly, the Bible describes death as sleep. When people are sound asleep, they are totally unaware of anything that goes on around them. More about this later, but for now, I want us to see that the redeemed (including the resurrected redeemed) go to heaven with Jesus at His second coming. This is the event that begins the 1,000-year period, often called "the millennium."

There are two deaths and two resurrections described in Revelation. The resurrection of the redeemed at Christ's second coming is called the first resurrection. With that said, what happens to the lost at that time? That will certainly not be the best day of their lives. They will be very remorseful for the sins that have caused them to miss out on eternal life, but they will not repent.

And the *kings* of the earth, the *great men*, the *rich men*, the *commanders*, the *mighty men*, every *slave* and every *free man*, *hid themselves* in the caves and in the rocks of the mountains, and said to the mountains and rocks, "*Fall on us and hide us from the face of Him who sits on the throne and from the wrath of the Lamb!*"[735]

The prophet Jeremiah also described what will happen to the lost when Jesus comes: "And at that day the *slain of the LORD* shall be from *one end of the earth even to the other end of the earth*. They shall *not* be *lamented*, or *gathered*, or *buried*; they shall become *refuse on the ground*."[736]

This is the first death. Those who die when Jesus comes will not be buried because there will not be anyone alive to bury them. When He comes, there will be only two classes of people: the saved and the lost. The saved will be taken to heaven with Jesus, but the lost will be destroyed by the brightness of His coming[737] and remain dead during the 1,000 years.

---

[734] 1 Thessalonians 4:13–17 (emphasis added)
[735] Revelation 6:15, 16 (emphasis added)
[736] Jeremiah 25:33 (emphasis added)
[737] See 2 Thessalonians 2:8

The description of the lost during the millennium continues: "But the *rest of the dead* did *not live again until* the *thousand years were finished*."⁷³⁸

Notice the resurrection of the saved is called the "first resurrection." "This is the *first resurrection. Blessed* and *holy* is he who has part in the *first resurrection*. Over such the *second death has no power*, but they shall be *priests* of God and of Christ, and shall *reign* with Him a *thousand years*."⁷³⁹

Everyone who has ever died will be resurrected in one of two resurrections. The first resurrection is the one we want to experience. Jesus said, "Do not marvel at this; for the hour is coming in which *all who are in the graves* will hear His voice and *come forth*—those who have done *good*, to the *resurrection of life*, and those who have done *evil*, to the *resurrection of condemnation*."⁷⁴⁰

Daniel also described these two resurrections: "And many of those who *sleep in the dust* of the earth shall *awake*, some to *everlasting life*, some to shame and *everlasting contempt*."⁷⁴¹ The resurrection of everlasting life takes place when Jesus comes in the brightness of His glory, with the sound of a trumpet that raises the dead to life again.

The apostle Paul described it this way:

Behold, I tell you a mystery: We shall not all *sleep*, but we shall all be *changed*—in a moment, in the twinkling of an eye, *at the last trumpet*. For the *trumpet will sound*, and the *dead will be raised incorruptible*, and we shall be *changed*. For this corruptible must put on incorruption, and this *mortal* must put on *immortality*. So when this corruptible has put on incorruption, and this mortal has put on immortality, then shall be brought

---

⁷³⁸ Revelation 20:5a (emphasis added)
⁷³⁹ Revelation 20:5b, 6 (emphasis added)
⁷⁴⁰ John 5:28, 29 (emphasis added)
⁷⁴¹ Daniel 12:2 (emphasis added)

to pass the saying that is written: *"Death is swallowed up in victory."* "O Death, where is your sting? O Hades, where is your victory?"[742]

What a wonderful day that will be for those who make spiritual preparation! Their battle with sin and evil will be over. Heaven will be their home during the 1,000 years. With that said, what will the redeemed do in heaven? As we already saw, they will not be sitting on clouds, strumming harps like the cartoons portray. Far from it! During the millennium, the redeemed will be engaged in a very important task. "And I saw *thrones, and they sat on them, and judgment was committed to them....* And they *lived* and *reigned with Christ* for a *thousand years.*"[743]

The redeemed will be involved in the work of judging, but who will they judge? The apostle Paul wrote of this judgment with which the redeemed will be involved: "Do you not know that the *saints will judge the world?...* Do you not know that *we shall judge angels*? How much more, things that pertain to this life?"[744]

What a fascinating thought! The redeemed will have the opportunity to review the record books (or maybe replay videos) and see for themselves why the angels fell, a favorite friend or relative is not in heaven, etc. God will not require them to accept His judgment without giving them the opportunity to evaluate the evidence themselves. What a wonderful God He is!

He has promised to "wipe away every tear from" our "eyes."[745] When we see that our favorite friend or relative would not be happy in the pure and holy atmosphere of heaven—that that person would be miserable in

> **Their battle with sin and evil will be over. Heaven will be their home during the 1,000 years. With that said, what will the redeemed do in heaven? As we already saw, they will not be sitting on clouds, strumming harps like the cartoons portray. Far from it! During the millennium, the redeemed will be engaged in a very important task.**

---

[742] 1 Corinthians 15:51–55 (emphasis added)
[743] Revelation 20:4 (emphasis added)
[744] 1 Corinthians 6:2, 3 (emphasis added)
[745] Revelation 21:4

the presence of God—we will acknowledge God's judgments are just and true. Understanding the reason why will help dry our tears of sorrow.

Therefore, if all the redeemed (including the resurrected ones) are living in heaven with Jesus and the lost are dead upon the earth, what is the condition of this planet during the millennium? Jeremiah gives us prophetic insight:

> I beheld the *earth*, and indeed it was *without form*, and *void*; And the heavens, they had no light. I beheld the mountains, and indeed they trembled, and all the hills moved back and forth. I beheld, and indeed *there was no man*, and all the birds of the heavens had fled. I beheld, and indeed the *fruitful land was a wilderness*, and *all its cities were broken down* at the *presence of the LORD*, by His fierce anger.[746]

When Jesus comes, not only will the lost be destroyed, but the world will be laid waste. It will be uninhabited and uninhabitable. It is interesting that Jeremiah described the earth during the millennium as "without form, and void." This directly parallels the description of the earth before creation week. "The *earth* was *without form*, and *void*; and *darkness* was on the face of the *deep*. And the Spirit of God was hovering over the face of the waters."[747]

The word "deep" in the Greek translation of the Old Testament (Septuagint) is ἄβυσσος (*abussos*), which is also the word used in the book of Revelation to describe where Satan will be bound during the millennium: the "bottomless pit." The apostle Paul used the same word, ἄβυσσος (*abussos*), to describe the grave, where no life exists.[748]

This destroyed planet will be Satan's home during the 1,000 years. He will have nothing at which to look except destruction and nothing to do except contemplate the results of his rebellion against God. This planet will be his "bottomless pit." Satan's only companions will be his host of fallen angels, and the chains that bind them on earth are the chains of darkness. "For if God did not spare the angels who sinned, but cast them down to hell and delivered them into *chains of darkness*, to be *reserved for judgment*."[749] The word for "hell" in this verse means "the deepest abyss, doleful and dark."

---

[746] Jeremiah 4:23–26 (emphasis added)
[747] Genesis 1:2 (emphasis added)
[748] See Romans 10:7
[749] 2 Peter 2:4 (emphasis added)

Satan and his angels remain bound to this dark, destroyed planet for 1,000 years. Notice what happens at the end of the millennium: "Now when the thousand years have expired, Satan will be released from his prison."[750]

Obviously, something happens on earth to release Satan, but as we already saw, he is only "released for a little while."[751] The redeemed who have died throughout the centuries will be resurrected at the beginning of the millennium, when Jesus comes in the clouds of heaven. That is the first resurrection—the resurrection of eternal life. Notwithstanding, what about the second resurrection—the resurrection of the lost—the resurrection of condemnation? When does that take place? "But the rest of the dead did not live again until the thousand years were finished."[752]

At the end of the 1,000 years, the "rest of the dead," the lost, live again. This is the second resurrection; and this is how Satan is released. He again will have multitudes of people to deceive and rally to his purposes. "Now when the *thousand years have expired*, Satan will be released from his prison and will go out to deceive the *nations* which are in the *four corners* of the *earth*, Gog and Magog, to gather them together to battle, whose *number is as the sand of the sea.*"[753]

The major events at the end of the 1,000 years will be the subject of the next chapter. Notice the millennium begins and ends with the two resurrections: the resurrection of life at the beginning and the resurrection of damnation at the end. The following chart reviews what we have discovered so far regarding the 1,000 years:

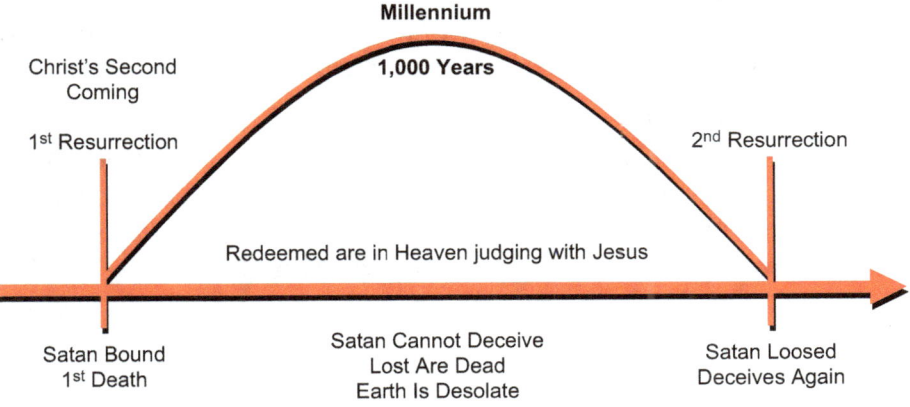

---

[750] Revelation 20:7
[751] Revelation 20:3
[752] Revelation 20:5
[753] Revelation 20:7, 8 (emphasis added)

What about this issue of death and the resurrection? How does the popular understanding of death fit the Bible teaching? It doesn't. The popular belief that when one dies, that person goes in spirit form directly to heaven or hell is not taught by the Bible. On the other hand, it has been taught by pagan religions since the beginning of Babylon.

The Tower of Babel, which was constructed by Nimrod, laid the foundation for all pagan religions. Nimrod, who was known as the sun god, died young, and his beautiful wife, Ishtar (also known as Semiramis), claimed the "miraculous birth" of her child was none other than the rebirth of Nimrod the sun god. She named her child Tammuz, and he was considered the sun god reborn. This was the beginning of sun worship.[754] "Cush begot Nimrod; he began to be a mighty one on the earth. He was a mighty hunter before the LORD; therefore it is said, 'Like Nimrod the mighty hunter before the LORD.' And the beginning of his kingdom was Babel."[755]

Ishtar claimed that when Nimrod died, he entered the spirit world and then returned in the form of her son Tammuz, which she claimed to be a miraculous birth. Of course, he was not the result of a miracle, but fornication instead.[756] From this beginning came the idea that when one dies, that person lives on in another form. This belief is in harmony with the first lie Satan told Eve in the Garden of Eden: "Then the serpent said to the woman, 'You will not surely die.'"[757]

Satan was not only successful in selling the idea to Eve, but he was also successful in selling it to God's people in the Old Testament, the Jews. Tammuz was also known as Baal, the sun god. Notice what the Bible says about Manasseh, who was one of the most sinful kings of Israel because he led God's people into worship of the sun god:

> But he did *evil* in the sight of the LORD, according to the *abominations of the nations* whom the LORD had cast out before the children of Israel. For he rebuilt the high places which Hezekiah his father had broken down; he raised up altars for the *Baals*, and made wooden images; and he *worshiped all the host of heaven* and served them.[758]

---

[754] See Alexander Hislop, The Two Babylons (Neptune, NJ: Loizeaux Brothers, 1959), pp. 19–90
[755] Genesis 10:8–10
[756] See Hislop, The Two Babylons
[757] Genesis 3:4
[758] 2 Chronicles 33:2, 3 (emphasis added)

The prophet Ezekiel was given a vision of what the leading women of Israel were doing: "And He said to me, 'Turn again, and you will see *greater abominations* that they are doing.' So He brought me to the door of the north gate of the *LORD's house*; and to my dismay, *women were sitting* there *weeping for Tammuz*."[759] He then described even greater abominations he was shown in vision:

> So He brought me into the *inner court* of the *LORD's house*; and there, at the door of the *temple of the LORD*, between the porch and the altar, were about twenty-five men with their *backs toward the temple* of the LORD and their *faces toward the east*, and they were *worshiping the sun toward the east*.[760]

The idea that a person lives on in another form after death began to find acceptance in the very heart of God's Old Testament church. This idea did not come from God or His prophets, but from paganism, and it is still being taught by spiritualists today.

> The *fundamental principle of spiritism* is that *human beings survive bodily death*, and that occasionally, under conditions not yet fully understood, *we can communicate* with those who have *gone before*.[761]

Spiritualism is defined as follows:

- It removes all fear of death, which is really the portal of the spirit world
- It teaches that death is not the cessation of life, but mere change of condition
- That those who have passed on are conscious—not asleep
- The communion between the living and the "dead" is scientifically proved[762]

> A *Spiritualist* is a person who is convinced (1) that *human personality survives beyond bodily death*, and (2) that *the surviving spirits can, and constantly do, communicate with living people* through the intermediacy of especially endowed individuals known as "mediums."[763]

---

[759] Ezekiel 8:13, 14 (emphasis added)
[760] Ezekiel 8:16 (emphasis added)
[761] Arthur Hill, Spiritism: History, Phenomena, and Doctrine (New York: George H. Doran Co., 1919), p. 25
[762] National Spiritualist Association of the United States of America Year Book (Washington, DC: National Spiritualism Association, 1946), p. 14
[763] C. E. Bechhofer Roberts, The Truth About Spiritualism (London: Eyre and Spottiswoode, 1932), p. 13

The Great Pyramids in Egypt were built because of the belief in the immortality of the soul—the belief that the soul never dies. Pagan ancestor worship is based on this doctrine as well. Unfortunately, the pagan doctrine of the immortality of the human soul has crept into the Christian church, just as it did with Israel of old. Nevertheless, what does the Bible say? Is the soul immortal, or is there a resurrection?

When Jesus appeared to the apostle John, as recorded in Revelation, He claimed to hold the keys of death.[764] If He holds the keys of death, He certainly knows what happens when a person dies and has revealed it in the Bible.

King Solomon wrote one of the plainest statements of Scripture regarding death: "For the living know that they will die; But the *dead know nothing*."[765] The last time I checked, nothing meant nothing. The Bible describes death as a sleep and the resurrection as the time when the dead are awakened out of that sleep. When you are sound asleep, you know nothing that goes on around you.

Daniel put it this way: "And many of those who *sleep in the dust* of the earth shall *awake*, some to *everlasting life*, some to shame and *everlasting contempt*."[766] There is no consciousness in death. The dead have no thought processes. The dead are dead—lifeless—waiting to be awakened at the resurrection. When a person dies, his or her brain ceases to function—stops thinking. "His breath goeth forth, he returneth to his earth; in that very day his thoughts perish."[767]

Over fifty times, the Bible calls death a sleep.[768] Death is like a deep sleep that lasts until Christ's second coming. The apostle Paul not only repeatedly called death a sleep, but he also made it clear that we do not receive immortality until the first resurrection:

> Behold, I tell you a mystery: We shall not all *sleep*, but we shall all be *changed*—in a moment, in the twinkling of an eye, *at the last trumpet*. For the *trumpet will sound*, and the *dead will be raised incorruptible*, and we shall be *changed*. For this *corruptible* must put on *incorruption*, and this *mortal* must put on *immortality*. So *when* this *corruptible* has put on *incorruption*, and this *mortal* has put on *immortality*, *then* shall be brought to pass the saying that is written: "*Death is swallowed up in victory*."[769]

---

[764] See Revelation 1:18
[765] Ecclesiastes 9:5 (emphasis added)
[766] Daniel 12:2 (emphasis added)
[767] Psalm 146:4, KJV
[768] See Psalm 13:3 for an example
[769] 1 Corinthians 15:51–54 (emphasis added)

No one possesses immortality now. Jesus will come in the clouds of heaven and raise the redeemed in the first resurrection at the beginning of the millennium. It is at that time that He will give them immortality. They will never die again! They will never experience the "second death." "*Blessed* and *holy* is he who has part in the *first resurrection*. Over such the *second death has no power*, but they shall be priests of God and of Christ, and shall reign with Him a thousand years."[770]

God alone has immortality now; we do not. However, He will give it to us at Christ's second coming. "He who is the blessed and *only Potentate*, the *King of kings* and Lord of lords, *who alone has immortality*."[771]

What about the soul? Does it continue living after death? The Bible uses the word "soul" 1,600 times and never once does it use the words "immortal soul." Notice how Jesus interchanges the words "life" and "soul": "For whoever desires to save his life will lose it, but whoever loses his life for My sake will find it. For what profit is it to a man if he gains the whole world, and loses his own soul? Or what will a man give in exchange for his soul?"[772]

We do not possess immortal souls. We are mortal souls or human beings. We individually must account for our lives. The father does not take the punishment of the son, and the son does not take the punishment of the father. "Behold, all *souls* are Mine; The *soul* of the father as well as the *soul* of the son is Mine; The *soul who sins shall die*."[773]

The apostle Peter used the word "souls" to describe the eight people who were saved from the flood. Those eight people were Noah, his wife, and their three sons and their wives. "Who formerly were disobedient, when once the Divine longsuffering waited in the days of *Noah*, while the ark was being prepared, in which a few, that is, *eight souls*, were saved through water."[774]

The word "soul" is a biblical term for living beings. When a person ceases to live, his or her soul ceases to exist. However, God has a record of one's life in His recording system in heaven, and in the resurrection, that life (soul) will be restored.

What is death like? Death is just the reverse of creation. By understanding how God created humanity in the beginning, we will understand what happens at death. "And the LORD God formed man of the *dust*

---

[770] Revelation 20:6 (emphasis added)
[771] 1 Timothy 6:15, 16 (emphasis added)
[772] Matthew 16:25, 26
[773] Ezekiel 18:4 (emphasis added)
[774] 1 Peter 3:20 (emphasis added)

of the ground, and breathed into his nostrils the *breath of life*; and man became a living being."[775]

We are made of two ingredients: dust and God's breath of life. The combination of these two ingredients creates a "living being," or as some translations put it, a "living soul." The word used in Hebrew is (*nephesh*), which means "a breathing creature."[776] When Jesus created Adam, He placed His breath of life, not an immortal soul, in him.

A light bulb is a good example of this. A shining light bulb is made up of two components: the bulb and electricity. When the bulb has electricity running through it, light is produced. When the switch is turned off, the light ceases to exist. So it is with us. If we have the breath of life from God, we are alive, but when we stop breathing (when God's breath of life returns to Him), we no longer have life.

What about the spirit? What happens to it at death? The Old Testament Hebrew word for "spirit" is חוּר (*rûach*), which means "breath." The spirit and the soul are different. A living soul is made up of dust plus the spirit, or breath of life, from God. Therefore, when a living soul (living person) dies, the opposite of creation takes place. The body returns to dust, and the spirit (breath of life), the power of life, goes back to God.

> Then the *dust* will return to the *earth* as it was, And the *spirit* will return to *God* who gave it.[777]
>
> And the *God who holds your breath in His hand* and owns all your ways, you have not glorified.[778]

The spirit about which the Bible is talking in this context is not the Holy Spirit, the third person of the Godhead. The spirit God places in us to make us live is His breath of life. Job declared, "All the while my *breath* is in me, and the *spirit of God* is in my *nostrils*."[779]

When one no longer breathes, that person can no longer live. The breath of life, the power of God to keep us alive, returns to Him, and that person sleeps the sleep of death. David wrote the following:

> Consider and hear me, O LORD my God; enlighten my eyes, *Lest I sleep the sleep of death*."[780]

---

[775] Genesis 2:7 (emphasis added)
[776] Strong's Greek and Hebrew Dictionary
[777] Ecclesiastes 12:7 (emphasis added)
[778] Daniel 5:23 (emphasis added)
[779] Job 27:3, KJV (emphasis added)
[780] Psalm 13:3 (emphasis added)

The *dead do not praise the LORD*, Nor any who go down into silence.[781]

King David was declared a man after God's own heart and is clearly among the redeemed, yet the New Testament makes it clear he is not in heaven. The apostle Peter declared he is asleep in the grave. "Men and brethren, let me speak freely to you of the patriarch *David*, that he is both *dead* and *buried*, and his tomb is with us *to this day*."[782] "For David did not ascend into the heavens."[783]

Jesus gave us one of the best illustrations of what happens at death and the resurrection. Mary, Martha, and Lazarus were very close friends of Jesus, and He often visited their home. One day, Jesus received a message that Lazarus was very ill. Instead of immediately going to heal him as requested, He waited four days, then told His disciples, "Our friend Lazarus sleeps, but I go that I may wake him up."[784] The disciples were puzzled. They thought if Lazarus was sleeping, he must be on the road to recovery and did not need Christ's attention. "Then Jesus said to them plainly, 'Lazarus is dead.'"[785] He clearly taught that death is like a deep sleep.

Jesus and His disciples went to Bethany and found out Lazarus had been dead and buried for four days. When Martha saw Jesus, she said to Him, "Lord, if You had been here, my brother would not have died."[786] "Jesus said to her, 'Your brother will *rise again*.' Martha said to Him, 'I know that he will *rise again in the resurrection at the last day*.' Jesus said to her, 'I am the resurrection and the life. He who believes in Me, *though he may die, he shall live*.'"[787]

Martha understood the truth about death. The resurrection of the redeemed will take place when Jesus returns. However, to give Martha and all believers an example of the resurrection, Jesus went to the tomb and, after praying to His Father in heaven, said, "Lazarus, come forth!"[788] He wanted to assure us death cannot snatch away our eternal life and He is the resurrection and life.

---

[781] Psalm 115:17 (emphasis added)
[782] Acts 2:29 (emphasis added)
[783] Acts 2:34
[784] John 11:11
[785] John 11:14
[786] John 11:21
[787] John 11:23–25 (emphasis added)
[788] John 11:43

"And *he who had died came out* bound hand and foot with grave clothes, and his face was wrapped with a cloth. Jesus said to them, 'Loose him, and let him go.'"[789] Jesus did not say, "Lazarus come down from heaven" or "Lazarus come up from hell." He simply said, "Lazarus come forth," and he came out of the tomb alive and well. In this way, Jesus gave us a practical illustration of death and the resurrection.

Biblical evidence that death is like a deep sleep is abundant. However, from a surface reading, there are three passages that seem to contradict the others, so let us study those three carefully to see if they really do contradict the others or not.

When Jesus was crucified, two thieves were crucified with Him, one on each side of Him. One of the thieves cursed Jesus, but the other expressed his faith in Him.

> Then *one of the criminals* who were hanged *blasphemed Him*, saying, "If You are the Christ, save Yourself and us." But *the other*, answering, rebuked him, saying, "Do you not even fear God, seeing you are under the same condemnation? And we indeed justly, for we receive the due reward of our deeds; but this Man has done nothing wrong." Then he said to Jesus, *"Lord, remember me when You come into Your kingdom."*[790]

Christ's response to this man's faith-filled request has caused confusion regarding the topic of death. "And Jesus said to him, 'Assuredly, I say to you, today you will be with Me in Paradise.'"[791]

Did Jesus promise this repentant criminal he would go to heaven with Him that very day? Why would He promise such a thing when He Himself did not go to heaven that day? How do we know that? Jesus Himself tells us. He was crucified and died on Friday, lay dead in the tomb on Sabbath, and came forth on Sunday morning a victor over death.

The first person to whom He appeared was His friend Mary. "Jesus said to her, 'Do not cling to Me, for *I have not yet ascended to My Father*; but go to My brethren and say to them, "I am ascending to My Father and your Father, and to My God and your God."'"[792]

Clearly, Jesus did not go to heaven on Friday. In fact, He didn't go to heaven until after He appeared to Mary on Sunday morning. Did He give

---

[789] John 11:44 (emphasis added)
[790] Luke 23:39–42 (emphasis added)
[791] Luke 23:43 (emphasis added)
[792] John 20:17 (emphasis added)

the repentant criminal a false hope? or did He not know what He was saying? Maybe there is a problem with the punctuation. You see, there was no punctuation in the original manuscript. The punctuation was added several hundred years later by translators.

Let us see what happens to this message if we move the comma. Most translations place the comma as follows: "Assuredly, I say to you, today you will be with Me in Paradise." Now, see what happens when the comma is moved to follow the word "today": "Assuredly, I say to you today, you will be with Me in Paradise."

With the comma following the word "today," the message to the thief is consistent with the rest of the Bible and in harmony with the fact Jesus did not go to heaven on the day of His death. The message Jesus gave the thief was as follows: I assure you right now (today) you will be with Me in Paradise. You will be saved and come forth in the first resurrection when I return. He was assuring the thief of the same thing the apostle Paul later assured all who have accepted Christ as their personal Savior:

> For the Lord Himself will descend from heaven with a shout, with the voice of an archangel, and with the trumpet of God. And *the dead in Christ will rise first.* Then *we who are alive and remain* shall be *caught up together with them* in the clouds to meet the Lord in the air. And *thus we shall always be with the Lord.*[793]

Some people claim that while Jesus was in the tomb, His spirit escaped His body and went and preached to the lost who were writhing painfully in the fires of hell. They misunderstand what Peter wrote:

> For Christ also suffered once for sins, the just for the unjust, that He might bring us to God, being put to death in the flesh but made alive by the Spirit, by whom also He went and preached to the spirits in prison, who formerly were disobedient, when once the Divine longsuffering waited in the days of Noah, while *the* ark was being prepared, in which a few, that is, eight souls, were saved through water.[794]

We need to clearly understand what Peter said. One thing is the gospel was preached to the people of Noah's day before the flood. However, who did the preaching, and who are the spirits in prison? Peter made it clear that Noah was the preacher: "And did not spare the ancient world, but

---
[793] 1 Thessalonians 4:16, 17 (emphasis added)
[794] 1 Peter 3:18–20

saved Noah, *one of* eight *people,* a preacher of righteousness, bringing in the flood on the world of the ungodly."[795]

Even though it was Noah who preached, it was the Holy Spirit who inspired him;[796] it was the Holy Spirit who spoke to their hearts and brought conviction;[797] it is the Holy Spirit who frees us from the bondage of sin through the blood of Jesus. This is the prison to which Peter referred regarding the people in Noah's day.[798] They were enslaved in sin to the point that only eight people were saved out of the many millions and maybe billions alive at that time. They were trapped and in slavery to sin and perished in the flood because of it.[799]

The word "spirit" has several meanings in the Bible. It can refer to the Holy Spirit; it can refer to evil spirits; it can also refer to the breath of life God gives each living being; it also can mean the mental attitude or disposition of a person.[800]

This misunderstood passage from Peter has nothing to do with Jesus preaching to lost people burning in hell while His body lay in the tomb. Besides that, this theory doesn't even make sense. In our next chapter, we will see why.

Another passage that has caused confusion was written by Paul: "So we are always confident, knowing that *while we are at home in the body* we are *absent from the Lord*. For we walk by faith, not by sight. We are confident, yes, well pleased rather to be *absent from the body and to be present with the Lord*."[801]

There are two ways people have interpreted these verses. One is that when one dies, that person's body remains in the grave, while in spirit form continues living and goes to heaven immediately. However, that does not agree with the rest of Scripture. When we go to heaven, our greatest emotion will be gratitude and praise to God, but remember what the Bible says:

> The dead do not praise the LORD, nor any who go down into silence.[802]

---

[795] 2 Peter 2:5
[796] See 2 Peter 1:21
[797] See John 16:7, 8
[798] See 2 Peter 2:19
[799] See Romans 6:16
[800] See Joshua 5:1; 1 Samuel 1:15; Psalm 34:18; 51:17; Daniel 7:15; Matthew 5:3; 26:41; Romans 11:8; 12:11
[801] 2 Corinthians 5:6–8 (emphasis added)
[802] Psalm 115:17 (emphasis added)

> For the living know that they will die; But *the dead know nothing*.[803]

The other way to interpret Paul's statement in 2 Corinthians 6 is that being "home in the body" means being a living person on this earth. While we are living here, we are not physically in Christ's presence because Jesus is in heaven. Paul longed for the day he would be in Christ's presence physically, but he knew he would die before that happened.

Paul was beheaded by Nero in Rome, but the very next thing he will experience will be the resurrection, when Jesus comes in the clouds of heaven. To Paul, it will seem like it has been a fraction of a second, even though around 2,000 years will have passed. He knows nothing of the passing of time.

The topic of death is directly connected to the topic of hell. We will look at the subject of hell in the next chapter. Let me just say the Church of Rome was the first church to embrace the false teaching of the immortality of the sinful human being. This mother church, Babylon the Great, has passed the teaching on to her daughter churches, and this is part of the reason God sends us such a strong warning in the fourth angel's message to come out of Babylon.

The teaching that the soul is immortal has laid the foundation for spiritualism, which takes on a variety of forms. Some people wonder about impersonations, ghosts, evil spirits, Ouija boards, tarot cards, Pokémon, etc. These are all manifestations of evil angels who were cast out of heaven with Satan in his rebellion. God warns us, "Give no regard to mediums and familiar spirits; do not seek after them, to be defiled by them: I am the LORD your God."[804]

If a spirit appears to you in the form of a dead loved one, you can know it is not your loved one; it is an evil angel. The Bible is clear that the dead will not return to us until the resurrection. "As the *cloud disappears* and *vanishes* away, So he who goes down to the *grave* does *not come up*. He shall *never return to his house*, Nor shall his place *know him anymore*."[805]

Halloween is becoming very popular in America today, even more so than Christmas. Yet it is Satan's holiday—evil angels working miracles.

> And I saw three *unclean spirits* like frogs coming out of the mouth of the dragon, out of the mouth of the beast, and out of

---
[803] Ecclesiastes 9:5 (emphasis added)
[804] Leviticus 19:31
[805] Job 7:9, 10 (emphasis added)

the mouth of the false prophet. For they are *spirits of demons*, performing *signs*, which go out to the kings of the earth and of the whole world, to gather them to the battle of that great day of God Almighty.[806]

In these last days of the battle between Christ and Satan, we cannot even trust our senses of sight, hearing, touch, taste, and smell. Satan's deceptions will be so great that the only way we can know the truth is by the Word of God.

And when they say to you, "*Seek* those who are *mediums* and *wizards*, who *whisper* and *mutter*," should not a people *seek their God*? Should they seek the dead on behalf of the living? To the *law* and to the *testimony*! *If they do not speak according to this word, it is because there is no light in them.*[807]

> *If a spirit appears to you in the form of a dead loved one, you can know it is not your loved one; it is an evil angel.*

This is also true regarding the reported near-death experiences where people see a beautiful light at the end of a long tunnel and themselves floating through space toward heaven. Drug addicts have the same out-of-body experiences when they overdose. It is a common phenomenon of the brain when it is deprived of oxygen. The Bible tells us there were many people resurrected from the dead by Jesus, but none of them reported having been in heaven.

In our world today, spiritualism has assumed a Christian front. When Christians profess to believe in the Bible and Jesus but refuse to obey all His commandments, the Bible equates that to spiritualism. "For rebellion *is as* the sin of witchcraft, and stubbornness *is as* iniquity and idolatry."[808]

Jesus made it clear that disobedience to God's law is the fatal issue with false Christian leaders.

> Not everyone who says to Me, "Lord, Lord," shall enter the kingdom of heaven, but he who does the will of My Father in heaven. Many will say to Me in that day, "Lord, Lord, have we not prophesied in Your name, cast out demons in Your name, and done many

---

[806] Revelation 16:13, 14 (emphasis added)
[807] Isaiah 8:19, 20 (emphasis added)
[808] 1 Samuel 15:23

wonders in Your name?" And then I will declare to them, "I never knew you; depart from Me, you who practice lawlessness!"[809]

They may be popular and attract large crowds to their churches; they may preach and teach many wonderful truths; but if they lead their followers to disregard a commandment of God, they are being used by the enemy.

> For such *are* false apostles, deceitful workers, transforming themselves into apostles of Christ. And no wonder! For Satan himself transforms himself into an angel of light. Therefore *it is* no great thing if his ministers also transform themselves into ministers of righteousness, whose end will be according to their works.[810]

Our faith needs to be rooted in the Bible and not in mystical experiences that Satan can manipulate. Death is an experience shrouded in mystery if you venture beyond what the Bible teaches. Hell can be also, but the Bible solves the mystery.

---

[809] Matthew 7:21–23
[810] 2 Corinthians 11:13–15

Chapter 14

The End of Sin

The Bible graphically depicts the last desperate struggle between Christ and Satan in this universal war that has been raging since Satan was cast out of heaven. Jesus and His armies are pictured as riding white horses. "Now I saw heaven opened, and behold, a *white horse*. And He who sat on him was called *Faithful and True*, and in *righteousness* He *judges* and *makes war*.... And the *armies in heaven*, clothed in *fine linen, white and clean*, followed Him on *white horses*."[811]

The other side of this battle is made up of the forces of Satan: the "kings of the earth," "their armies," the "beast," and "false prophet." Notice what happens when these massive armies engage in the last great battle of the universe:

> And I saw the *beast*, the *kings of the earth*, and *their armies*, gathered together to *make war* against *Him who sat on the horse and against His army*. Then the *beast* was *captured*, and with him the *false prophet* who *worked signs in his presence*, by which he *deceived* those who received the *mark of the beast* and those who *worshiped his image*. These two were *cast alive* into the *lake of fire burning with brimstone*.[812]

It is the first beast (the sea beast—the papacy) of Revelation 13 that is cast into the lake of fire. With him is the "false prophet." Who is the false prophet? It is none other than the second beast (the land beast—Protestant America) of Revelation 13. Notice the description of the false prophet in 19:20 (above). The same description is given for the land beast.

> And he exercises all the authority of the first beast *in his presence*, and causes the earth and those who dwell in it *to worship the first beast*, whose deadly wound was healed. He performs great signs, so that he even makes fire come down from

---

[811] Revelation 19:11, 14 (emphasis added)
[812] Revelation 19:19, 20 (emphasis added)

The End of Sin

heaven on the earth in the sight of men. And *he deceives those who dwell on the earth*—by those signs which he was granted to do in the sight of the beast, telling those who dwell on the earth to *make an image to the beast* who was wounded by the sword and lived. He was granted power to give breath to the image of the beast, that the image of the beast should both speak and cause as many as would not *worship the image of the beast* to be killed.[813]

The final battle against Jesus and His faithful followers will be led by the union of Protestant America and the Vatican and ends with Satan and his forces being cast into a lake of fire. This is the decisive and final end of evil. Nevertheless, Revelation 20 adds a disturbing detail to this lake of fire—a detail we must study carefully. "The *devil*, who deceived them, was cast into the *lake of fire* and brimstone where the *beast* and the *false prophet* are. And they will be *tormented day and night forever and ever*."[814]

This is a description of hell, but when does hell take place? Where is hell? And how long do the fires of hell last? This topic has caused multitudes to hate and reject God, and understandingly so.

Most people consider Adolf Hitler a very evil man because he tortured and killed millions of people during World War II. However, his tortures lasted only a few years. Could you genuinely love a God who would keep people alive for all eternity, torturing them with excruciating pain in fire and never allowing them to die? Would heaven be a pleasant place to live if you could witness the tortures of loved ones for ceaseless ages?

What does the topic of hellfire teach us about the Godhead? Does this understanding of hellfire match what we have already discovered about the character of God, revealed by Jesus?

To answer these and other questions, we will return to the study of the millennium that we began in the last chapter. The following chart will refresh our memory of where we left off:

---

[813] Revelation 13:12–15 (emphasis added)
[814] Revelation 20:10 (emphasis added)

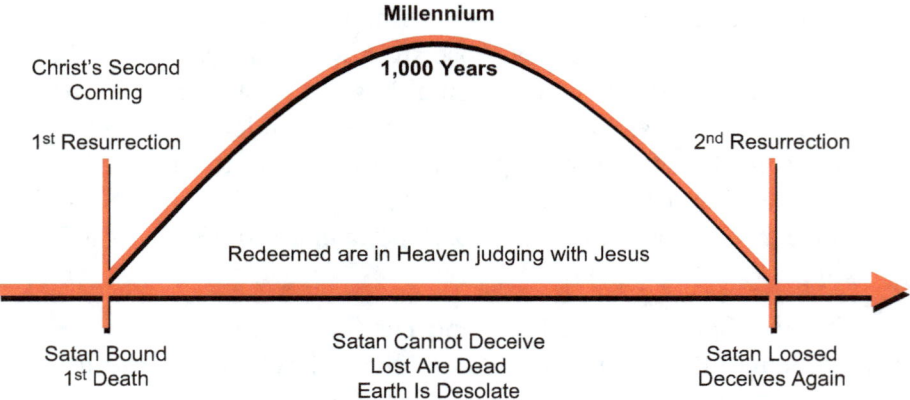

The second resurrection (the resurrection of the lost) takes place at the end of the 1,000 years, causing Satan to be released. He again will have multitudes to deceive and rally to his purposes. "Now when the *thousand years have expired*, Satan will be released from his prison and will go out to deceive the *nations* which are in the *four corners* of the *earth*, Gog and Magog, to gather them together to battle, whose *number is as the sand of the sea*."[815]

It is also at the end of the 1,000 years that Jesus brings the New Jerusalem (the fantastically beautiful home of the redeemed) to this earth. "Then I, John, saw the holy city, New Jerusalem, coming down out of heaven from God, prepared as a bride adorned for her husband."[816]

The New Jerusalem, along with the redeemed, will descend from heaven to the earth. At the same time, the countless lost will be resurrected in the second resurrection. The stage will be set for the great and final battle between Christ and Satan, and Satan and his forces will make the first move. "They went up on the *breadth of the earth* and *surrounded the camp of the saints* and the *beloved city*. And *fire came down from God* out of heaven and *devoured them*."[817]

This verse tells us several things about hellfire:

- It is on the surface of the earth
- God, not Satan, is in charge and control of hellfire
- It will devour Satan and the lost (to devour is to leave nothing behind)

---

[815] Revelation 20:7, 8 (emphasis added)
[816] Revelation 21:2
[817] Revelation 20:9 (emphasis added)

- It will happen at the end of the 1,000 years (hellfire is not burning now)

How does this verse match the very next verse? We have read it before, but let us read it again: "The *devil*, who deceived them, was *cast into the lake of fire* and brimstone where the beast and the false prophet are. And they will be *tormented day and night forever and ever*."[818]

Being tormented day and night forever and ever does not seem the same as being "devoured." Is John the revelator contradicting himself, or is there a deeper meaning that will take some study to understand? First, notice hellfire produces the "second death." "Then *Death* and *Hades* were cast into the *lake of fire*. This is the *second death*. And anyone *not found written in the Book of Life* was cast into the *lake of fire*."[819]

The word "Hades" means "the grave," the place where dead people sleep until one of the two resurrections. Therefore, the second death is the end of death and the grave. This is in harmony with God's promise to the redeemed. Once the lake of fire has finished its work of devouring and God has created this world new again, death will be forever gone.

> And I heard a loud voice from heaven saying, "Behold, *the tabernacle of God is with men*, and He will dwell with them, and they shall be His people. *God Himself will be with them* and be their God. And God will *wipe away every tear* from their eyes; there shall be *no more death*, nor *sorrow*, nor *crying*. There shall be *no more pain*, for the *former things* have *passed away*."[820]

If the lost burn in the fires of hell for eternity, this passage would not be true. There would be many tears, much sorrow, plenty of crying, endless pain, and therefore, the suffering we have known in this life would not be "passed away."

I believe God will weep when He sends the fire upon Satan and his followers. God hates sin but loves the sinner. He has provided abundant grace, salvation, and power over sin. When we refuse His grace, salvation, and power, we are sold out to the carnal, sinful, selfish nature with which we are all born. If we were taken to heaven in that condition, the sinless and holy atmosphere would be a living torture to us.

---

[818] Revelation 20:10 (emphasis added)
[819] Revelation 20:14, 15 (emphasis added)
[820] Revelation 21:3, 4 (emphasis added)

Therefore, destroying the lost is an act of mercy, but it is God's "strange act," according to the prophet Isaiah: "For the LORD shall rise up as in mount Perazim, he shall be wroth as in the valley of Gibeon, that he may do his work, *his strange work*; and bring to pass his act, *his strange act*."[821] God's intentions are to give life, not destroy it. That is why the destruction of the wicked is called His "strange act."

Jesus told a parable that illustrates that hellfire will take place at the very end; it is not happening now. He told of a farmer who sowed good wheat seeds in his field, but an enemy sowed weed seeds. The wheat and weeds began to grow up together, and his farm workers asked why there were weeds.

> He said to them, "*An enemy has done this.*" The servants said to him, "Do you want us then to go and gather them up?" But he said, "No, lest while you gather up the tares you also uproot the wheat with them. *Let both grow together until the harvest*, and at the *time of harvest* I will say to the reapers, 'First gather *together the tares and bind them in bundles to burn them*, but *gather the wheat into my barn*.'"[822]

Jesus goes on to describe the meaning of this parable:

> The *enemy* who sowed them is the *devil*, the *harvest is the end of the age*, and the *reapers* are the *angels*. Therefore as the *tares* are gathered and *burned in the fire*, so it will be at the *end of this age*. The Son of Man will send out His angels, and they will gather out of His kingdom all things that *offend*, and *those who practice lawlessness*, and will *cast them into the furnace of fire*. There will be wailing and gnashing of teeth.[823]

Hellfire is not happening now, but it will happen, just as Revelation described it, at the end of the 1,000 years, when this experiment with rebellion against God's law is brought to an end. Nevertheless, how are we to understand those passages of Scripture that indicate the lost will burn for eternity? Is there a deeper meaning? Let us look at the seven passages that bring this question to our attention:

---

[821] Isaiah 28:21, KJV (emphasis added)
[822] Matthew 13:28–30 (emphasis added)
[823] Matthew 13:39–42 (emphasis added)

1. "And they will be tormented day and night forever and ever."[824]

It may come as a surprise to some that the word "forever" in the Bible does not always mean never-ending. It is sometimes used as a figurative form of speech, much like we use it frequently today. How many times have you heard someone say, "That took forever to do"?

That is exactly how it was used by the reluctant prophet Jonah when he was describing the three days he spent in the belly of a huge fish. If I spent three days in the belly of a whale, I would think it was forever. Notice how Jonah described his experience: "I went down to the moorings of the mountains; The earth with its bars closed behind me *forever*."[825] Nevertheless, the reality is he was only there three days.

Another way the word "forever" is used in the Bible is to mean "as long as life shall last." One of the regulations regarding setting servants free illustrates this:

> But if the servant plainly says, "I love my master, my wife, and my children; I will not go out free," then his master shall bring him to the judges. He shall also bring him to the door, or to the doorpost, and his master shall pierce his ear with an awl; and he shall *serve him forever*.[826]

In other words, he would serve his master for as long as he had life. Another illustration of this was when Hannah, the prophet Samuel's mother, dedicated him to the service of God.

> But Hannah did not go up, for she said to her husband, "Not until the child is weaned; then I will take him, that he may appear before the LORD and *remain there forever*."[827]

> Therefore I also have lent him to the LORD; *as long as he lives* he shall be lent to the LORD.[828]

Samuel served the Lord as long as he lived. Likewise, when the fire falls on the lost, it will not be extinguished until they are

---

[824] Revelation 20:10
[825] Jonah 2:6 (emphasis added)
[826] Exodus 21:5, 6 (emphasis added)
[827] 1 Samuel 1:22 (emphasis added)
[828] 1 Samuel 1:28 (emphasis added)

consumed and there is nothing left. The prophet Malachi speaks of this clearly:

> "For behold, the day is coming, *burning like an oven*, and all the proud, yes, all who do wickedly will be *stubble*. And the day which is coming shall *burn them up*," says the LORD of hosts, "That will *leave them neither root nor branch*."[829]
>
> "You shall *trample the wicked*, for they shall be *ashes under the soles of your feet* on the day that I do this," Says the LORD of hosts.[830]

Satan and his followers will be cremated in the lake of fire, and their ashes will be mixed in with the dirt when God creates this earth again. The result of the fire will be eternal.

2. He shall be *tormented* with *fire* and *brimstone* in the presence of the holy angels and in the presence of the Lamb. And the *smoke* of their *torment ascends forever and ever*; and they have *no rest day or night*, who worship the beast and his image, and whoever receives the mark of his name.[831]

This is part of the third angel's message and highly symbolic in nature. For example, it contains the symbols of beast, image, mark, etc. Symbolic prophecy cannot be taken literally. We have to decode the symbols by the rest of the Bible, which is its own best interpreter. Most of Revelation makes direct references to the Old Testament, and this passage is no exception. The prophet Isaiah used the same symbolic language to describe the complete and permanent destruction of the nation of Edom:

> For it is the day of the LORD's vengeance, the year of recompense for the cause of Zion. Its streams shall be turned into *pitch*, and its dust into *brimstone*; its land shall become *burning pitch*. It shall *not be quenched night or day*; its *smoke shall ascend forever*. From generation to generation *it shall lie waste*; no one shall pass through it forever and ever.[832]

Isaiah described the destruction of Edom in this symbolic language in order to highlight the fact that it would be totally

---

[829] Malachi 4:1 (emphasis added)
[830] Malachi 4:3 (emphasis added)
[831] Revelation 14:10, 11 (emphasis added)
[832] Isaiah 34:8–10 (emphasis added)

destroyed and never be a nation again. It was clearly symbolic because Edom was destroyed by war, not by burning pitch and brimstone that is still burning and smoking today. In using this symbolic language, Isaiah is referring back to the destruction of the wicked cities of Sodom and Gomorrah. The destruction of these cities is an example of how totally and permanently Edom would be destroyed. "Then the LORD rained *brimstone* and *fire* on *Sodom* and *Gomorrah*, from the *LORD out of the heavens*. So He overthrew those cities, all the plain, *all the inhabitants* of the cities, and what *grew on the ground*."[833]

If you go to Israel today, you can see where Sodom and Gomorrah used to be. There is nothing there—they are totally gone! Isaiah used the burning of Sodom and Gomorrah as an illustration of Edom's destruction, even though the destruction was by the sword, not by fire and brimstone from heaven.

John, the author of Revelation, used Isaiah's symbolic language to describe that the lost will be utterly destroyed and never live again. The fire will burn, and the smoke will ascend as long as there is fuel to burn, but when the fuel is turned into ashes, the fire will go out. The destruction of Jerusalem is an example of this: "But if you will not heed Me to hallow the Sabbath day, such as not carrying a burden when entering the gates of Jerusalem on the Sabbath day, *then I will kindle a fire* in its gates, and it shall *devour the palaces of Jerusalem*, and *it shall not be quenched*."[834]

Jerusalem is not burning today. Jeremiah explained that the destruction of Jerusalem was an example of unquenchable fire. The destruction of Sodom and Gomorrah by fire and brimstone was also used by Peter and Jude to serve as an illustration of hell-fire at the end of time:

> As *Sodom* and *Gomorrah*, and the cities around them in a similar manner to these, having given themselves over to sexual immorality and gone after strange flesh, are set forth as an *example*, suffering the vengeance of *eternal fire*.[835]

---

[833] Genesis 19:24, 25 (emphasis added)
[834] Jeremiah 17:27 (emphasis added)
[835] Jude 1:7 (emphasis added)

> And turning the cities of *Sodom* and *Gomorrah* into *ashes*, condemned them to destruction, making them an *example* to those who *afterward would live ungodly*.[836]

King David wrote about the destruction of the wicked and illustrated it as smoke vanishing away. "But the *wicked* shall *perish*; And the enemies of the LORD, like the splendor of the meadows, shall *vanish*. Into *smoke* they shall *vanish away*."[837]

God knew there would be great confusion about hellfire, so He gave us a powerful example of what it will be like. The results of the fire are eternal; the burning is not. Sodom and Gomorrah are not burning today. However, the Bible does describe God as a "consuming fire,"[838] and He is eternal.

For those who allow God, the eternal fire, to consume the sin in their lives, His fire will be lifegiving; but for those who cling to their sin, His eternal fire will be death-dealing.

> The *sinners* in Zion are *afraid*; *fearfulness* has seized the *hypocrites*: "Who among us shall dwell with the devouring fire? Who among us shall *dwell with everlasting burnings*?" He who walks *righteously* and speaks *uprightly*, he who despises the gain of oppressions, who gestures with his hands, refusing bribes, who stops his ears from hearing of bloodshed, and shuts his eyes from seeing evil: He will dwell on high; his place of defense will be the fortress of rocks; *bread will be given him, his water will be sure*.[839]

This presents a different picture from what has been typically presented from Christian pulpits. It is the redeemed who will dwell with the everlasting fire because God is everlasting, and His presence is a consuming fire. However, to the righteous, His presence gives life, but to the wicked, it brings death.

3. Jesus also used the concept of "everlasting fire," but notice He did not say "everlasting burning." The fire is everlasting because God is everlasting and the results of the fire will be everlasting. "Then He will also say to those on the left hand, 'Depart from Me,

---

[836] 2 Peter 2:6 (emphasis added)
[837] Psalm 37:20 (emphasis added)
[838] Hebrews 12:29 (see also Psalm 50:3; Exodus 24:17; Deuteronomy 4:24; Isaiah 33:14–16)
[839] Isaiah 33:14–16 (emphasis added)

you cursed, into the *everlasting fire* prepared for the *devil and his angels*."[840]

4. A few verses later, Jesus used the term "everlasting punishment" to describe the reward of the wicked. Again, notice He didn't say "everlasting punishing." The punishment takes place relatively quickly, as in the case of Sodom and Gomorrah, but the results of the punishment will be everlasting. "And these will go away into *everlasting punishment*, but the righteous into eternal life."[841]

> *For those who allow God, the eternal fire, to consume the sin in their lives, His fire will be lifegiving; but for those who cling to their sin, His eternal fire will be death-dealing.*

5. The apostle Paul used this same concept by saying "everlasting destruction": "These shall be punished with everlasting destruction from the presence of the Lord and from the glory of His power."[842]

6. Some people wonder what Jesus meant when He talked about the worm that does not die. "If your hand causes you to sin, cut it off. It is better for you to enter into life maimed, rather than having two hands, to go to *hell*, into *the fire that shall never be quenched*—where 'Their *worm does not die* and the *fire is not quenched*.'"[843]

The fire that burned the Twin Towers on September 11, 2001 was unquenchable. The firefighters were unable to put it out, and all that was left was a pile of rubbish and ashes. The "worm" that does not die is not referring to a soul or spirit that lives on after death. We learned in the last chapter that dead people are unaware of anything—they know nothing. The word "worm" means "maggot."[844] Maggots eat dead things, so this is another way of saying the lost will be destroyed in the lake of fire and never live

---

[840] Matthew 25:41 (emphasis added)
[841] Matthew 25:46 (emphasis added)
[842] 2 Thessalonians 1:9
[843] Mark 9:43, 44 (emphasis added)
[844] See Strong's Greek and Hebrew Dictionary

again—the maggot eating their remains will not die until there is nothing more to eat.

Eternal life is the gift of God to those who are in Christ. Those who are not in Christ will not have eternal life—they will not live forever in hell. The wage of sin is death—knowing nothing. "For the wages of sin is death, but the gift of God is eternal life in Christ Jesus our Lord."[845]

7. Jesus told a parable that has been misunderstood and used to promote the idea that the lost burn in hell forever. Therefore, we need to look at it as well and understand what Jesus was trying to teach. I will quote the entire parable here:

There was a certain *rich man* who was clothed in purple and fine linen and fared sumptuously every day. But there was a certain *beggar named Lazarus*, full of sores, who was laid at his gate, desiring to be fed with the crumbs which fell from the rich man's table. Moreover the dogs came and licked his sores. So it was that the *beggar died*, and was carried by the angels to *Abraham's bosom*. The *rich man also died* and was *buried*. And being in *torments in Hades*, he lifted up his *eyes* and *saw Abraham* afar off, and *Lazarus* in his bosom. Then he *cried and said*, "Father *Abraham*, have mercy on me, and *send Lazarus* that he may *dip the tip of his finger in water and cool my tongue*; for I am tormented in this flame." But Abraham said, "Son, remember that in your lifetime you received your good things, and likewise Lazarus evil things; but now he is comforted and you are tormented. And besides all this, *between us and you there is a great gulf fixed, so that those who want to pass from here to you cannot, nor can those from there pass to us*." Then he said, "I beg you therefore, father, that you would *send him to my father's house*, for I have *five brothers*, that he may *testify to them*, lest they also come to this place of torment." Abraham said to him, "They have *Moses and the prophets*; let them hear them." And he said, "No, father Abraham; but *if one goes to them from the dead*, they will *repent*." But he said to him, *"If they do not hear Moses and the prophets, neither will they be persuaded though one rise from the dead."*[846]

---

[845] Romans 6:23
[846] Luke 16:19–31 (emphasis added)

The End of Sin

The parable of the rich man and Lazarus is the fifth in a series of Jesus' parables. It was a commonly known Jewish story. As we study the passage, we will see it is not the details that are important. The lesson Jesus was trying to teach is what is important:

- The rich man was buried, but Lazarus was carried physically to "Abraham's bosom." We know that when people die, whether saved or lost, they are buried. If all the redeemed are physically transported to Abraham's bosom, it must be very large. This is obviously symbolic, not literal.
- The rich man and Abraham carried on a conversation. However, the Bible clearly forbids trying to communicate with the dead.

> Give no regard to mediums and familiar spirits; do not seek after them, to be defiled by them: I am the LORD your God.[847]
>
> The dead do not praise the LORD, nor any who go down into silence.[848]
>
> For the living know that they will die; but the dead know nothing.[849]
>
> As the cloud disappears and vanishes away, so he who goes down to the grave does not come up. He shall never return to his house, nor shall his place know him anymore.[850]

- The rich man, Lazarus, and Abraham have body parts, showing they are not bodiless spirits. They have eyes, tongues, fingers, and voice boxes and can obviously think, reason, and respond to arguments. You get into trouble when you try to match this parable with the idea of the immortal soul. It was obviously a symbolic parable, not literal.

By this parable, Jesus was not trying to teach about hellfire and what happens when a person dies, for the details contradict what the rest of the Bible teaches on those topics. Instead, He used familiar folklore to teach at least four important lessons:

- Riches are not a sign of God's favor, as the Jewish rabbis taught
- Poverty is not a sign of God's displeasure, as was commonly believed

---

[847] Leviticus 19:31
[848] Psalm 115:17
[849] Ecclesiastes 9:5
[850] Job 7:9, 10

- After death, there is no second chance for salvation
- Those who reject the Scriptures will not be convinced by miracles, even by someone who has been resurrected from the dead

Jesus did raise a man by the name of Lazarus from the dead—a man who testified of Christ's Messiahship. This was the crowning miracle of His ministry, which made the religious leaders decide that Jesus must be killed in order to stop His growing popularity; otherwise, they would lose their authority. Lazarus did come back from the dead and testify to the house of Israel, but because they had refused to listen to Moses and the prophets, they also did not believe him, even though he had been raised from the dead. Lazarus was not raised as a spirit. He was raised as a fully living human being, just like he had gone into the grave: physical, mental, spiritual, and social.[851]

As we studied in the last chapter, the redeemed will be involved in the judgment of the fallen angels and the lost during the millennium. At the conclusion of the 1,000 years, the final phase of the judgment will take place: the public sentencing and execution of the sentences. Revelation calls this the judgment of the great white throne.

Then I saw a *great white throne* and Him who sat on it, from whose face the *earth and the heaven fled away*. And there was found *no place* for them. And I saw the *dead*, small and great, standing before God, and *books were opened*. And another book was opened, which is the *Book of Life*. And the *dead were judged according to their works*, by the things which were *written in the books*.[852]

The fact that earth and heaven fled away from God and no place was found for them is reminiscent of Nebuchadnezzar's dream in Daniel 2. The stone cut out without hands (which represented the kingdom of heaven) struck the image of gold, silver, bronze, iron, and clay (which represented the nations of this world).

Then the *iron*, the *clay*, the *bronze*, the *silver*, and the *gold* were *crushed* together, and became like *chaff* from the summer threshing floors; the *wind carried them away* so that *no trace of them was*

---

[851] See John 11:43, 44
[852] Revelation 20:11, 12 (emphasis added)

found. And the **stone** that struck the image became a great mountain and *filled the whole earth.*[853]

During the millennium, the books of record will be reviewed by the redeemed. Every question they have ever had regarding God's treatment of the sin problem will be answered. The lost will be dead during the 1,000 years, but they stand before the judgment through the record of their lives found in the books of heaven. At the end of the millennium, the lost will be resurrected to receive the execution of the sentence determined in the judgment.

The sea gave up the *dead* who were in it, and Death and Hades delivered up the *dead* who were in them. And *they were judged*, each one *according to his works*. Then Death and Hades were cast into the lake of fire. This is the *second death*. And anyone *not found written in the Book of Life* was cast into the *lake of fire*.[854]

The Bible is consistent with its message regarding death and hell. There is no burning hell today, but it will come at the end of the millennium. "But the *cowardly, unbelieving, abominable, murderers, sexually immoral, sorcerers, idolaters*, and *all liars* shall have their part in *the lake which burns with fire and brimstone*, which is the *second death*."[855]

The lake of fire will not go out until all the fuel is burned up, but once that happens, sin will be no more, and "affliction will not rise up a second time."[856] Self-sacrificing love will be the atmosphere of the universe, and God will embark on a new creation. He will create this world again. "Now I saw a new heaven and a new earth, for the first heaven and the first earth had passed away."[857]

> *Society's freefall will be reversed! God will recreate this planet, and sin will never enter it again—only righteousness. That is why God desires we understand and accept the everlasting gospel of Jesus Christ.*

---

[853] Daniel 2:35 (emphasis added)
[854] Revelation 20:13–15 (emphasis added)
[855] Revelation 21:8 (emphasis added)
[856] Nahum 1:9
[857] Revelation 21:1

In conclusion, because I am a visual learner and know many others are as well, I am completing the millennium chart here:

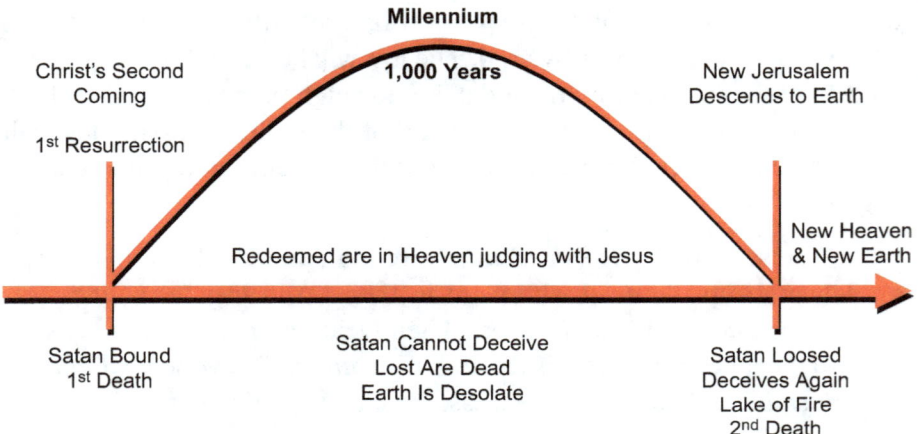

Society's freefall will be reversed! God will recreate this planet, and sin will never enter it again—only righteousness. That is why God desires we understand and accept the everlasting gospel of Jesus Christ. "Nevertheless we, according to His promise, look for new heavens and a new earth in which righteousness dwells."[858]

Do you want to be there? I do, and I want you there as well. The new heaven and earth is the topic of the final chapter in this book, so keep reading.

---

[858] 2 Peter 3:13

Chapter 15

Society's Rebirth

Before Jesus returns, society will fall so low, it can only be compared to either the days of Noah, before God destroyed the earth with a global flood, or Lot, before God destroyed Sodom and Gomorrah with fire and brimstone.[859] The Bible describes what society was like in Noah's day: "The earth also was corrupt before God, and the earth was filled with violence."[860]

That is an accurate description of our society today: corrupt and violent. Sodom and Gomorrah were notorious for their sexually perverted lifestyle,[861] which also describes our society today.

God is in control, and there is a line past which He will not allow society to fall. When the decree goes forth to kill His people (those who refuse to worship the image to the beast and receive his mark),[862] society will have passed that line, and God will intervene to save His people. Jesus will come in the clouds of heaven and interrupt society's freefall.

Then, at the end of the millennium, after this world is cleansed by fire, God will restore the world to its original beauty and purity. It will again be like the Garden of Eden. "And that He may send Jesus Christ, who was preached to you before, whom heaven must receive until the times of restoration of all things, which God has spoken by the mouth of all His holy prophets since the world began."[863]

The Bible gives us word pictures of what heaven and the earth made new will be like. Heaven will be glorious, breathtaking, and awe-inspiring! The society there will be based on the eternal principles of love and righteousness—a society that will last for all eternity!

It may surprise you, but God has revealed in His Word:

1. Where heaven will be
2. What heaven will be like
3. Where its capital city will be

---

[859] See Matthew 24:38; Luke 17:26–30
[860] Genesis 6:11
[861] See Romans 1:26, 27; Genesis 19:1–26; "Sodomy," The Free Dictionary, legal-dictionary.thefreedictionary.com/sodomy (accessed February 9, 2021)
[862] See Revelation 13:15–17
[863] Acts 3:20, 21

4. What people will do there
5. What people will be like
6. Where the saved will live
7. What the capital city will look like

The apostle John was given a vision of these things and wrote what he saw in the last two chapters of Revelation. Interestingly, the first two chapters of the Bible describe the earth as it came from the Creator's hand: perfect, pure, and sinless. The last two chapters of the Bible describe the earth made new again by our great Creator, restored to its original perfection, purity, and sinlessness. Everything between the first two and last two chapters of the Bible describes God's work of restoration.

> Now I saw a *new heaven* and a *new earth*, for the *first heaven* and the *first earth* had *passed away*. Also there was no more sea. Then I, John, saw the *holy city, New Jerusalem*, coming down out of heaven from God, *prepared as a bride adorned for her husband*.[864]

John talked about a new heaven as well as a new earth. There are three heavens mentioned in the Bible. One is the place where God dwells and Jesus will take the redeemed during the millennium.[865] Another heaven is outer space, where the constellations exist.[866] Then there is the atmosphere around our planet, which is also called "heaven."[867]

When God makes heaven and earth again, He will make the atmosphere completely new and cleanse our solar system of all the spacecraft and satellite debris we have scattered abroad. The new heaven and earth will be restored to their original perfection.

---

[864] Revelation 21:1, 2 (emphasis added)
[865] See Psalm 115:3; John 14:1–3
[866] See Genesis 22:17; Psalm 19:1
[867] See Genesis 1:8

All the patriarchs and prophets looked forward to living in the New Jerusalem. Notice what the Bible says about Abraham, the father of the faithful:

> By faith *Abraham* obeyed when he was called to go out to the place which he would receive as an inheritance. And he went out, not knowing where he was going. *By faith* he dwelt in the land of promise as in a foreign country, *dwelling in tents* with Isaac and Jacob, the heirs with him of the same promise; *for he waited for the city which has foundations, whose builder and maker is God.*[868]

This was not only Abraham's faithful expectation, but that of his descendants as well.

> These all died in *faith*, not having received the promises, but having *seen them afar off* were assured of them, embraced them and confessed that they were *strangers and pilgrims on the earth....* But now they desire a *better*, that is, a *heavenly country*. Therefore God is not ashamed to be called their God, *for He has prepared a city for them.*[869]

They were all looking forward to the new heaven, new earth, and New Jerusalem made by God. The prophet Isaiah was also given a vision of these things: "For behold, I create new heavens and a new earth; And the former shall not be remembered or come to mind."[870]

What are the former things that will not be there? Violence was a prominent characteristic of society in Noah's day as well as Lot's day, and society has again fallen into violence. However, God has something better in store for us: "Violence shall no longer be heard in your land, neither wasting nor destruction within your borders; but you shall call your walls Salvation, And your gates Praise."[871]

In fact, even the dangerous things in nature will not be dangerous there! There will be nothing to cause fear and anxiety! Notice this beautiful word picture of what it will be like!

> The wolf also shall dwell with the lamb, the leopard shall lie down with the young goat, the calf and the young lion and the fatling together; and a little child shall lead them. The cow and the

---

[868] Hebrews 11:8–10 (emphasis added)
[869] Hebrews 11:13–16 (emphasis added)
[870] Isaiah 65:17
[871] Isaiah 60:18

bear shall graze; their young ones shall lie down together; and the lion shall eat straw like the ox. The nursing child shall play by the cobra's hole, and the weaned child shall put his hand in the viper's den. They shall not hurt nor destroy in all My holy mountain, for the earth shall be full of the knowledge of the LORD as the waters cover the sea.[872]

To our society filled with cancer, heart disease, stroke, diabetes, COVID-19, and many other deadly diseases, God's promise of heaven and the new earth is incredibly good news. "And the inhabitant will not say, 'I am sick'; The people who dwell in it will be forgiven their iniquity."[873]

The handicapped and impaired will rejoice to see that day. The day Jesus comes will be the best day of their lives. There will be no need for eyeglasses, hearing aids, braces, crutches, wheelchairs, prostheses, or any other devise. Even the desolate parts of the earth will be no more.

> Say to those who are *fearful-hearted*, "Be *strong*, do *not fear*! Behold, *your God will come* with vengeance, with the recompense of God; *He will come and save you.*" Then the *eyes* of the *blind* shall be *opened*, and the *ears* of the *deaf* shall be *unstopped*. Then the *lame* shall *leap like a deer*, and the *tongue* of the *dumb sing*. For waters shall burst forth in the *wilderness*, and streams in the *desert*. The *parched ground* shall become a pool, and the *thirsty land* springs of water; in the habitation of jackals, where each lay, there shall be grass with reeds and rushes. A highway shall be there, and a road, and it shall be called the *Highway of Holiness*. The *unclean shall not pass over it*, but it shall be for others.[874]

Some people have the mistaken idea that heaven will be a boring place where everyone sits around on clouds, strumming harps for eternity. The truth is just the opposite. We will be forever learning more about God, nature, and the universe. We will even have the opportunity to build our dream house. Just think about what you can build if you have eternity. "They shall build houses and inhabit them; they shall plant vineyards and eat their fruit. They shall not build and another inhabit; they shall not plant and another eat."[875]

---

[872] Isaiah 11:6–9 (emphasis added)
[873] Isaiah 33:24
[874] Isaiah 35:4–8 (emphasis added)
[875] Isaiah 65:21, 22

The greatest joy of heaven and the new earth will be gathering each Sabbath and every month to worship our great God! Just think of the truths Jesus will unfold to us each week. It will be thrilling as our minds grasp new facets of truth and we explore new horizons of understanding. What a blessed fellowship we will have as we experience the true meaning of Sabbath for eternity!

> "For as the *new heavens* and the *new earth* which I will make shall remain before Me," says the LORD, "so shall your descendants and your name remain. And it shall come to pass that from *one New Moon to another*, and from *one Sabbath to another*, all flesh shall come to *worship before Me*," says the LORD.[876]

The joys of heaven and the new earth will be far more than perfect health, delicious food, exciting learning, and beautiful surroundings. To be in the presence of Jesus, the One who died for our sins, will thrill our hearts more and more as time passes and we understand more of God's love and what it took to redeem us from the curse of sin—death. "And there shall be *no more curse*, but the throne of God and of the Lamb shall be in it, and His servants shall serve Him. *They shall see His face*, and *His name* shall be on their *foreheads*."[877]

A particular gospel hymn catches this thought: "Face to face with Christ my Savior, face to face, what will it be, when with rapture I behold Him, Jesus Christ, who died for me?"[878] Have you ever been in the presence of someone who loved, respected, and valued you so much that you never wanted to leave that person's presence? That is what it will be like with Jesus through all eternity!

Society will be perfect there. There will be no need to lock doors or hide belongings; no need for fear or feeling lonely, neglected, or unloved. All bad experiences, thoughts, words, and feelings will be pleasantly absent.

> But there shall *by no means enter it* anything that *defiles*, or causes *an abomination* or a *lie*, but only those who are *written in the Lamb's Book of Life*.[879]

---

[876] Isaiah 66:22, 23 (emphasis added)
[877] Revelation 22:3, 4 (emphasis added)
[878] Frank A. Breck, "Face to Face with Christ My Savior" (No. 206) in The Seventh-day Adventist Hymnal (Washington, DC: Review and Herald Publishing Association, 1985)
[879] Revelation 21:27 (emphasis added)

> And I heard a loud voice from heaven saying, "Behold, the *tabernacle of God is with men*, and *He will dwell with them*, and they shall be His people. God Himself will be with them and be their God. And God will *wipe away every tear from their eyes*; there shall be *no more death, nor sorrow, nor crying*. There shall be *no more pain*, for the former things have passed away."[880]

Some people wonder if we will know our friends and loved ones there just like we know them here? The apostle Paul gives us a hint: "For now we see in a mirror, dimly, but then face to face. Now I know in part, but then I shall know just as I also am known."[881]

We do not have the slightest idea of what God has in store for the redeemed. Our wildest imaginations fall far short of the wonderful things He is preparing. There are many spectacular mansions here on earth, but they are nothing in comparison to what Jesus is preparing for you.

> Let not your heart be troubled; you believe in God, believe also in Me. *In My Father's house are many mansions*; if it were not so, I would have told you. *I go to prepare a place for you*. And if I go and prepare a place for you, *I will come again* and receive you to Myself; that *where I am, there you may be also*.[882]

> Eye has not seen, nor ear heard, nor have entered into the heart of man the things which God has prepared for those who love Him.[883]

John was taken into vision and shown the New Jerusalem as it will descend to this earth after the millennium. Let your imagination run wild as you read what he saw:

> And he carried me away in the Spirit to a great and high mountain, and showed me the great city, the *holy Jerusalem*, descending out of heaven from God, *having the glory of God*. Her *light* was like a most precious stone, *like a jasper* stone, *clear as crystal*. Also she had a *great and high wall* with *twelve gates*, and twelve angels at the gates, and names written on them, which are *the names of the twelve tribes of the children of Israel*: three gates on the east, three gates on the north, three gates on the south, and three gates on the west.

---

[880] Revelation 21:3, 4 (emphasis added)
[881] 1 Corinthians 13:12
[882] John 14:1–3 (emphasis added)
[883] 1 Corinthians 2:9

> Now the *wall* of the city had *twelve foundations*, and on them were the *names of the twelve apostles of the Lamb*. And he who talked with me had a gold reed to measure the city, its gates, and its wall. The city is *laid out as a square*; its length is as great as its breadth. And he *measured the city* with the reed: *twelve thousand furlongs*. Its length, breadth, and height are equal. Then he *measured its wall: one hundred and forty-four cubits*, according to the measure of a man, that is, of an angel. The construction of its *wall* was of *jasper*; and the *city was pure gold*, like clear glass. The *foundations of the wall* of the city were adorned with all kinds of precious stones: the first foundation was *jasper*, the second *sapphire*, the third *chalcedony*, the fourth *emerald*, the fifth *sardonyx*, the sixth *sardius*, the seventh *chrysolite*, the eighth *beryl*, the ninth *topaz*, the tenth *chrysoprase*, the eleventh *jacinth*, and the twelfth *amethyst*. The *twelve gates* were *twelve pearls*: each individual gate was of *one pearl*. And the *street of the city* was *pure gold*, like transparent glass.[884]

A cubit is 18 inches, so the wall is 216 feet high. A furlong is one-eighth of a mile, so the city is 375 miles per side and 1,500 miles in circumference. Though hard to imagine, it is also 375 miles high because its length, breadth, and height are equal. If this city were on earth today with society as it is, it would soon be destroyed. However, since society will be perfectly sinless, completely unselfish, and totally honest, the city will remain pristine for eternity. There will be no need for locks on doors, police patrols, jails, prisons, fire departments—and no taxes!

There will be no night in the city because the glory of God will outshine the sun. No clouds will obscure the brilliance of His glory. "The city had no need of the sun or of the moon to shine in it, for the glory of God illuminated it. The Lamb is its light.... Its gates shall not be shut at all by day (there shall be no night there)."[885]

I would like to make an appointment with you to meet under the tree of life next to the river of life on the first Sabbath we are in heaven. What do you say?

> And he showed me a *pure river of water of life*, clear as crystal, proceeding from the throne of God and of the Lamb. In the middle of its street, and on either side of the river, was the *tree of life*, which

---

[884] Revelation 21:10–21 (emphasis added)
[885] Revelation 21:23, 25

bore *twelve fruits*, each tree yielding its fruit *every month*. The leaves of the tree were for the healing of the nations.[886]

Do you long to go to heaven but feel you are too sinful and there is no hope for you? Do you feel you have gone too far in a life of sin and moral failure to receive forgiveness? Do you fear you have committed the unpardonable sin? We need to understand what this is:

- It cannot be murder because Moses murdered a man, and we know he is saved.[887]
- Neither is it lying or deception because Jacob lied and deceived his father, but he is accounted as saved.[888]
- It is not denying Christ because Peter denied Him, yet we know he was forgiven and wrote two books of the New Testament.[889]
- Is it persecuting God's people? No, because the apostle Paul persecuted the early Christian Church, yet God chose him to be His missionary to the Gentiles, and he wrote almost half the New Testament.[890]

You may be a great sinner, but you have a greater Savior! *"If we confess our sins*, He is *faithful* and *just* to *forgive* us our sins and to *cleanse* us from *all unrighteousness.*"[891]

With that said, what is the unpardonable sin if God is willing to forgive and cleanse us from "all unrighteousness"? Jesus said the following:

> Therefore I say to you, every sin and blasphemy will be forgiven men, but the *blasphemy against the Spirit will not be forgiven* men. Anyone who speaks a word against the Son of Man, it will be forgiven him; but *whoever speaks against the Holy Spirit, it will not be forgiven* him, either in this age or in the age to come.[892]

The unpardonable sin is not a specific type of sin; instead, it is the continual rejection of the prompting of the Holy Spirit. Let us see what the Bible says about the work of the Holy Spirit and how we can reject His work in our lives. Jesus was talking about the Holy Spirit when He said,

---

[886] Revelation 22:1, 2 (emphasis added)
[887] See Hebrews 11:23–28; Luke 9:30
[888] See Exodus 3:6, 15; Luke 13:28
[889] See John 21:15–19; Acts 2:1–47
[890] See Acts 9:15
[891] 1 John 1:9 (emphasis added)
[892] Matthew 12:31, 32 (emphasis added)

"And when He has come, He will *convict* the world of *sin*, and of *righteousness*, and of *judgment*."[893]

Our natural, sinful hearts, like Nebuchadnezzar's, do not like to be convicted of sin, righteousness, or judgment, yet this is the work of the Holy Spirit. It is easy to resist or even reject His convictions if we do not act upon them at the point of conviction. The longer we delay, the easier it is to resist and the weaker and weaker the convictions become, until we can no longer hear His pleadings.

In this condition, we are unable to overcome the temptations and traps laid by the enemy. However, those who open their hearts to the work of the Holy Spirit have a different experience. "But he who does the truth comes to the light, that his deeds may be clearly seen, that they have been done in God."[894]

Therefore, it is essential to be born again, and that new-birth experience only happens by opening our hearts to the transforming power of the Holy Spirit. "Most assuredly, I say to you, *unless* one is *born* of *water* and the *Spirit*, he *cannot enter the kingdom of God*. That which is born of the flesh is flesh, and that which is born of the Spirit is spirit. Do not marvel that I said to you, 'You must be born again.'"[895]

Water baptism is a symbol of dying to self, being buried with Christ, and rising to a new life in Him through the Holy Spirit. It is a symbol of being baptized by the Holy Spirit. If you have not been baptized by immersion, I invite you to do so as soon as possible.

> *If this city were on earth today with society as it is, it would soon be destroyed. However, since society will be perfectly sinless, completely unselfish, and totally honest, the city will remain pristine for eternity. There will be no need for locks on doors, police patrols, jails, prisons, fire departments—and no taxes!*

Another aspect of the work of the Holy Spirit is to lead us into all truth. In our world today, even within many Christian churches, biblical truth is considered dispensable. Instead, a sentimental "love" and outward show

---

[893] John 16:8 (emphasis added)
[894] John 3:21
[895] John 3:5–7 (emphasis added)

of "unity," or at least "compliance," are more highly valued than biblical truth is. However, that is not in harmony with what Jesus said:

> However, when He, the *Spirit of truth*, has come, *He will guide you* into *all truth*; for He will not speak on His own authority, but whatever He hears He will speak; and *He will tell you things to come*. He will glorify Me, for *He will take of what is Mine and declare it to you*.[896]

When we reject or downplay the importance of biblical truth, we reject or downplay the Holy Spirit because it was He who inspired the biblical writers. And it is the work of the Holy Spirit to bring Jesus, who is "the way, the truth and the life,"[897] into our hearts and minds. Therefore, by rejecting the work of the Holy Spirit, we are also rejecting Jesus.

When we studied Daniel 8, we discovered it was the antichrist power that cast truth to the ground. "Because of transgression, an army was given over to the horn to oppose the daily sacrifices; and he cast truth down to the ground. He did all this and prospered."[898] This is the work of the enemy of God. He wants to entrap us in sin so we will be lost along with him.

Nevertheless, Jesus emphasized the importance of biblical truth:

> If you *abide in My word*, you are My disciples indeed. And *you shall know the truth*, and *the truth shall make you free*.[899]
> *Sanctify* them by Your *truth*. Your *word is truth*.[900]

Notice to whom the Holy Spirit is given. Knowing the truth does us no good unless we believe and obey the truth through the indwelling power of the Holy Spirit. "And we are His witnesses to these things, and so also is the Holy Spirit whom God has given to those who obey Him."[901]

Therefore, when truth is presented to us and we do not act upon it, we are silencing the still small voice of the Holy Spirit. It is when we are content to remain in disobedience to God's Word that we are in danger of rejecting the Holy Spirit, because known sin silences the Spirit of God. After King David's sins of adultery and murder, he pled with God in deep, humble repentance, saying, "Create in me a clean heart, O God, and

---

[896] John 16:13, 14 (emphasis added)
[897] John 14:6
[898] Daniel 8:12
[899] John 8:31, 32 (emphasis added)
[900] John 17:17 (emphasis added)
[901] Acts 5:32 (emphasis added)

renew a steadfast spirit within me. Do not cast me away from Your presence, and do not take Your Holy Spirit from me."[902]

The sin that is unpardonable is the sin we do not want pardoned; the sin we do not want to confess and forsake; the sin to which we want to hang on. The unpardonable sin occurs when we repeatedly say "NO" to God—when we put Him off to another time—a better day. However, *today* is the day of salvation! "Today, if you will hear His voice, do not harden your hearts."[903]

To harden one's heart is to refuse to accept and obey the truth of God's Word through faith in Jesus. "Behold, *the LORD's hand is not shortened, that it cannot save*; nor His ear heavy, that it cannot hear. But *your iniquities have separated you from your God*; and your sins have hidden His face from you, so that He will not hear."[904]

Obedience is not a popular concept today, but it is central to the Word of God, especially for those who wish to live with Jesus for eternity.

> *Do not love* the *world* or the *things in the world*. If anyone loves the world, the *love of the Father is not in him*. For all that is in the world—the *lust of the flesh*, the *lust of the eyes*, and the *pride of life*—is not of the Father but is of the world. And *the world is passing away*, and the lust of it; but *he who does the will of God abides forever*.[905]

Jesus has prepared a most glorious place for you in His kingdom! There is nothing in this world for which it is worth exchanging heaven and the new earth. When Jesus comes again, there will be only two groups of people: those who have opened their hearts to the convictions of the Holy Spirit through the Word of truth and those who reject the pleadings of God's Spirit.

> Blessed are those who *do His commandments*, that they may have the right to *the tree of life*, and may *enter through the gates into the city*. But *outside* are dogs and sorcerers and sexually immoral and murderers and idolaters, and whoever *loves and practices a lie*.[906]

---

[902] Psalm 51:10, 11
[903] Hebrews 4:7 (cf. Psalm 95:7, 8)
[904] Isaiah 59:1, 2 (emphasis added)
[905] 1 John 2:15–17 (emphasis added)
[906] Revelation 22:14, 15 (emphasis added)

The only way we can do His commandments is by the faith of Jesus.[907] The Holy Spirit is appealing to you right now! How will you respond to His invitation? Please do not put Him off for a better time. That time may never come. Do not silence the voice of conviction. Your eternal life is at stake! "And the Spirit and the bride say, 'Come!' And let him who hears say, 'Come!' And let him who thirsts come. Whoever desires, let him take the water of life freely."[908]

Will you accept the truth of God's Word and step out in faith to obey? After going over fool's hill and returning to God, King Solomon admonished, "Buy the truth, and do not sell it, also wisdom and instruction and understanding."[909] Some people sell the truth for a job, money, fame, family, friends, relationships, pleasure, entertainment, houses, possessions, etc. I appeal to you to buy the truth as it is in Jesus and not sell it!

Please let me know your response to God's invitation to you by sending me an email when you enter the following link in your web browser: https://1ref.us/i9457056. I would love to hear from you and pray with you. There is more in God's Word that I would love to share with you.

> Now to Him who is able to keep you from stumbling, and to present *you* faultless before the presence of His glory with exceeding joy, to God our Savior, who alone is wise, *be* glory and majesty, dominion and power, both now and forever. Amen.[910]

---

[907] See Revelation 14:12
[908] Revelation 22:17
[909] Proverbs 23:23
[910] Jude 24, 25

Appendix A

Why Antiochus IV Epiphanes Is Not the Little Horn of Daniel 8

In 167 BC, Antiochus IV (Epiphanes) conquered Jerusalem. In the temple, he set up a pagan idol, even going so far as to offer a pig upon the altar in disdain for the Hebrew religion and mock their God. Down through the centuries, the Jews have not forgotten his terrible desecrations. They have hated Antiochus IV with a passion and tried to make him fit into the ominous prophecies of Daniel 7 and 8. Most Christians agree with this mistaken interpretation. However, many see a future antichrist being pictured in Daniel 7. Though we can understand why the Jews could have such feelings of revulsion against him, we have to look at the evidence and accept God's Word as the authoritative answer to the question of who this historical individual may be.

Below are reasons why many serious Bible students have rejected the interpretation of Antiochus IV as a fulfillment of these prophecies.

1. **Horns are typically symbols for kingdoms** (see Daniel 7:7, 8; 8:3, 6, 7, 22), not individual kings, as was Antiochus IV. When it represents an individual king, it states that (see 8:21).
2. A **comparison of the greatness** of the ram (v. 4—"became *great*"), goat (v. 8—"grew *very great*), and little horn (vs. 9–11—"grew *exceedingly great*") does not fit Antiochus IV, as will be discussed below. Notice the "little horn" grows in two directions: horizontally and vertically.
3. **Activities of the little horn**
   A. Daniel 8:9—Conquests in the:

   > **South** (Egypt): Antiochus IV conquered part of the Delta. The next year, he began to besiege Alexandria, but he was then told by a Roman diplomatic mission to leave Egypt and go back to Palestine or else. The Roman ambassador, C. Popilius Laenas, drew a circle around Antiochus IV and told him not to leave it until he had given his answer. Antiochus decided to leave Egypt. It must have been terribly humiliating!

East: His father, Antiochus III, had conquered much of the east, as far as India, but lost it again after he was defeated by the Romans at Magnesia. Antiochus IV tried to retake it. He achieved some initial diplomatic and military success in Armenia and Media, but met resistance on the part of the Parthians, who stopped him "dead in his tracks,"—literally! Antiochus died of natural causes while in a campaign against the Parthians circa 164 BC.

Glorious Land (Palestine): Antiochus' father had already conquered Palestine from the Ptolemies in 198 BC. He actually lost control of it. His army suffered significant defeats there toward the end of his reign, which eventually led to the complete independence of Judea from the Seleucids during the period of the Maccabees.

*In summary, Antiochus' military conquests were very few and short lived. We would have to say that his "career" was a failure as a military conqueror and a ruler in general. He had referred to himself as "Epiphanes" (an appearance or manifestation of God). His contemporaries sarcastically called him "Epimanes" ("the mad man"). To say he "grew exceedingly great" (Daniel 8:9) just does not fit the facts.

B. **Anti-temple Activities**

Antiochus IV never did anything to the temple that would qualify as "casting down its place" (Daniel 8:11). He did not physically deface or destroy it in any way. He desecrated it for three years to the day (actual sacrifices he offered on the altar) or three years and ten days (the time he had an idol erected in the temple).

Clifford Goldstein mentions that in Daniel 8:11–12, the little horn took away the daily (Hebrew *tamid*), but it does not say anything about taking away the yearly (see *1844 Made Simple* [pub info], pp. 62, 71). However, Antiochus IV did both during his three-year reign. The papacy could only affect the daily because his power was broken at the end of the 1,260 years of persecution (AD 538–1798). Thus, the papacy had no effect upon the antitypical yearly, which began in 1844. Though this is an "argument from silence," it still fits the papacy, but not Antiochus IV.

4. **Time factors** for the little horn
   A. **Time of origin**

   The Seleucid dynasty, of which Antiochus IV was a part, existed from 311–65 BC and had twenty kings ruling during its duration. Antiochus IV ruled from 175–164/3 BC and was the eighth of these kings. In either case, he can hardly be said to come up "at the latter end of their rule" (Daniel 8:23). He ruled during the middle or before. It just does not fit.

   B. **Duration**

   His desecration of the temple lasted three years (or three years and ten days), as explained above. There is no way to fit the 2,300-day prophecy within this time period, even if the "2,300 days" is understood to represent "sacrifices," which were offered twice a day. Dividing 2,300 in half yields 1,150, not the 1,080 (or 1,090) days in which the sanctuary was desecrated by Antiochus IV. Again, it does not fit.

   C. **The End**

   Gabriel came to explain the *"mareh"* (literally, "appearing," used to describe theophanies or appearances of heavenly beings). Daniel defines this appearing as the appearing of the two angelic beings found in 8:13–14 (see 8:26). This is the part of the vision (*chazon*) Daniel could not understand. Verse 17 states categorically that the *mareh* ("appearing") "is for the time of the end." Verse 19 calls this "the appointed time of the end." The little horn still exists in "the time of the end" (vs. 12, 17).

   This "time of the end" cannot be made to fit Antiochus or the Seleucid dynasty of which he was a part. At a bare minimum, Daniel's time prophecies extend to the coming of the Anointed One or Messiah (see Daniel 9:24–27). This "time of the end" had to extend until after the fulfillment of the seventy-week prophecy, which was to be cut off (*chathak*—literally, "to cut off," derived from a word meaning "to amputate") from the 2,300 days. The reign of Antiochus IV does not come close to extending to the time of the Messiah.

5. **Nature of the end** of the little horn

He was to come to his end "by no human hand" (Daniel 8:25). In Daniel 2, 7, 8, and 11, these prophecies are all brought to their climax by the direct intervention of God in human history. Antiochus IV died of natural causes. It was not even in battle or from some extraordinary circumstances, as we would expect from Daniel 8:25.

6. **Origin** of the little horn

Daniel 8:8 states the he-goat's great horn (Alexander the Great) would be broken and in its place "came up four conspicuous horns toward the four winds of heaven(s)." (The Hebrew is actually understood as being plural.) A major question arises at this point: Did the little horn come from one of the four conspicuous horns, (which could conceivably apply to Antiochus IV if we disregard what we have already discussed above) or from one of the four winds of heaven(s)? Daniel 8:9 says the little horn came "out of one of them" (literally, "*from* the one *from* them"). The question is, To whom or what is the "them" a reference?

"Them" in the Hebrew has a masculine plural ending. "Horns" and "winds" from verse 8 both have feminine plural endings. If "them" refers to either "horns" or "winds," we have a problem. The gender does not match. Any commentary that does not deal with this is shirking its duty to be true to the text! To make this even more interesting, the numerals "one" in verse 9 and "four" in verse 8 have feminine endings. Therefore, the "them" does not match here either. Here is the only solution to this problem in the syntax:

<u>Feminine Masculine</u>

    v. 8—"to the four *winds* of the *heavens*
    v. 9—"from the *one* from *them*

When this is recognized, the genders match perfectly. Consequently, we have the little horn arising not from the "horns" but from the "heavens." That is the Hebraic way of saying the little horn comes from one of the compass directions. He is not a Seleucid king after all! This would agree with all that is indicated above.

THE ABOVE FACTS MAKE IT CLEAR: ANTIOCHUS IV IS NOT THE LITTLE HORN OF DANIEL 8![911]

Material gleaned from *Selected Studies*, William Shea, pp. 35–43

---

[911] Material gleaned from William H. Shea, Selected Studies on Prophetic Interpretation, revised ed. (Silver Spring, MD: Biblical Research Institute, 1992), pp. 35–43

Appendix B

Some Critical Hebrew Words in Understanding and Connecting Daniel 8 and 9

1. *chazon* ("**vision**")—Comes from a word that means "to see as a prophet" and is often translated "seer."
   KJV, NKJV, NIV, RSV, etc.—translated "vision": Daniel 8:1, 2 [twice], 13, 15, 17, 26; 9:21, 24 (also 1:17; 10:14; 11:14)
   Strong's Definition:
   H2377—*chazown* (*khaw-zone'*); from 2372; a sight (mentally), i.e., a dream, revelation, or oracle.
   H2372—*chazah* (*khaw-zaw'*); a primitive root; to gaze at; mentally, to perceive, contemplate (with pleasure); specifically, to have a vision of—behold, look, prophesy, provide, see.
2. *mareh* ("**vision**")—Comes from a word that means "to see." It is sometimes translated "appearance" as it refers to seeing the appearance of heavenly beings, either God or angels (as Daniel does in 8:13).
   KJV, NKJV, NIV, RSV—translated "vision": Daniel 8:16, 26, 27; 9:23; 10:1 (10:7 [twice], 8, 16 [uses *marah*], feminine ending)
   Strong's Definition:
   H4758—*mar'eh* (*mar-eh'*); from 7200; a view (the act of seeing); also, an appearance (the thing seen), whether a (real) shape (especially if handsome, comely; often plural—the looks), or a (mental) vision.
   (Please note, *Strong's* mistakenly lists *chazon* as the word used in 9:23 in earlier editions, but this mistake has been corrected in recent editions. Also, see *Young's Concordance* for the correct listing of this word, *mareh*, used in 9:23)
3. *chathak*—This occurs only once in the Bible; the word is used frequently in rabbinic Hebrew (extra-biblical sources) and means "to cut off" or "amputate."

KJV—"determine": Daniel 9:24
Strong's Definition:
H2852—*chathak* (*khaw-thak'*); a primitive root; properly, to cut off, i.e., (figuratively) to decree.

Daniel uses *chazon* to refer to the "entire vision," while *mareh* refers *only* to the part involving the "appearance" of the two angels in 8:13–14, a small part of the vision. Recognizing how these two words for "vision" are used clearly points to the fact that the portion of the vision of Daniel 8, which the prophet did not understand, was the *mareh* of verses 13–14 (see also vs. 26, 27).

Notice, Gabriel is told to "make this man understand the vision" (*mareh*, v. 16) but was unable to do so at that time. After Daniel becomes sick for "some days" (v. 27), Gabriel returns in 9:23 to do what he was commanded to do: explain the *mareh*, the part about the 2,300 days. This is the part that Daniel did not and would not understand until 9:24 and onward. In 8:26, the only portion of the vision (*mareh*) that Daniel did not understand—and therefore the whole vision (*chazon*) was sealed up—was the part where the two angels "appeared" in verses 13–14, the *mareh* ("appearing").

By Daniel's own designation, the *mareh* refers to the part of the vision regarding the "evenings and mornings" (8:26). This is the part that makes Daniel "sick." Twelve or thirteen years pass from the end of chapter 8 to the beginning of chapter 9, where we find Daniel studying the prophecy of the seventy-year captivity because it was nearly at its end. If the 2,300 days were talking about a literal six-plus years (as modern-day Protestants and Catholics believe), Daniel should have been delighted because the prophesied captivity would have been shortened and should have ended six years earlier! Of course, the captivity was not over. Obviously, Daniel understood the 2,300 days as years, and the explanation in 9:24–27 verifies this!

At the end of chapter 8, Daniel was sickened by what he saw, but he did not understand it. Twelve or thirteen years later, the same angel, Gabriel, would return and give him understanding. Notice how he does it in 9:24: He uses the seventy-week (490-year) prophecy to explain the 2,300-day (year) prophecy—one time period is "cut off," amputated, from the other time period (see 8:14). Just as the 2,300 years is a unit, the 490 years ("seventy weeks of years"—RSV) is "cut off" as a unit. The one provides the explanation of the starting date for the other. It is obvious to Daniel that both have the same starting date.

Critical Conclusion—You cannot understand Daniel 8:14 without understanding 9:24, which is given to explain 8:14. When we understand these two chapters as being a completely connected unit, we then have the basis to understand the essence of Daniel 7 and the cosmic judgment scene presented therein.

*Keep in mind the first word translated "vision" in 8:26 is the Hebrew *mareh*. The second word translated "vision" is *chazon*.

Material provided via email by Jim Anderson, one of my pastoral friends.

TEACH Services, Inc.
P U B L I S H I N G

We invite you to view the complete
selection of titles we publish at:
www.TEACHServices.com

We encourage you to write us
with your thoughts about this,
or any other book we publish at:
info@TEACHServices.com

TEACH Services' titles may be purchased in
bulk quantities for educational, fund-raising,
business, or promotional use.
bulksales@TEACHServices.com

Finally, if you are interested in seeing
your own book in print, please contact us at:
publishing@TEACHServices.com

We are happy to review your manuscript at no charge.

www.ingramcontent.com/pod-product-compliance
Lightning Source LLC
Chambersburg PA
CBHW050846230426
43667CB00012B/2162